QuickTime

Macintosh Multimedia

Dan Parks Sydow

MIS:
PRESS

A Subsidiary of
Henry Holt and Co., Inc.

First Edition—1994

ISBN 1-55828-338-2

Printed in the United States of America.

10 9 8 7 6 5 4 3 2 1

MIS:Press books are available at special discounts for bulk purchases for sales promotions, premiums, fund-raising, or educational use. Special editions or book excerpts can also be created to specification.

For details contact: Special Sales Director
MIS:Press
a subsidiary of Henry Holt and Company, Inc.
115 West 18th Street
New York, New York 10011

Publisher, Steve Berkowitz
Development Editor, Cary Sullivan
Production Editor, Patricia Wallenburg
Associate Production Editor, Kevin Latham
Copy Editor, Peter Bochner
Technical Editor, Ray Valdes

Acknowledgements

Carole McClendon, WaterSide Productions, for introducing me to MIS:Press.

Ray Valdes—thanks for another helpful technical edit.

Peter Bochner, copyeditor—once again a copy editor saves me from looking foolish. Thanks for catching any droll mistakes I might have made.

Patty Wallenburg, MIS:Press, for all the work involved in the page layout of the book.

Cary Sullivan, MIS:Press, for being patient at the onset of this project!

Dedication

To my wife, Nadine…
Dan

Table of Contents

Introduction

About This Book   xv

What's In This Book xvi

What's On the Disk xvii

    For Both Nonprogrammers and Programmers xvii

    For Nonprogrammers xvii

    For Programmers xviii

What You Need xviii

    Using the Book xviii

    Using the Software xviii

Extracting the Disk Contents xix

CHAPTER 1

Introduction to QuickTime   **1**

Installing QuickTime 2

    If You Don't Have QuickTime 2

    If You Already Have QuickTime 3

What QuickTime Can Do For You 4

    The Everyday User 4

    The Business User 5

    The Novice Programmer 5

    The Advanced Programmer 7

QuickTime Terminology 8

    QuickTime Itself 8

    QuickTime Movies 8

    Types of Movies 9

    Movie Compression 10

Chapter Summary 10

CHAPTER 2

QuickTime Basics   **13**

The "For Nonprogrammers" Folder 14

Playing Movies 15

    The Movie Controller: User Interface for Movies 15

    Using the MovieViewer Program 17

    Using Apple's Movie Player 21

    Playing a Startup Movie 23

Making Movies 25

    Creating PICT Files 25

    PICTs to Movie: Using MovieMaker 32

Image Compression 34

    Apple's Movie Converter 35

Using Standard Compression Settings 38

Chapter Summary 44

CHAPTER 3

Using Movies   **45**

Including Movies in Documents 46

Movies in Microsoft Word 47

Movies in ClarisWorks 49

Movies in Other Application Documents 58

Wild Magic: Movies in Any Document? 61

Getting and Installing Wild Magic 61

Using Wild Magic 61

Providing Others with Wild Magic 64

Programs Written for QuickTime 64

Morph 64

TheaterMaker 69

Chapter Summary 75

CHAPTER 4

Capturing Video   **77**

Digitizing Video 78

Why Digitize? 78

Capture Rates 78

Digitizers 79

Capturing Video with a Digitizer 79

Using ComputerEyes/RT to Capture Video 80

Hooking Up the ComputerEyes/RT Hardware 80

Making a Movie Using
the ComputerEyes/RT Software 80

Using VideoSpigot to Capture Video 86

Hooking Up the VideoSpigot Hardware 86

Making a Movie Using the VideoSpigot Software 87

Capturing Still Images 91

Using ComputerEyes/RT to Capture an Image 91

Using VideoSpigot to Capture an Image 103

Chapter Summary 104

CHAPTER 5

Adding Sound 105

Movie Tracks 106

Capturing Sound through a Built-in Sound Port 107

Making the Connection 108

Making the Movie 109

Capturing Sound with MacRecorder 113

Making the Connection 114

Making the Movie 116

Using SoundEdit to Create and Edit Sounds 117

Using SoundEdit Pro—The Basics 118

Using SoundEdit Pro to Edit Sounds 122

Using SoundEdit Pro to Mix Multiple Soundtracks ... 126

Using SoundEdit Pro to Capture Music 128

Using SoundEdit Pro to Capture
and Edit the Soundtrack of a Tape 129

Other Sources of Sounds 129

Obtaining Sounds from Information Services 130

Purchasing Sounds 134

Chapter Summary 135

CHAPTER 6

Editing Movies 137

Editing Sounds—Advanced 138

Cue Points 138

Labels 142

Using Premiere to Edit Movies 145

Premiere Basics 145

Editing 150

Special Effects 151

Filters 154

Using Files Other than PICTS in Movies 157

Obtaining Pictures 158

Obtaining Pictures from Others 162

Graphics to Movies: With the Help
of Corel Converters 162

Using Graphics You Can't Read 167

Chapter Summary 168

CHAPTER 7

Introduction to QuickTime Programming

169

Playing a Movie—Now! 170

The Movie Toolbox 171

Initializing Movies 172

Checking for QuickTime 172

Initializing the Movie Toolbox 174

Opening a Movie File 176

File Pathnames 176

Opening the File 179

Loading a Movie 179

Closing a Movie File 182

Opening a Display Window for a Movie 182

Creating a Display Window 183

Resizing the Display Window 183

Showing the Window 187

Setting the Movie Graphics World 187

Playing a Movie 188

Example Program: QuickTrivia 190

  Program Project: QuickTrivia.π 192

  Program Resources: QuickTrivia.π.rsrc 192

  Program Listing: QuickTrivia.c 195

  Stepping Through the Code 202

Adding to QuickTrivia—Without Programming! 217

  Making Changes with ResEdit 217

  Adding to QuickTrivia's Lists of Movies 218

  Adding to QuickTrivia's Questions 218

Chapter Summary 221

CHAPTER 8

Programming with Movie Controllers   223

QuickTime Components 224

The Movie Controller Component 225

Opening a Movie File 227

  The Standard Get File Dialog Box 228

  Displaying the Standard Get File Dialog Box 230

Attaching a Controller to a Movie 233

Movies and the Event Loop 236

Changing Controller Features 239

  Movie Looping With MCDoAction() 240

  Enabling Keystrokes with MCDoAction() 240

Movie Editing 241

  Enabling Movie Editing 241

  Using Movie Editing Routines 242

  The Application Editing Function 244

Saving a Movie 246

Example Program: MovieViewer 247

  Program Resources: MovieViewer.π.rsrc 248

Program Listing: MovieViewer.c 248

Stepping Through the Code 259

Chapter Summary 272

CHAPTER 9

More Movie Toolbox   **275**

Changing the Look of a Controller 276

Hiding Controller Buttons 276

Hiding the Controller 277

Movie Frames 279

Determining the Length of a Movie 279

Copying a Single Frame as a 'PICT' 280

Changing the Movie Playing Rate 282

The Fixed Data Type 283

Changing the Rate of Play 283

Playing Movie Selections 285

Looping, Revisited 286

Sample Program: MovieFeatures 287

Program Resources: MovieFeatures.π.rsrc 288

Program Listing: MovieFeatures.c 288

Stepping Through the Code 302

Chapter Summary 312

APPENDIX

Appendix of QuickTime Products   **313**

Audio and Video Clips 314

Hardware 315

Software 316

Online Services 321

About This Book

his book is for casual Mac users, serious Mac users, novice programmers, and the more dedicated Macintosh programmers. Quite a claim—but then, QuickTime is quite a program. In brief, QuickTime is a tool that allows you to easily add multimedia features to anything you presently do on your Macintosh. The purposes of QuickTime are as varied as those of multimedia itself. The uses for QuickTime cross boundaries—and so must the topics in this book.

A casual Macintosh user may want to take a video clip from a home movie they filmed with a camcorder and transfer it to their computer. Maybe even paste that clip right inside a word processing document, copy the document to a floppy disk, and mail it to a relative for viewing. QuickTime lets a user do just that—easily.

A worker who uses the Macintosh may want to spice up a report by showing a sales trend—not as a series of graphs on paper, but as a short movie embedded in an electronic version of the report. The report is then distributed to other Macintosh users, who can view the monthly graphs, one after the other, on their computer screens. This same business user might even want to include a video clip of the highlights of a speech the company's CEO recently gave. Again, QuickTime makes such tasks easy to do.

Anyone who knows how to program the Macintosh—even at the simplest level—would love to be able to include multimedia features in their Macintosh programs. Almost any program would be enhanced by allowing the program's user to—at a click of the mouse—open a window that displays and runs a movie. With Apple's QuickTime, multimedia features like this are no longer a dream. This kind of animated programming trick is available and accessible to anyone with any level of programming skill.

Which category of Macintosh user do you fall into? You could very well belong to more than one. Business people may be able to write a minimal program. Programmers may need to create reports. And everyone who uses a Macintosh soon finds themself tinkering, exploring, and testing their creativity.

Users can't be pegged into a single category—that's why this book crosses the artificial lines that separate one type of use from another. No matter what you use your Macintosh for, you'll find tips, techniques, and ideas in this book that will interest and intrigue you.

What's In This Book

QuickTime: Macintosh Multimedia is full of ideas, examples, and step-by-step instructions on how to make the most of QuickTime—Apple's revolutionary multimedia tool.

In *QuickTime: Macintosh Multimedia*, we introduce you to the basics of QuickTime—what it is, how to install it, and how to play an existing QuickTime movie.

This book shows you the different ways to make QuickTime movies. You can use a Macintosh paint or draw program, a camcorder, a VCR, or your TV. We'll cover each method in detail.

We'll show you how to improve, or completely change, a QuickTime movie using QuickTime editing programs.

QuickTime: Macintosh Multimedia shows you what to do with QuickTime movies once you have them—whether you made them yourself or got them from any one of a variety of sources. (We'll tell you those sources too!)

Finally, if you program on the Macintosh, *QuickTime: Macintosh Multimedia* will show you how to open a window and play a QuickTime movie from within your own program. We'll take a few chapters to cover this topic so that both intermediate and more advanced programmers can do it.

What's On the Disk

The disk that comes bundled with this book has three folders on it: one for non-programmers, one for programmers, and one for both. Here's what's in them.

For Both Nonprogrammers and Programmers

In order to play movies, programmers and nonprogrammers alike need the QuickTime program. The latest and greatest edition, QuickTime version 1.6.1, is on the disk.

For Nonprogrammers

You get three ready-to-run programs, a sample movie, and six PICTs (Macintosh pictures).

MovieStartUp plays a movie when your Macintosh starts up. As your Mac boots up, a window will be centered on the screen and a movie—any movie you've previously specified—will play. Now you can have a startup screen that moves!

MovieViewer lets you play any QuickTime movie you have. It will also let you edit movies by copying, cutting, and pasting parts of them to create new ones.

MovieMaker lets you create your own QuickTime movies by combining pictures you draw, or clip art you have, into animated sequences.

Just in case you don't have any QuickTime movies, we start you off with one. That way you can test MovieViewer to see that it really does work!

To speed you through your first attempt at making a moving using Macintosh pictures, we've included a series of six pictures that can be strung together using MovieMaker.

For Programmers

If you know how to program the Mac in C language, you'll really appreciate what's in this folder. Not only can you use the MovieViewer and MovieMaker applications found in the For Nonprogrammers folder, you get the complete source code for both programs.

Chapters 7, 8, and 9 of this book walk you through the source code of three complete Macintosh QuickTime programs. One of the programs is a trivia game. The other two are movie viewers—userful applications that allow you to open and play any QuickTime movie. We've saved you wear and tear on your keyboard by providing the source code files for these three programs. We've also included the THINK C project files for each. You can experiment with the code and then, if you own either the THINK C or Symantec C++ compiler, you can compile your own versions of these three programs.

What You Need

Just about everything you'll need to make full use of QuickTime is included in this package. Here, specifically, is just what you should have.

Using the Book

For those of you who use the Macintosh, but don't program on it, all you need is curiosity and a willingness to learn all about QuickTime. That's it!

If you're a programmer and you want to learn how to include QuickTime movies in your own programs, you'll need a basic understanding of how to write a C language program for the Macintosh.

Using the Software

The disk that comes with this book contains QuickTime itself and source code for three programs. Here's what you need to make use of what we've given you.

Using QuickTime

To play movies using QuickTime, you need a Macintosh with a 68020 CPU or better. The Macs that meet this criteria include:

- any Macintosh with a "II" in its name
- Macintosh SE/30
- any Macintosh LC
- any Centris
- any Quadra
- Powerbooks numbered 140 or greater

All Macs have system software; you'll need to have System 6.0.7 or any version of System 7.

Graphics require a lot of memory. QuickTime movies are composed of graphics. You'll need to have 4Mb or better of RAM.

Using the Source Code

If you aren't a programmer, or don't plan on trying to be one, skip this section. If you do program, read on!

The source code files on the included disk are written in C language. If you have THINK C or Symantec C++, you can compile and run the source code.

Extracting the Disk Contents

The disk that comes bundled with this book is a 1.4Mb disk that contains a single file. Because we wanted to pack as much helpful stuff onto the disk as we could, we compressed the software. To gain access to everything in this one file you have to decompress it. That process is simple because the file is *self-extracting*, which means you don't need any special software to decompress, or extract, everything.

To extract the files, first copy the file titled **QTstuff.sea** from the floppy disk to your hard drive. Then remove the floppy disk and store it (you won't be needing it again).

Double-click on the **QTstuff.sea** icon that is now on your hard drive. You'll see the dialog box shown in Figure 1. (The names in the list will be different—the ones shown in Figure 1 are from our hard drive.)

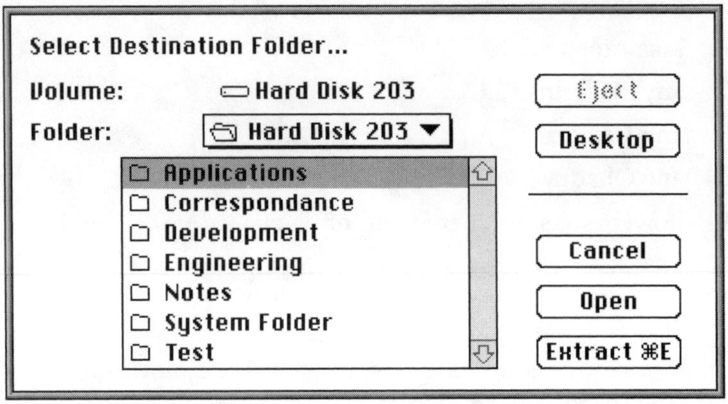

Select Destination Folder...

Volume: ⊂⊃ Hard Disk 203   [Eject]

Folder: [🗁 Hard Disk 203 ▼]   [Desktop]

    🗀 **Applications**
    🗀 Correspondance
    🗀 Development   [Cancel]
    🗀 Engineering
    🗀 Notes   [Open]
    🗀 System Folder
    🗀 Test   [Extract ⌘E]

FIGURE 1

Dialog Box You'll See After Double-Clicking on QTstuff.sea

Click the **Extract** button in the dialog box of Figure 1. File extraction will start, as shown in Figure 2.

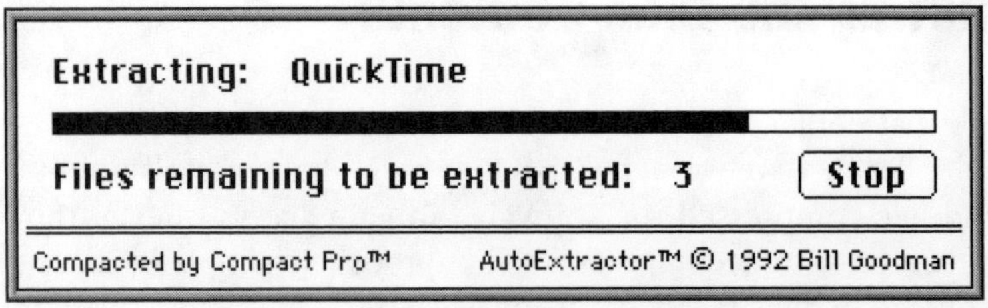

Extracting: QuickTime

Files remaining to be extracted: 3   [Stop]

Compacted by Compact Pro™   AutoExtractor™ © 1992 Bill Goodman

FIGURE 2

Extracting the Files

Once the operation is completed, you'll have a new folder on your hard drive, titled MIS QuickTime. The contents of that folder are shown in Figure 3.

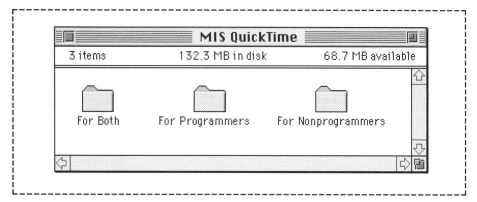

FIGURE 3

The New Folder Resulting from the Extraction

Drag the QTstuff.sea icon to the Trash can. The files have been extracted from it—you're all done with it. Now, read the book to see just how to make use of all the things in the new MIS QuickTime folder!

Introduction to QuickTime

he Macintosh, like any computer, needs an operating system in order to run. Part of the operating system is programmed into chips inside the Macintosh, and other parts exist in the System file. You'll find the System file in the System folder of your Mac. When Apple adds code that expands the capabilities of the Macintosh, you don't have to buy a new computer. Instead, you upgrade your System file. That's exactly what you did if you switched from, say, System 6.0.7 to System 7.

There's another way you can expand the capabilities of your Mac. You can add a system software *extension*. Like the System file itself, an extension contains code that adds features to your computer. You don't ever actually open or double-click on an extension to run it. When you start up your computer, the Macintosh takes note of all the extensions you have. It can then use the code within them whenever necessary.

In case you haven't guessed by now, QuickTime is just such a system software extension. Like all extensions, you place it in the Extensions folder that is inside your System folder. Once it's there, you never have to do anything with it. Every time you start your Mac, QuickTime will be running in the background, ready for your use.

Figure 1.1 shows the Extensions folder on our hard drive. It shows a few of the extensions in the folder, including QuickTime. The contents of your Extensions folder will be different, but should include the QuickTime icon. If not, don't be alarmed. We've included a copy of QuickTime on the disk.

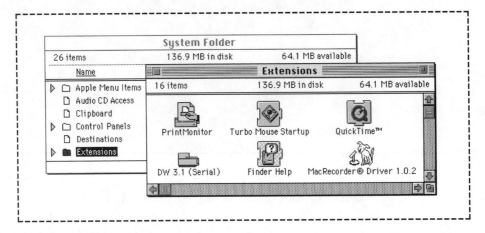

FIGURE 1.1
QuickTime Resides in the Extensions Folder

Installing QuickTime

If you didn't have QuickTime, you do now. And if you already had QuickTime, we might have supplied you with a more recent version. If you haven't extracted the files from the disk, do so now. Instructions on how to do this appear in the introductory pages of this book.

If You Don't Have QuickTime

If you don't have QuickTime in your Extensions folder, add it to the folder now. Open the MIS QuickTime folder. You'll see three more folders; open the one titled For Both. Simply drag the QuickTime icon to your System folder. You'll get a dialog box that asks you if it should be put into the Extensions folder. Click the **OK** button. Now to make your Macintosh know that you've added a new extension, restart your Mac.

You must restart your Macintosh in order for it to recognize QuickTime.

Once QuickTime has been installed, it will be available for your use every-time you start your Mac.

If You Already Have QuickTime

The latest version of QuickTime (as of this writing)—1.6.1—is included on the disk. If you have QuickTime, but aren't sure which version, here's what you can do.

1.   Click once on the **QuickTime** icon in your Extensions folder.
2.   Select **Get Info** from the File menu. You'll see a dialog box like the one shown in Figure 1.2.
3.   Check the version number in the dialog box.

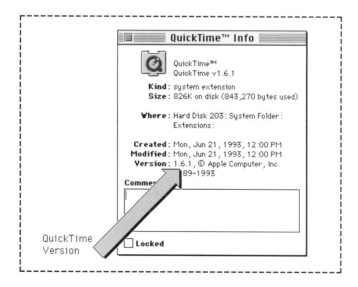

FIGURE 1.2
Using Get Info to Check the Version of QuickTime

If your version of QuickTime is older than the one on the disk, copy our version into your Extensions folder. If you have a version even newer than ours, send us a copy and tell us where you got it!

What QuickTime Can Do For You

QuickTime sounds interesting, but just what can you do with it? Its potential is limitless. The following sections are examples of how different users might use QuickTime.

The Everyday User

If you write letters, you probably use a word processing program on your Mac. Instead of printing the letter, you can copy it to a floppy disk and mail the disk to a friend or relative who also has a Macintosh. When the person receives the disk, they open the file and read the letter on screen. Why should you send a letter this way? Imagine the surprise of your friend or relative when their mouse-click on the letter results in the playing of a home-movie you shot of yourself, your children, or your vacation. Figure 1.3 is an example.

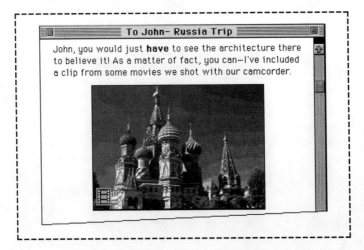

FIGURE 1.3

Including a QuickTime Movie in a Personal Letter

The Business User

Just as you can include a QuickTime movie in a personal letter, you can also do so in a business letter or report. If your company has a monthly newsletter, you could distribute it in its normal printed format, and have an electronic version available for employees that have Macintoshes. In the electronic version you can include a QuickTime clip of the company CEO giving a speech. Figure 1.4 is an example. If you want to keep things on the light side, you could include a movie of highlights of a company picnic or gathering.

You can include QuickTime movies in most major applications now on the market, such as Microsoft Word and Excel, Aldus Persuasion, and HyperCard. That makes the insertion of QuickTime movies a natural for training, educational, and promotional materials.

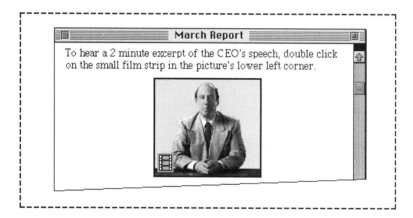

FIGURE 1.4
Including a QuickTime Movie in a Business Report

The Novice Programmer

If you've dabbled in programming, and can write a very simple Macintosh C language program, you might feel left out of the multimedia trend sweeping the industry. You'd love to write a program that makes use of multimedia, but you're afraid that the programming skills necessary to do so are way beyond your current level. Not so. QuickTime provides the tools that do much of the work for you.

Perhaps you'd like to write a Macintosh program that would amuse your children. But after seeing the high-tech special effects in movies, and the slick animation in kid's video games, you feel that anything you could program wouldn't thrill a three-year-old! That might have been true before, but not with QuickTime. If you have any knowledge of programming at all, you can write a program that will run QuickTime movies from within your program—movies of your kids, of cartoon characters, or any film clip at all. Whether it's from a VCR tape or a scene you've filmed with your camcorder, you can have your own program open a window and play it. Even Sega and Nintendo can't do that!

Figure 1.5 shows the type of program you might write. It's a simple trivia game that displays a question, then lets the user select the correct answer by clicking on a button. In response to the user's choice, the program opens a window and plays a QuickTime movie—one movie for the correct answer, a different one for a wrong response.

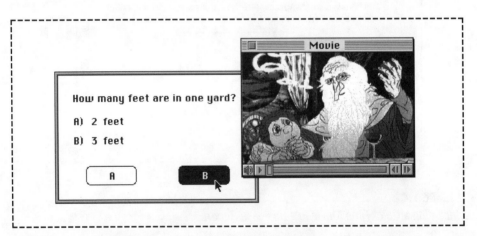

FIGURE 1.5
Playing QuickTime Movies from within Your Own Program

You might wonder how you, a novice Mac programmer, could possibly write code that will make use of such advanced technology as the display of video images. We'd like to take all the credit for that, but we can't. Most of it goes to Apple Computer.

When you start your computer, the QuickTime extension loads all sorts of code into the operating system of your Macintosh. Think of this code as a set of tools, or utilities, capable of performing different QuickTime-related tasks. One utility finds a QuickTime movie on your hard disk and displays it. Another utility plays that movie in a window. Where do you come in? You write only the code that tells the Macintosh which task to perform, such as playing a movie. We said above that Apple gets most of the credit, but not all of it. We get a little. We tell you what code to write to make use of Apple's utilities.

We provide you with sample code and detailed explanations of what we're doing each step of the way. To complete the picture, we provide the entire source code for a simple program that makes use of your newfound QuickTime knowledge. In fact, it's the code for the trivia game we just described. You'll find all this information in Chapter 7. And to save some time, you'll find all the source code already typed in for you on the included disk. If you own either THINK C or Symantec C++ (two popular Macintosh compilers from Symantec Corp.), you're all set to test the source code.

The Advanced Programmer

If you're an experienced programmer, everything we just stated in the previous section applies to you. Additionally, you'll be able to intertwine QuickTime movies into your programs in a more sophisticated way (see Figure 1.6). You can write programs that not only play movies, but *make* movies. The last chapters in this book contain the source code, fully explained, for two QuickTime movie players.

You may be familiar with Apple's *Inside Macintosh* series of reference books. The two books in that series dealing with QuickTime comprise over 1500 pages of technical material—not for the faint of heart. If you're serious about programming, you may want to work your way up to these manuals. But before jumping in, you'll appreciate a good introduction that summarizes and fully explains the most useful and important QuickTime programming topics.

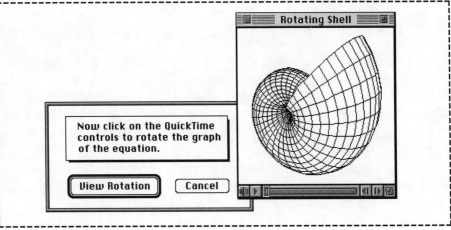

FIGURE 1.6
Using QuickTime Movies in Advanced Programming

QuickTime Terminology

Like any new technology, QuickTime has terms associated with it that may be new to you. We'll cover them here so they don't surprise you later on.

QuickTime Itself

QuickTime is an *extension*—software added to the system software already present in your computer.

QuickTime Movies

QuickTime works with *dynamic data*. The word "dynamic" means motion, or change. The "data" in dynamic data is the movie itself. A QuickTime movie is stored in a file on disk, just as other forms of data are stored. All QuickTime movie files have the same icon, just as any other type of data file has its own unique icon. Figure 1.7 shows files for a QuickTime movie, Microsoft Word, and TeachText.

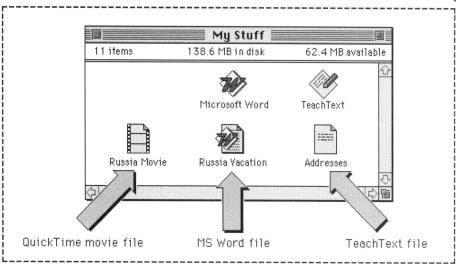

FIGURE 1.7
QuickTime Movies Have Their Own Icon Type

Figure 1.7 shows the icons for the programs that created two of the three files: Microsoft Word and TeachText. It doesn't show the icon of the program that created the QuickTime movie file. That's because there are many different programs you can use to create a QuickTime movie. Apple's Movie Player and the MovieMaker program included with this book are just two of them. We'll have more to say about the different ways to make a movie throughout this book.

A QuickTime movie is made up of *frames*. A single frame is one still image in a movie. To play a movie, QuickTime displays a sequence of frames in rapid succession.

Types of Movies

When you transfer part of a VCR tape or a home movie to a QuickTime movie, you have a *motion video* movie. The other common type of QuickTime movie is created using *animation*. In animation you use a program that allows you to string together a series of graphic pictures into a movie. These pictures can be drawings you've made using a Macintosh drawing program, or pictures from a clip art collection.

The processes of creating these two types of movies, motion video and animation, are different. The processes of playing them back, however, are the same.

Movie Compression

Graphics, whether a picture or figure in a document or a QuickTime movie, take up a lot of disk space. But, because QuickTime movies are composed of sequences of graphic images, they take up an enormous amount of disk space. In fact, the amount of disk space a movie required was a major stumbling block to the release of a product that worked with motion video. QuickTime overcame this obstacle by incorporating built-in *image compressors*. An image compressor can reduce the file size of a movie up to 20 times. Image compression, like much of what goes on in QuickTime, requires little technical knowledge on your part. That's no accident—QuickTime was made to be easy!

Chapter Summary

QuickTime is an extension—a piece of software containing code that is added to your Mac's system software each time you start up your computer. To install QuickTime, you simply copy the QuickTime extension from a floppy disk to the Extensions folder in the System folder of your hard drive.

What can you do with QuickTime? Too many things to sum up in just a few sentences. This book will show you how to make and play your own movies, and how to include movies in the documents of popular programs such as Microsoft Word. If you program the Macintosh, this book will show you how to use QuickTime movies from within your programs.

A QuickTime movie is saved to disk just as any other type of file. A movie is made up of several frames. Each frame is a single still image. QuickTime plays a movie by displaying these images one after the other.

A QuickTime movie that contains footage from a VCR tape or home movie, or any other "live action" source, is called a motion video movie. A QuickTime movie made up of a sequence of pictures, such as those drawn in a Macintosh paint or draw program, is an animated movie.

Graphic images take up large amounts of disk space. By using image compression to greatly reduce the space requirements of a movie, Apple has found a way to bring computer movie technology to the home computer user.

QuickTime Basics

o play a QuickTime movie, you need a movie-playing utility. This chapter discusses MovieViewer, the movie-playing program included with this book. You'll see how you can use MovieViewer to open a movie, play any movie, loop through a movie, or change the size of it. A Macintosh equipped with QuickTime is capable of playing a movie every time it starts up. Here we'll show you a couple of ways to get your Mac to do just that.

Anyone can create movies for QuickTime. You don't have to be a computer programmer, you don't have to own fancy video hardware, and you don't need additional, expensive software. If you have access to a Macintosh drawing program, you can draw a series of pictures. If you save each picture as an individual file, you can then use a movie-making program, such as the MovieMaker software included with this book, to turn this set of files into one QuickTime movie. It really is that easy—and this chapter shows you in detail how to create these files and make them into a QuickTime movie.

The "For Nonprogrammers" Folder

For QuickTime users, Apple sells a disk/CD-ROM package called the QuickTime Starter Kit. The disk contains the QuickTime extension and utilities for playing movies, creating movies, and compressing images. The CD-ROM contains no utilites, but has hundreds of video clips you can view.

For those of you who don't have the Starter Kit, or don't want to pay roughly $150 to get it, we've included a few utilities that provide much of the functionality of the programs found in the Starter Kit. Our utilities are in the For Nonprogrammers folder of the disk included with this book. Figure 2.1 shows the contents of this folder.

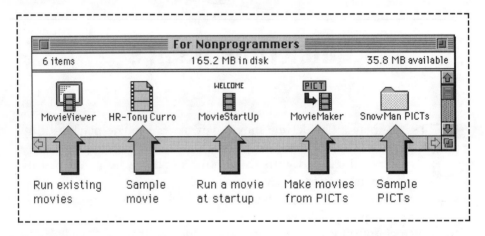

FIGURE 2.1

The Contents of the For Nonprogrammers Folder

The MovieViewer program allows you to run existing QuickTime movies. Once you open a movie with MovieViewer, you can play it as often as you want. You can also step through it, or set it to loop repeatedly. MovieViewer lets you resize the movie to half or double its original size. MovieViewer also allows you to edit movies by copying, cutting, and pasting frames. You can edit a single movie, or copy frames from one movie and paste them into another.

MovieStartUp is a program you put in your System folder, and then forget about. Every time your Macintosh starts up, a movie will play. Which movie? Any one you choose.

MovieMaker allows you to compile a movie from graphic images you create. Use a draw or paint program to create a series of pictures. Then run MovieMaker to string these pictures together into a single QuickTime movie. You'll be able to play the movie using any movie player, such as MovieViewer. We've included a folder with six pictures in it so you can quickly test out MovieMaker for yourself.

All three of the included utilities, MovieViewer, MovieStartUp, and MovieMaker, are discussed in detail in this chapter.

Playing Movies

Applications that allow the user to play QuickTime movies use a standardized method of letting the user control when and how often the movie is played. In this section we'll discuss this type of movie controller, and two programs that use it: MovieViewer and Movie Player. MovieViewer is a movie-playing utility included with this book. Movie Player is a popular movie-playing program that can be purchased from Apple.

The Movie Controller: User Interface for Movies

The *movie controller*, also called the *standard controller* or *control bar*, is the means of controlling the playing of a QuickTime movie. You'll find the movie controller at the bottom of a movie. Some movie-playing programs allow you to resize a movie window. As shown in Figure 2.2, when a movie is resized, the controller is also resized automatically.

Figure 2.3 shows the buttons found on a movie controller. Because not all movies contain a sound track, the Speaker button can take on different looks, as illustrated in Figure 2.4.

Because Apple provides an easy way for developers to add a movie controller to a movie, you'll probably never see any other means of controlling the playing of a movie.

FIGURE 2.2

The Movie Controller is Resized along with a Movie

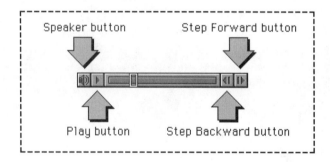

FIGURE 2.3

The Movie Controller for QuickTime Movies

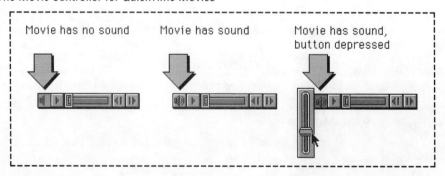

FIGURE 2.4

The Speaker Button of a Movie Controller

Using the MovieViewer Program

When installed in the System folder of your Macintosh, the QuickTime extension gives your Mac the ability to play movies. But as a system software extention, QuickTime runs things from behind the scenes. To play a movie, you need an interface to QuickTime. For that, you'll use a movie-playing utility. If you haven't bought one, don't worry. MovieViewer is included on the disk.

Besides the Apple menu, MovieViewer has three menus in its menu bar. The items in each are shown in Figure 2.5.

File		**Edit**		**Movie**
Open...	⌘O	Undo	⌘Z	Loop
Close	⌘W			
		Cut	⌘X	Half Size
Save	⌘S	Copy	⌘C	Normal Size
		Paste	⌘V	Double Size
Quit	⌘Q	Clear		

FIGURE 2.5
The Menus of MovieViewer

The File menu allows you to open, close, and save a movie. After selecting **Open**, you'll see a dialog box like the one shown in Figure 2.6. It lists QuickTime movies and folders.

At the bottom of the dialog box is a check box titled Show Preview. Clicking in this box expands the dialog box. If you click once on the name of a movie file, the expanded portion of the dialog box displays, as a preview, a single picture from the movie. Figure 2.7 shows an expanded dialog box.

After clicking once on the movie you'd like to view, click the **Open** button. The movie will open, complete with a movie controller. To run the movie, click the **Play** button of the controller. Figure 2.8 shows the sample movie included with this book.

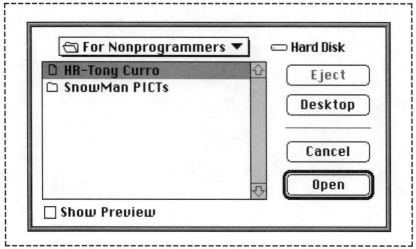

FIGURE 2.6
MovieViewer's Open Dialog Box

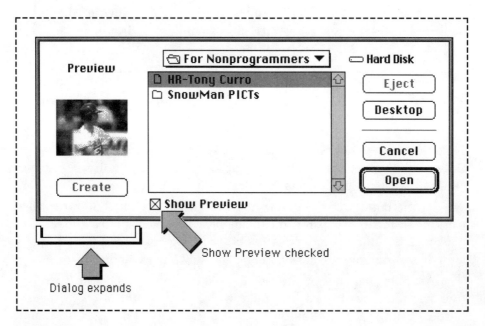

FIGURE 2.7
The Expanded Open Dialog Box

FIGURE 2.8

A Sample Movie Viewed in MovieViewer

MovieViewer allows you to resize a movie to half or double its normal size. Its normal size is the size it was recorded at, and the size it initially opens to. Figure 2.9 shows the sample movie at half size. Note that if a half-sized movie gets small enough, one or more buttons will be lost. But they'll return when the movie is reset to its normal size.

FIGURE 2.9

A Sample Movie Viewed at Half Size

When the size of a movie doubles, image quality is reduced—Figure 2.10 shows the graininess that occurs when a movie is enlarged. The playing speed of an enlarged movie will also be affected, because it takes the Mac longer to calculate and display the larger images.

FIGURE 2.10
A Sample Movie Viewed at Double Size

The Loop item in the Movie menu lets you set a movie to loop. When set to loop, and the **Play** button is clicked on, the movie will play repeatedly until you click the mouse. Select **Loop** again to return the movie to its normal playing mode.

MovieViewer allows you to use standard editing commands to edit a movie. You can use the commands in the Edit menu to copy, cut, or paste frames of a movie. The editing commands perform their action on the *current selection* of a movie. By holding down the **Shift** key, and then moving the slider or clicking on a **Step** button, you select a portion of a movie. The portion will appear black in the slide bar, as shown in Figure 2.11.

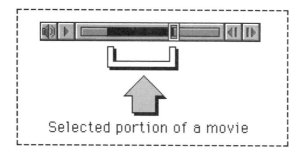

Selected portion of a movie

FIGURE 2.11
Selecting Part of a Movie

When you cut or copy a movie selection, that portion of the movie will be placed on the Clipboard. You can paste it back into the movie, or you can open the Scrapbook and paste it there. Once in the Scrapbook, you can copy and paste it into other movies at any time.

If you make editing changes to a movie, and you want to save those changes, select **Save** from the File menu. Note that this isn't a **Save As** command—the changed movie will replace the original one.

Using Apple's Movie Player

Movie Player is a movie-playing utility that is available as part of Apple's QuickTime Starter Kit. It works much as the MovieViewer utility does—so much, in fact, that we'll just cover a couple of the features found in Movie Player, but not in MovieViewer.

When you select **Open** from the File menu, you'll see the same dialog box that you saw in MovieViewer. If you click the **Show Preview** check box, you'll see the preview for a selected movie. A preview is a single picture, or frame, of a movie. This one frame of the movie is called its *poster frame.* Figure 2.12 shows where the poster frame is displayed.

When a movie is created, the first frame in it is used as the poster. Movie Player lets you change the poster of a movie by selecting **Set Poster Frame** from the Movie menu. First, open the movie. Then click either **Step** button until you get to the movie frame that is to be the new poster. Then select **Set Poster Frame**. Before closing the movie, select **Save** from the File menu to save the change. From now on, this new frame will be used as the movie's poster frame.

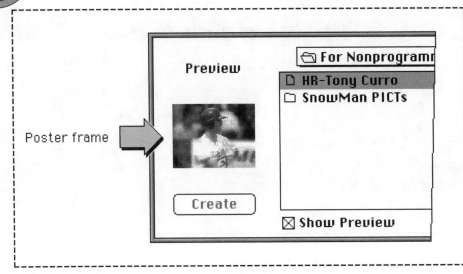

FIGURE 2.12
A Movie's Poster Frame is Displayed in the Open Dialog Box

Movie Player allows you to edit a movie using the standard editing commands. If you want to save the changed movie as a new movie, while retain-
ing the original movie, select **Save As** from the File menu. When you do,
you'll see a dialog box like that shown in Figure 2.13. A pair of radio buttons
in the Save As dialog box gives you two ways to save a movie.

If you save the movie *normally*, the saved movie contains only the
changes from the original. Because a movie file saved in this manner only
contains information about the differences between the movie and the original on which it is based, it is much smaller than the original. When played,
the saved movie will run just as any other movie would. That's because
Movie Player will be using both the new movie and the original when it
plays back the new movie. Therein lies the drawback to saving a movie in
the normal manner—the original movie *must* be present on disk for the new
movie to run.

If you're going to be copying the new version of a movie to another
disk, either to store or give to someone else, save the movie as a *self-contained movie*. Using this method, the entire movie is saved, not just the
changes. A self-contained movie doesn't need any information from the original movie.

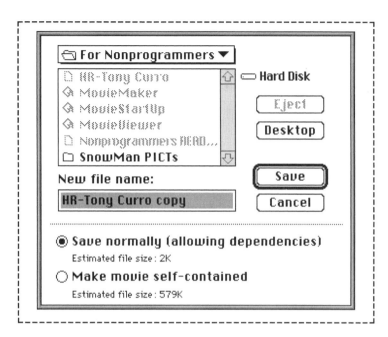

FIGURE 2.13
Movie Player's Save As Dialog Box

Playing a Startup Movie

We've covered movie-playing utilities—the standard means of playing movies. Now, we'll look at a more obscure method.

When you start up your Mac, extensions are loaded and you're greeted by the message "Welcome to Macintosh." With QuickTime, you can add to this introduction by having your computer automatically play a movie.

If you have Apple's Movie Player program, simply select any movie and name it Startup Movie. Place the movie in the Startup Items folder found in the System folder. Now, every time you restart your Mac, that movie will be played.

The above method of playing a startup movie requires that you have Movie Player. If you don't, the movie titled Startup Movie will not be played. For readers who don't have Apple's program, we've included a very small program that allows you to play a startup movie. The program is called MovieStartUp, and can be found in the For Nonprogrammers folder of the included disk. Here are the steps to set up your Mac to play a startup movie:

1. Move the MovieStartUp program into the Startup Items folder in the System folder.

2. Create a new empty folder in the Startup Items folder (select **New Folder** from the File menu).

3. Name the new folder MovieStartUp Folder (use upper and lower-case, as shown).

4. Move the movie you want to play at startup into this MovieStartUp Folder. Any movie will work.

5. Rename the movie MovieStartUp.Movie. Again, use upper and lowercase.

Figure 2.14 shows what your folders should look like. Now, restart your Macintosh. As your Mac finishes booting up, the startup movie opens, centered on an all-gray Desktop. The movie will play once, and your Desktop will then appear as it normally does.

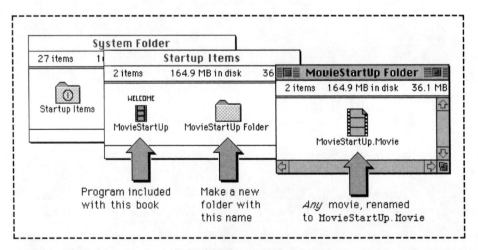

FIGURE 2.14
Folder Setup for Playing a Startup Movie Using MovieStartUp

Any time you want a new movie to be used as the startup movie, just move the old startup movie out of the MovieStartUp Folder. Copy or move a new movie into the MovieStartUp Folder and rename it MovieStartUp.Movie. From then on, that movie will play at startup. If you want to discontinue using MovieStartUp, move the MovieStartUp program out of the Startup Items folder.

Making Movies

You can use two basic techniques to make a QuickTime movie. *Animation* involves stringing together a series of computer drawings, each one a little different than the previous one, to give the illusion of movement. Imagine that the four figures in Figure 2.15 were displayed one after another, very quickly. The elephant's ears and trunk would move down, and his eyes would shut. That's animation.

FIGURE 2.15
Animation is the Displaying of Pictures in Sequence

The second method of creating a movie is by *digitizing* video. Digitizing takes the output of a video source, such as the tape from a camcorder or VCR, and transforms it into something recognizable by your Macintosh. A QuickTime movie made in this way looks like the source it came from—a video tape. Figure 2.16 shows one such frame from a QuickTime movie.

In this chapter we'll look at animation. In Chapter 4 we'll take an in-depth look at creating movies from video sources.

Creating PICT Files

Creating a digitized movie requires special digitizing hardware. Movies made from video also require additional software that may or may not come with the digitizing hardware you purchase. An animated movie, on the other hand, requires no extra hardware, and, most likely, you have the necessary software. Almost any Macintosh draw or paint program can create the animated graphics, and you'll need a program that converts these graphics into the QuickTime movie. If you have a program like MacDraw, MacPaint, or Canvas, you have the graphics software. We've included the other program you need—MovieMaker converts graphics files into a movie.

FIGURE 2.16

Digitizing Video Creates a Movie from Video Output

In this section we'll explain how to make a sequence of drawings and how to save each as a PICT or PICT2 file. A PICT file contains a black-and-white picture, while a PICT2 file holds a color picture.

For our example we'll use Claris Corp.'s popular MacDraw Pro program. The techniques used to create a PICT or a PICT2 with MacDraw are similar to those used with most other draw or paint programs.

Start by running MacDraw. In the window that opens, draw a rectangle the size of the picture you'll want to create. Figure 2.17 illustrates an example. This will serve as a border that forces you to draw each picture in the sequence the same size. If they aren't the same size, and you string them together into one QuickTime movie, each frame of the movie will appear to be in a different scale. You'll see the full importance of this in the next section when you actually create the movie.

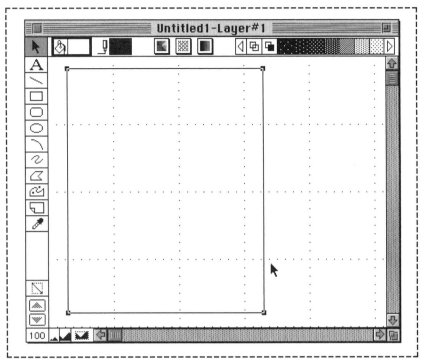

FIGURE 2.17
Creating a Boundary Rectangle for the Picture

With your final picture in mind, draw one part of it. For this example we're going to draw a simple snowman. For the first drawing we drew the base of the snowman. To turn the background rectangle and the snowman's base circle into one object, we **Shift**-clicked on each. Then we chose the **Group** option from the Arrange menu. Figure 2.18 shows what the first picture might look like.

The program you'll use to make QuickTime movies recognizes both PICT and PICT2 formats. The PICT format is for black-and-white drawings. The PICT2 format can store either color or black-and-white drawings. If your drawing is black-and-white use the PICT format—the resulting file will be smaller than if you use the PICT2 format. Since this example contains no color, use the PICT type. To do this, choose **Save As...** from the File menu. When you do, you'll see a dialog box like that shown in Figure 2.19.

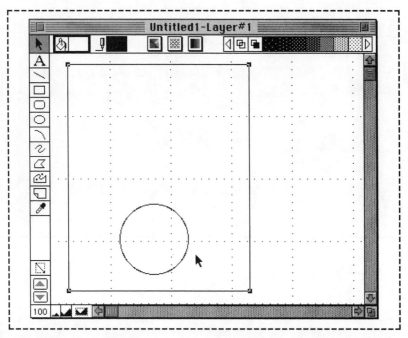

FIGURE 2.18
The First of Several Pictures

FIGURE 2.19
The "Save As" Dialog Box in MacDraw Pro

In a *draw* program, like MacDraw, you draw by creating objects. In a *paint* program, such as PixelPaint, you turn on individual bits to create a picture. If you're more comfortable using a paint program you can create a picture in your favorite paint program, select the area you want as your picture, and paste it into the Scrapbook. Then run a draw program, copy the picture from the Scrapbook, and paste it in a window of the draw program. Next, use the draw program's **Save As...** command to save it as a PICT or PICT2 file.

If your paint program is capable of saving to a PICT format, why can't you just save the picture in your paint program? You can, but more than likely it saves the entire page as a PICT, including all of the white page you didn't draw to. When you paste your drawing to a draw program, it turns the pasted section into an object that it will save independently of the rest of the blank page.

Each picture in the series will have a name. The first part of the name will be the same, and the end of the name will be a two-digit number, such as 01. Give this first picture the name of SnowMan01. Except for the end number, the name of each picture in the sequence *must* be the same. Otherwise, when it comes time to turn the pictures into a movie, not all the pictures will be included in the movie.

The name of each picture in the sequence *must* be the same. And each picture must end with a number. Follow closely the file-naming convention just described.

And now, another important step. The drawing program you use will save drawings in a format it recognizes—not as a PICT file. But in almost every drawing program you can override the program's desire to use its own special formatting. In MacDraw Pro, click on the pop-up menu in the Save As dialog box to see the different formats available. Fortunately, the PICT format is in the list, and so is the PICT2 format, should you want to use color in future movies. Figure 2.20 shows this pop-up menu. In Figure 2.20 the format is being changed from the default MacDraw Pro format, which is checked, to the PICT format.

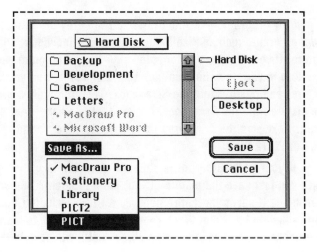

FIGURE 2.20
Saving a Picture in PICT Format

Select the **PICT** format, then click the **Save** button. Congratulations—you've just created a PICT file.

Now, create a second file in the same manner as the first. Simply add a little more of the snowman to the first file—the one you currently have on the screen. Then save it as SnowMan02. Remember to choose **Save As...** from the File menu, not Save. When you do, note that the file type pop-up has reverted back to the MacDraw Pro type. It's important that you change it to the PICT type *every* time you save a file.

 Any drawings that don't have a file type format of PICT will not be found by the program that makes the movie from the pictures. This gap in the sequence will cause an error, and a movie won't be made.

We've created a series of six PICTs in the exact same manner as the first two. Figure 2.21 shows them, reduced to fit on a page of this book, of course. We've included these six files on the disk. They're in the SnowMan PICTs folder in the For Nonprogrammers folder. If you'd like to see what one of them looks like, run your draw program. Select **Open** from the File menu. Make sure you select the **PICT** format, or the file names might not be displayed in the list of files.

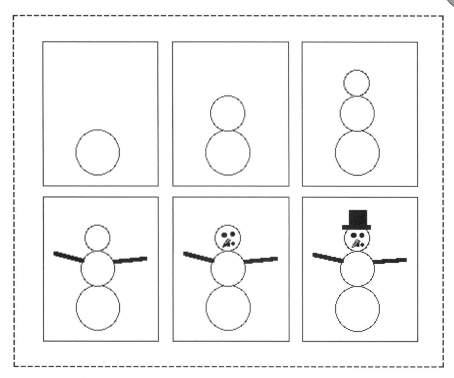

FIGURE 2.21

Six Pictures, Ready to Be Made into a Movie

Figure 2.21 should make one thing clear to you. No, not that we are professional graphic artists! Rather, that if these six figures were to be displayed, one after another, it would give the appearance of a snowman being built. In the next section you'll create a QuickTime movie that does exactly that.

It's important that each picture in your series of pictures have the same background. Our snowman pictures all have a plain white background. For a richer effect, create one picture for the background, and make multiple copies of it. Then overlay a foreground figure on top of one copy of the background. Save it as a PICT file. Then repeat the process. This time, place the foreground figure in a slightly different position over a copy of the background. Figure 2.22 gives an example. By placing the man in different positions over the cityscape background, a series of pictures would create the effect of the cartoon man walking through the city.

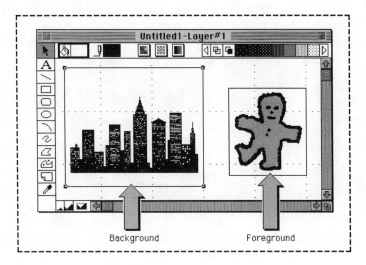

FIGURE 2.22
Background and Foreground Figures

PICTs to Movie: Using MovieMaker

To turn a sequence of PICT files into a movie, you need a picture converter program. The MovieMaker program does just that. Apple sells a program that does just what MovieMaker does, and a little more. It's called Movie Converter. We describe its use in the next section. If you don't want to spend the money for it, try using the MovieMaker program included with this book. Like the MovieViewer program that came on the disk, MovieMaker has one advantage over Apple's comparable product—it's free!

When you run MovieMaker, you'll see a dialog box like the one shown in Figure 2.23. Move to the folder that contains the pictures to be made into a movie. Click once on any of the picture files, and then click the **Open** button.

Once you select one file, MovieMaker will look for all PICT files with the same base name (SnowMan in our example). It then strings each of these files together, starting with the file that has a name ending in 01, such as SnowMan01. Now you can see why you named all your PICT files in this manner.

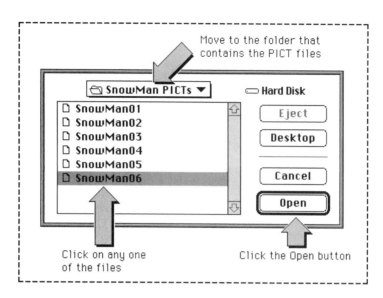

FIGURE 2.23
Telling MovieMaker Which Files to Use

Next, MovieMaker displays the dialog box shown in Figure 2.24. Enter the number of PICT files that are in the sequence. For our snowman example, there are six picture files: SnowMan01 through SnowMan06. Click the OK button.

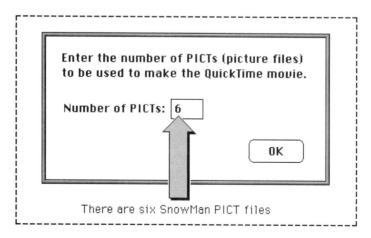

FIGURE 2.24
Telling MovieMaker How Many PICTs to Use

Finally, MovieMaker gives you the opportunity to name the movie. The dialog box that lets you do this appears in Figure 2.25. If you don't type in a name, MovieMaker will simply call the movie Movie File. Type in a more appropriate name, then click on the **Save** button.

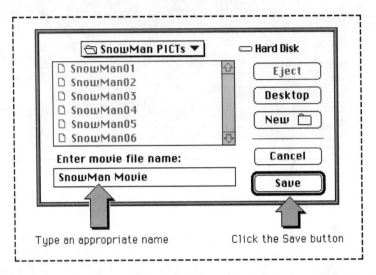

FIGURE 2.25
Naming the Movie

After you click the **Save** button, MovieMaker will take a few seconds to convert the selected PICT files into a QuickTime movie. The program then quits. Run MovieViewer, or any other movie-playing program, to view the new movie. We ran MovieViewer, selected **Open** from the File menu, and opened the SnowMan Movie that MovieMaker had created and placed in the SnowMan PICTs folder. The result is shown in Figure 2.26.

Image Compression

In Chapter 1 we mentioned image compression, the technology that greatly reduces the amount of disk space a graphic image occupies. In this chapter you've seen that QuickTime movies consist of a series of graphic images. Our snowman demonstration used just six images, but longer movies can use hundreds of them.

FIGURE 2.26
The New Movie Running in MovieViewer

Image compression is a complex science because of the short time frame in which compression must take place. Images are compressed as they are recorded to a movie, and then decompressed each time the resulting movie is played. A common *frame rate*—the rate at which frames are recorded or displayed—is 30 frames per second. At this rate, each frame, or image, must be compressed or decompressed in 1/30th of a second. Achieving this sophisticated level of compression on a home computer did not come quickly or easily. That's why software like QuickTime is a recent development.

Apple's Movie Converter

Some QuickTime programs allow you to open a *standard compressor dialog box*. This dialog box allows you to adjust compression settings to change the way a movie is stored and played back. It's called a "standard" dialog box

---

because Apple has made the way it looks, and the settings in it, easy to duplicate. Accordingly, many programs use the very same dialog box.

Apple's Movie Converter utility uses the standard compressor dialog box. This program, available in Apple's QuickTime Starter Kit, allows you to make a movie from a series of PICT files, just as the MovieMaker utility included with this book does. Unlike MovieMaker, the Movie Converter program also lets you change some of the compression settings. In this section we'll quickly step through the process of making a movie with Movie Converter—it's similar to making one using MovieMaker. In the next section we'll discuss using the standard compressor dialog box available in Movie Converter.

After running Movie Converter, select **Open** from the File menu. A dialog box will display a list of files. As you did in MovieMaker, click on any **PICT** file in a sequence of files, then click on the **Open** button. Movie Converter also lets you create a movie from a PICS file. The PICS file format is used by many animation programs. Figure 2.27 shows how you can display different file formats in the file list of the Open dialog box.

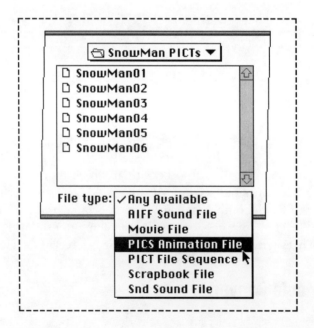

FIGURE 2.27
Listing Different File Types in Movie Converter

After clicking on a file name, and then the **Open** button, you'll see a movie conversion window like that shown in Figure 2.28. We'll again use our snowman sequence of PICT files for an example. Movie Converter tells you how many PICT files it will be using. You can preview the contents of any or all of the files by using the scroll bar found at the bottom of the window.

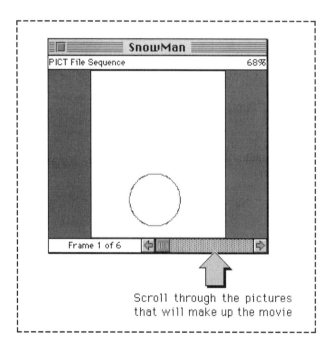

FIGURE 2.28
Movie Converter's Conversion Window

When you're ready to make a movie, select **Convert** from the Conversions menu. You'll see a dialog box just like the one used by MovieMaker (shown back in Figure 2.25). It lets you give the movie file a name. Type in a name, then click on the **Save** button. Movie Converter will let you see the progress of the conversion in a dialog box like that shown in Figure 2.29.

When the conversion is complete, a window displaying the first frame of the movie will open, just as it did when you made a movie using MovieMaker.

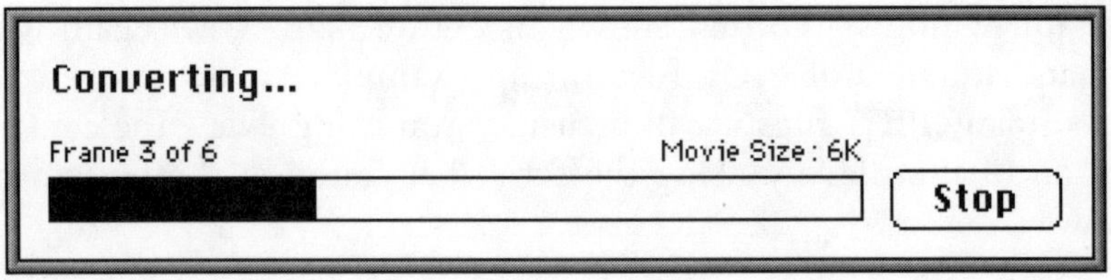

```
Converting...

Frame 3 of 6                              Movie Size : 6K

[█████████████          ]              [ Stop ]
```

FIGURE 2.29
The Conversion Progress Indicator

Using Standard Compression Settings

If you aren't pleased with the movie that Movie Converter creates, you might want to change one or more of the compression settings. Selecting **Compression Settings** from the Conversion menu displays the standard compressor dialog box mentioned a few pages back. It's shown in Figure 2.30.

In the next several sections we discuss the various settings found in the standard compressor dialog box. One thing is common to all settings: Once you make a change, you must again select **Convert** from the Conversion menu to recreate the movie. Compression changes have no effect on movies already displayed on the screen—they only affect movies you make after the compression setting change.

Before discussing compression settings, we'll comment on one subtle but important point. Any time you select the **Convert** menu option, the movie made is created from the contents of the *active* window. For your first movie, that means the movie will be made from the conversion window that allows you to preview the pictures used for the movie. But after you've created a movie, you'll have two windows on the screen: the conversion window and the new movie window. This situation is shown in Figure 2.31. You should now activate the proper window before selecting **Convert**.

If the first movie is based on the pictures in the conversion window, why does it matter which window is used to make subsequent movies? Movie Converter allows you to edit a movie. If you cut or paste frames in the new movie, then leave it as the active window, the next movie will be based on the new set of pictures in the movie, not on the original set shown in the conversion window.

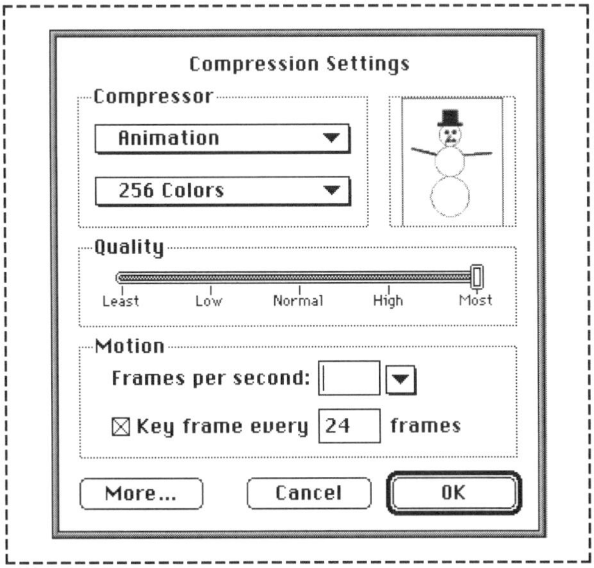

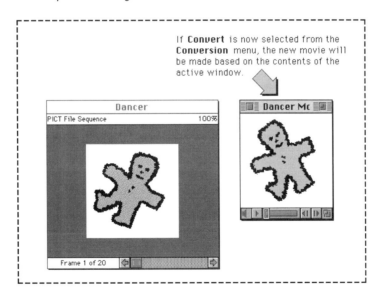

FIGURE 2.30

The Standard Compressor Dialog Box

FIGURE 2.31

New Movies Are Always Based on the Active Window

Compressor and Quality Settings

Image compression is achieved through the use of one of several *image compressors*. An image compressor is a program that performs the compression. When you add QuickTime to your system, you get a half dozen compressors—they're internal to QuickTime. Programs such as Movie Converter choose the proper compressor based on features of the images to be compressed. One such feature is the level of color in an image.

For the conversion of PICT files to a movie, Movie Converter will select the Animation compressor. When it does, it will set the quality-level to Most, as shown on the slider scale in Figure 2.32. Different compressors may move the quality-level slider. That's because the more compression that's applied, the lower the quality—some information gets lost during compression.

For any set of files or movie, Movie Converter estimates the best compression method and chooses the appropriate compressor. You should seldom need to override Movie Converter's selection.

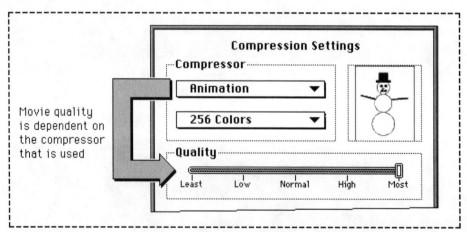

FIGURE 2.32

Movie Quality is Dependent on the Compressor Used

Color Settings

The standard compressor dialog box lets you choose how many colors should be used in the movie. Figure 2.33 shows the pop-up menu that lets you make changes. As always, changes affect only subsequent movies you make, not ones currently on the screen. If you use fewer colors than are present in the PICT files, you'll notice a loss of quality.

One instance where you might change the color level is if you are converting color PICTs to a movie that you know will only be run on a grayscale monitor. You can set the color level to a level of gray, then select **Convert** to make a movie. Since grayscale images hold less information about each pixel than color images, the resulting grayscale movie will be smaller than a color movie made from the same PICT files.

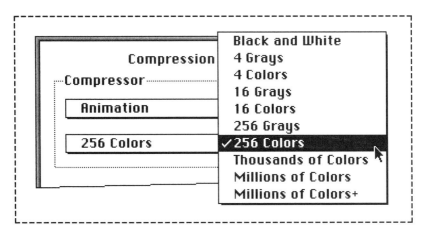

FIGURE 2.33
Choosing the Number of Colors to Use in the Movie

Motion Settings

If your converted movie runs too fast or too slowly, you can change the frame rate and then recreate the movie. The Compression Settings dialog box has an edit text box labeled Frames per second. You can type in a number, or select one from the pop-up menu. Figure 2.34 shows this part of the Compression Settings dialog box.

When making a movie from a set of PICT files, the frames-per-second figure influences the length of the movie. For our six-frame snowman movie, a frames-per-second rate of six will result in a movie that lasts one second. A frames-per-second setting of 12 will result in a movie that is just half a second long. Each time you change the frames-per-second rate, you'll have to again select **Convert** from the Conversion menu to create a new movie.

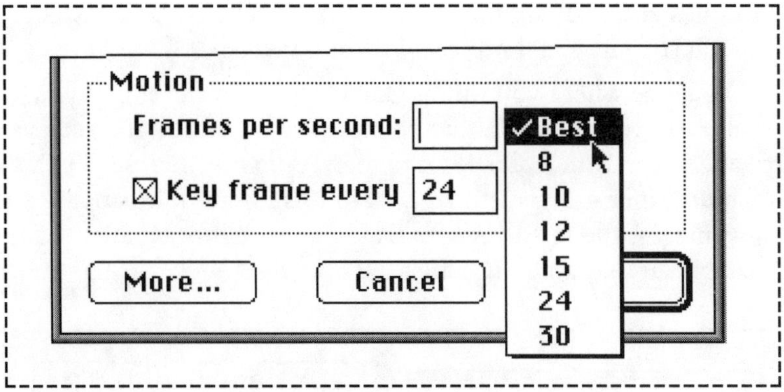

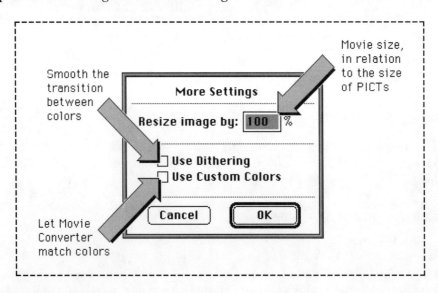

FIGURE 2.34
Selecting the Movie Frames-Per-Second Rate

Additional Settings

If you click the **More** button in the Compression Settings dialog box, you'll see a second, smaller dialog box that provides a few more conversion options. That dialog box is shown in Figure 2.35.

FIGURE 2.35
The More Settings Dialog Box

Normally, when a movie is made from PICT files, each frame of the movie will be the same size as the image in the first PICT file in the sequence. You can scale the movie to a different size by entering a new percentage in the edit text box of the More Settings dialog box. We resized the snowman image to 50 percent and then again selected **Convert** from the Conversion menu. This created a second snowman movie. Figure 2.36 shows both movies.

FIGURE 2.36

Two Different-sized Movies Made from the Same PICT Files

If you are creating a movie using fewer colors than found in the original PICT file, you can use *dithering*. Dithering involves attempting to match original colors by adding patterns to the pixels, rather than using solid colors. A movie created using dithering will be closer in look to the original than one created without dithering. There is a trade-off though—the dithered movie will occupy more disk space.

Many Macintoshes are capable of displaying millions of different colors, but not at the same time. When you create a color picture, you choose from *palettes* of colors. A palette holds a set of colors. If you don't specify a particular palette in your drawing program, that program will use the System palette—a default set of 256 colors. Like drawing programs, Movie Converter uses the System palette, unless you check **Use Custom Colors** in the More Settings dialog box. In that case, Movie Converter will make up a custom palette of colors that best match those in the original pictures used to make the movie.

 For the best color match, why wouldn't you always select **Use Custom Colors?** When a movie made in this manner is played back, QuickTime will switch from the System palette to this custom palette. If other windows are being displayed, the graphics in them will be affected by the palette change. Whether that is bothersome is up to you.

Chapter Summary

QuickTime gives your Mac the ability to work with movies, but you also need movie-playing software to control the playing and editing of movies. Apple's Movie Player is one such software utility. For readers without Movie Player, the MovieViewer program included with this book allows you to play and edit any QuickTime movie.

You can set your Mac to play a movie every time it's turned on. If you have Movie Player, you can name any movie Startup Movie and place it in your System folder. If you don't have Movie Player, the small utility we've given you called MovieStartUp allows you to have a movie of your choice play automatically upon startup.

An easy way to make a movie of your own is to draw a sequence of pictures using a Macintosh drawing program. If each picture is saved as an individual PICT file, a movie-converting utility can be run to string these files into one QuickTime movie. Apple's Movie Converter does that. If you don't have Movie Converter, you can use MovieMaker to turn pictures into QuickTime movies.

Using Movies

n the previous chapter we discussed making movies. But after you've played a movie a few times, what else can you *do* with a movie? In this chapter we look at several ways you can make practical use of movies—and a couple of not-so-practical ways too!

Many programs now allow you to paste movies right into the documents they generate—just as easily as you paste in text or a picture. Word processors, graphics programs, and many other applications support movies. Presentation software (programs that produce on-screen "slide shows") is a practical vehicle for showing off movies. In this chapter we discuss the generalities of using movies in all of these types of programs, and the specifics of using movies in some of the more popular applications on the market. For owners of older versions of programs—applications that weren't designed to support movies—we discuss a handy utility that lets almost any program add working movies to its documents.

We end the chapter with a look at a couple of programs designed just for QuickTime movies. Morphing is the eye-catching special effect of transforming one image into another. There's a new product on the market that allows Mac owners to easily make QuickTime movies that include this exciting technology. To run QuickTime movies normally requires a movie player. But one utility allows you to make any movie self-contained—playable *without* a movie player. In this chapter we cover both these interesting products.

45

Including Movies in Documents

With the release of QuickTime, many software vendors added movie-handling features to their products. In this section we'll cover several of the more popular programs that now give you the power to incorporate QuickTime movies in their documents.

When you include a movie in a document, regardless of the program you're using, keep one fact in mind. The movie itself does not actually become part of the document, as text and pictures do. Instead, a single frame—a *poster*—of the movie appears in the document. A movie in a document has a *badge* in its lower left corner; you click on the badge to open a standard movie controller for the movie. When you play a movie from within a document, the program will search your hard disk for the movie itself. Figure 3.1 illustrates how a Microsoft Word document follows this procedure.

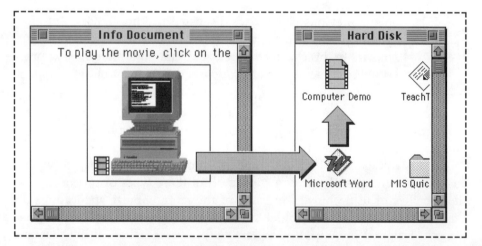

FIGURE 3.1

Movies in Documents Rely on the Original Movie on Disk

After the program finds the movie file, it will use information from within it to display a movie controller and play the movie, as shown in Figure 3.2. This process is transparent to the user who is reading the document and playing the movie.

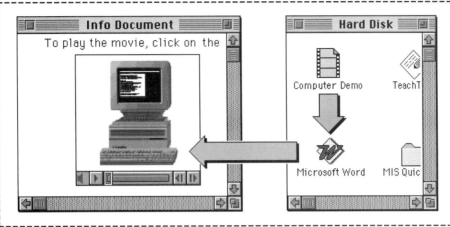

FIGURE 3.2
The Movie on Disk Provides Information Used by the Document

If the events behind the playing of a movie are invisible to the user, why do we bother to mention them? For one very important reason: If you transfer a document that includes QuickTime movies in it, you *must* also transfer the movie itself. You must copy not only the document to a floppy disk, but also the movie or movies.

Movies in Microsoft Word

Microsoft Word 5.1, the latest version of this word processor, has a movie-insertion feature built into it. You can directly paste a movie from the clip-board to a document, or you can select **Movie** from the Insert menu. Using the second method, you'll see a dialog box that lets you select any movie you have. After you select a movie, it will appear in its own window, complete with movie controller. When you close the window, the movie will appear in the document. To play the movie, anyone reading the document merely double-clicks on the movie's badge, and a movie controller appears.

If you click once on a movie that's in a Microsoft Word document, a new item will be added to the Edit menu: **Edit Movie**. Selecting this option opens a dialog box that lets you control the behavior of the movie. Figure 3.3 shows this dialog box.

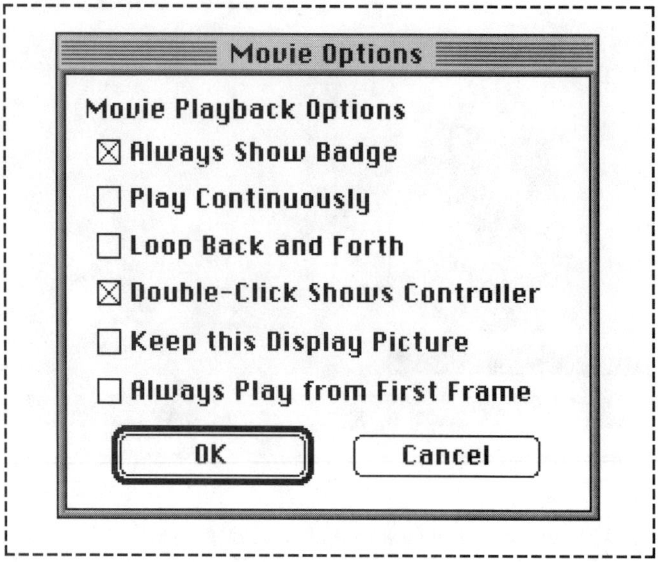

Movie Options

Movie Playback Options

☒ Always Show Badge

☐ Play Continuously

☐ Loop Back and Forth

☒ Double-Click Shows Controller

☐ Keep this Display Picture

☐ Always Play from First Frame

[OK]   [Cancel]

FIGURE 3.3

The Movie Options Dialog Box Sets Movie Playing Options

If you have version 5.0 of Microsoft Word, you too can paste QuickTime movies into documents. It will take a one-time effort to make this possible, though. To add movie-handling capabilities to your version of Microsoft Word—which doesn't normally accommodate movies—you'll need Microsoft's Movie PIM. A *PIM*, or plug-in-module, is Microsoft's method of providing users of its programs with intermediate updates. A PIM is added to the Commands folder of the Microsoft product it was made for. The PIM adds functionality without forcing you to replace the entire program. Besides the QuickTime Movie PIM, there are also Spell Checker, Equation Editor, and other function-adding PIMs.

Microsoft posts PIMs on information services such as CompuServe and America Online—they're free for the downloading. Once you have the Movie PIM, simply place it in the Word Commands folder. Figure 3.4 shows a few of the PIMs, including the Movie PIM, in the Word Commands folder. Then restart your Macintosh. After that, your version 5.0 of Microsoft Word will handle movies just like version 5.1.

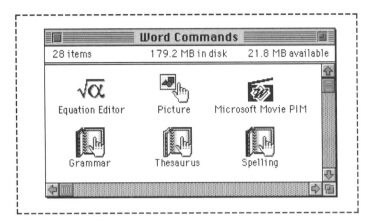

FIGURE 3.4
Some of the Plug-in-Modules Used by Microsoft Word

Movies in ClarisWorks

Several graphics programs and presentation software packages now support QuickTime movies. We'll discuss both types of programs here as we cover ClarisWorks. This popular and inexpensive integrated package allows you to select the environment you want for a document. Figure 3.5 shows the New Document dialog box that appears when you select **New** from the File menu.

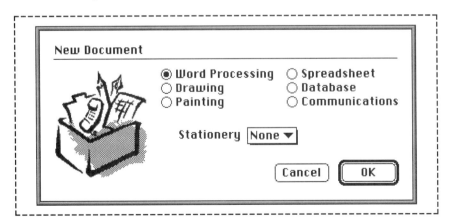

FIGURE 3.5
The New Document Dialog Box in ClarisWorks

Adding a Border to a Movie

You can use the Drawing portion of ClarisWorks to add a border to a movie—as plain or as fancy as you want. When viewed from within ClarisWorks, the movie can be played by clicking on its badge. When printed, the badge will be omitted from the hardcopy.

To add a border to a movie, first select **New** from the File menu. Click on the **Drawing** radio button to open a new Drawing document. Now, create two rectangular objects, one white, one with a gradient fill. Figure 3.6 shows the rectangle tool used to draw each object, and the tool used to change the fill effect of whatever object is selected.

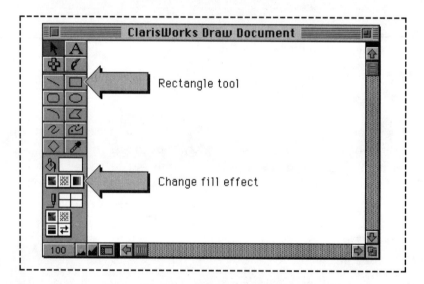

FIGURE 3.6

The Rectangle Tool and Gradient Fill Tool in ClarisWorks

Next, paste a QuickTime movie into the document. Figure 3.7 shows the three objects. Note that the QuickTime movie, which is selected, has a badge in the lower-left corner.

In Figure 3.8 we've moved the three objects on top of one another. Even though the QuickTime movie is seated on top of other objects, clicking on its badge will still open a movie controller that allows anyone viewing the document to play the movie.

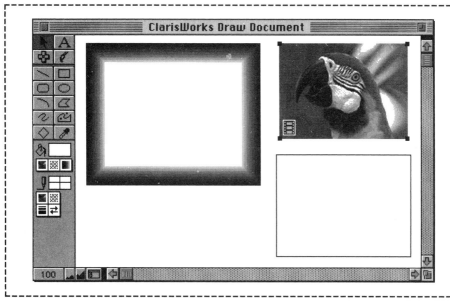

FIGURE 3.7
Creating a Frame for a Movie

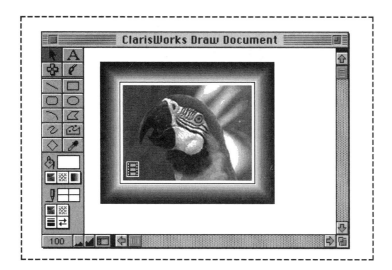

FIGURE 3.8
A Framed Movie

To move several objects at one time, you can **Shift**-click on each, and select **Group** from the Arrange menu. In the above example, that results in the two drawn objects and the movie being grouped together into one object. You can then move, or copy and paste, all the objects together. After you've positioned them in their final location, however, you must click on the object and then select **Ungroup** from the Arrange menu. Why? Once a movie is grouped with other objects, it won't be recognized as a movie. Clicking on the badge will have no effect.

Using the above method you can even group together two or more movies, as shown in Figure 3.9. Clicking on the badge of either one displays a movie controller for that movie.

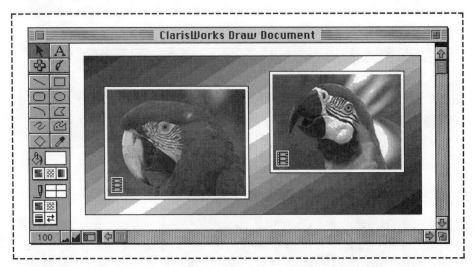

FIGURE 3.9
Framing Two Movies

Adding Movies to Slide Shows

One interesting and easy-to-use feature of ClarisWorks is its ability to transform documents into presentations—on-screen slide show presentations. Starting with ClarisWorks 2.0, you can easily include QuickTime movies in presentations. While the incorporation of movies in some types of documents may seem frivolous, movies are a very practical means of spicing up a presentation. Movement catches a person's attention. And if the movie fits well into the topic of the presentation, it can also hold the attention of the audience well beyond the end of the movie.

You can create a ClarisWorks Drawing document that consists of a number of pages, then display those pages one after the other to form a presentation. To give your presentation a professional look, ClarisWorks provides a simple method for creating a common background for each page. When you're ready to run the slide show, the program will run it with a single click of the mouse button, displaying each page in turn, and providing a fade out and fade in between each page.

In the next few pages we'll describe how to make a simple presentation that includes a QuickTime movie. As we do so, we'll make use of just three ClarisWorks menu items (highlighted in Figure 3.10).

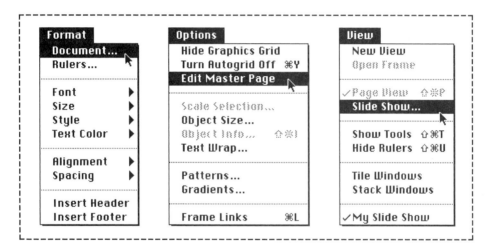

FIGURE 3.10
The Menu Items used to Create a ClarisWorks Slide Show

ClarisWorks allows your Drawing document to span more than one page. For a slide show presentation, each page of the document will be considered a slide. To specify the number of pages, or slides, you'll use, select **Document** from the Format menu. You'll encounter a dialog box like the one shown in Figure 3.11. Type in the number of slides you'll be making. You won't be interested in printing the document—the slide show is going to take place right on your monitor. Set all the margins to zero to eliminate any white space around the edges of the slides. Click the **OK** button to dismiss the dialog box.

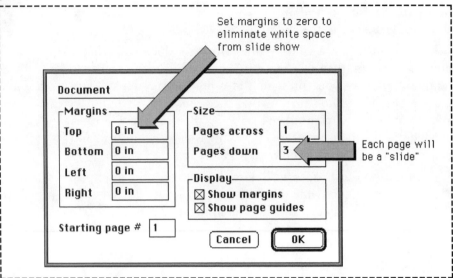

FIGURE 3.11

Establishing the Number of Slides for the Slide Show

ClarisWorks 2.0 lets you design a Master Page that will serve as the background for each slide. You create the page just once, and it will be used as the backdrop for every slide you make thereafter. A company logo is one suggestion for the Master Page. Or you can just create a shaded rectangle that covers the entire page. Figure 3.12 shows a Master Page being created—this one is simply a full-page rectangle filled with a gradient fill effect. The figure shows the gradient palette.

After the Master Page is completed, deselect the **Edit Master Page** menu choice. Instead of a blank white background, each page you draw to will have the Master Page background pattern. In Figure 3.13 we created a slide by adding a little text to a page and then inserting a QuickTime movie.

Figure 3.14 shows a different Master Page, and three slides created using it. We created a page-sized rectangle and filled it with solid black. We then added a white diamond to it. Then we deselected **Edit Master Page** from the Options menu. Now, every page, or slide, that we create will have this background. After completing a page, scroll down to the next page. It will be blank except for the Master Page background. Figure 3.14 shows a reduced view of the Master Page and the pages we created for our demonstration presentation.

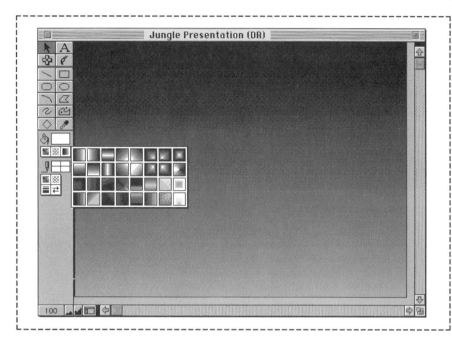

FIGURE 3.12
A Master Page for a Slide Show

FIGURE 3.13
Creating a Slide with the Master Page Background

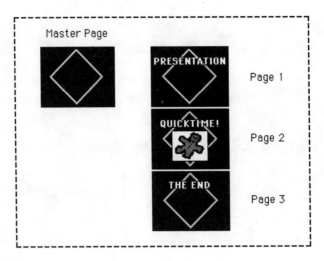

FIGURE 3.14

The Master Page is Used as the Background for All Slides

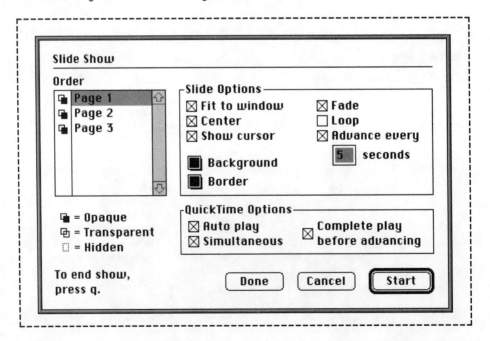

FIGURE 3.15

The Slide Show Settings Dialog Box

With your pages completed, select the **Slide Show** option from the View menu. You'll encounter a Slide Show dialog box like the one shown in Figure 3.15.

Figure 3.16 shows the part of the Slide Show dialog box that pertains to QuickTime movies. If you check the **Auto play** check box, movies will automatically play as a slide is displayed. Otherwise, the viewer will have to click on the movie. If you're using Auto play, and any slide contains more than one movie, check the **Simultaneous** check box. That causes all movies on a page to play simultaneously.

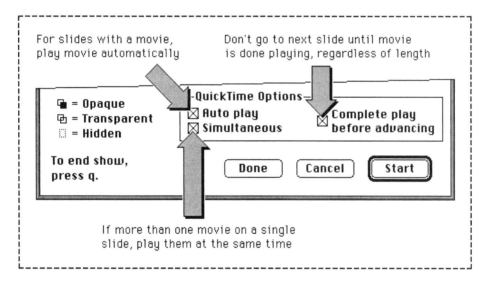

FIGURE 3.16
Slide Show Settings that Pertain to QuickTime Movies

When done with the slide show settings, click the **Start** button to start the slide show. Your monitor will slowly dim until the screen is black. Then there will be a fade-in to the first slide. The first slide is the first page in your Drawing document. After a period set by you in the Slide Show dialog box, the first slide will dim and the next will appear. As shown in Figure 3.17, this process will appear until each slide in the series has been shown.

Slide shows in ClarisWorks are easy to create and dramatic to view. Multimedia presentation software is one of the most intuitive vehicles for QuickTime movies, which are themselves products of the multimedia revolution.

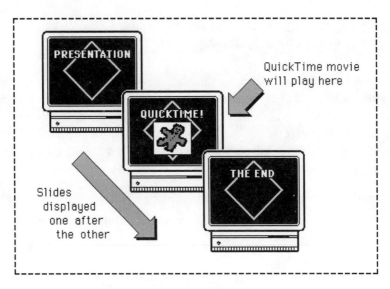

FIGURE 3.17
Slides are Simply Pages Displayed One after the Other

Movies in Other Application Documents

We provided detail about QuickTime movies in drawing programs, word processors, and presentation software because each is a common, practical use for movies. But there are several other types of software packages that allow movies to be imported into them. The following is a representative sample.

Movies and Databases: Claris FileMaker Pro

Starting with version 2.0, of you can include QuickTime movies in FileMaker Pro databases. Support for movies is simple—you create a field, define it as a graphics field, select it, and then choose **Import Movie**. This menu option is in a submenu attached to the Import/Export option found in the File menu. Figure 3.18 shows this menu in FileMaker Pro 2.0.

Databases traditionally held text, such as names, addresses, and product or ordering information. That started to change when Macintosh databases made it simple to import pictures into layouts. Now many companies include a company logo in their databases. Movies are simply an extension of this ability for databases to hold graphics.

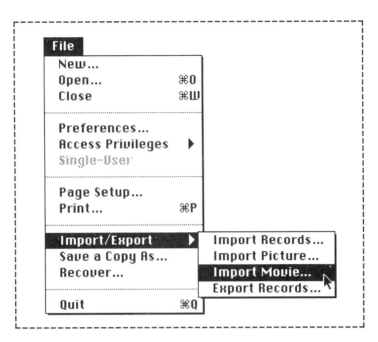

FIGURE 3.18
Importing a Movie into FileMaker Pro

Why would you want to include a movie in a database? A database of company employees could have a short clip of each employee (this would be especially helpful for new employees who are being oriented). A database of animals could include a digitized clip of each one. A database of automobiles could show footage of each car. A database of music groups could include a short clip of each group in concert. And on and on.

Movies and Office Mail: WordPerfect Office

With the WordPerfect Office package you can attach a QuickTime movie to a mail message. A company CEO could E-mail a message addressed "to all" that included a film clip of his latest address to stockholders. Any employee could send a video to any other employee, such as the edited highlights of a presentation that another employee missed.

Movies are large, and they can bottleneck networks as they are transferred. But networking technology is rapidly improving, and this limiting factor will soon disappear.

Movies and Animation: Director and PROmotion

Many programs were designed to created animated sequences long before the arrival of QuickTime. Now, several of these programs allow you to save an animation as a QuickTime movie as well as an animation in the program's own native format. Two such programs are PROmotion by Motion Works, and MacroMind Director 3.1.

We tested PROmotion by turning a simple animation into a QuickTime movie. Once an animation is created in PROmotion, select the **Movie** option from the submenu attached to the **Export** command in the File menu. Figure 3.19 shows this option. The result? A QuickTime movie file that can be run using any movie viewer.

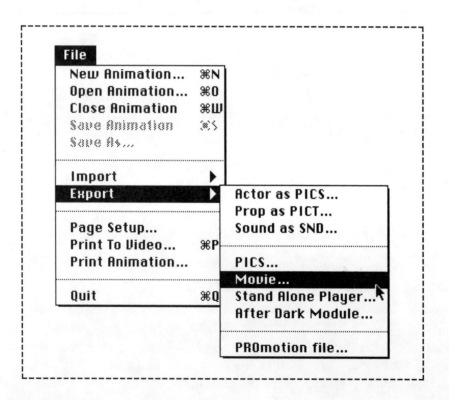

FIGURE 3.19

Creating a QuickTime Movie from a PROmotion Animation

Wild Magic: Movies in Any Document?

You've seen in the previous sections of this chapter that many Macintosh applications now support QuickTime movies in their documents. But many still don't. If one of your favorite programs doesn't make use of QuickTime movies, or has an upgrade that costs too much, you still may be able to include movies in the documents of that program. To do this you'll need a free software program called Wild Magic.

Getting and Installing Wild Magic

Wild Magic is available from bulletin boards such as CompuServe. If you, or anyone you know, accesses one of these services, take a few minutes to download this program.

Wild Magic is a control panel that runs on any Macintosh running System 7.0 or later, and QuickTime. To install it, simply drag the file to your System folder. Then restart your computer.

Using Wild Magic

Once you have Wild Magic in your System folder, it's turned on. You can turn it off by selecting **Control Panels** from the Apple menu, then double-clicking on the Wild Magic icon. Figure 3.20 shows the Wild Magic control panel and the dialog box that opens when you double-click the control panel.

Once Wild Magic is turned on, you can forget about it. You won't notice its effect until you paste a QuickTime movie in the document of an application that doesn't support QuickTime. Normally, an attempt to paste a movie in an older application results in the pasting of just a single picture of the movie. With Wild Magic, the movie will be pasted. You can tell the difference because a movie in a document has a badge in its lower left corner. Now, clicking on the badge opens a movie controller that allow you to run the movie. Figure 3.21 illustrates how Wild Magic changes things.

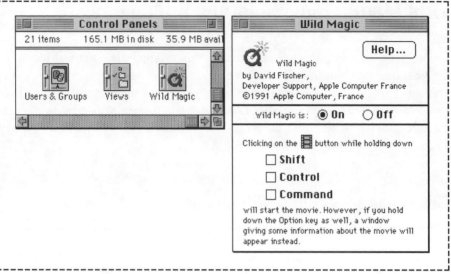

FIGURE 3.20

The Wild Magic Control Panel

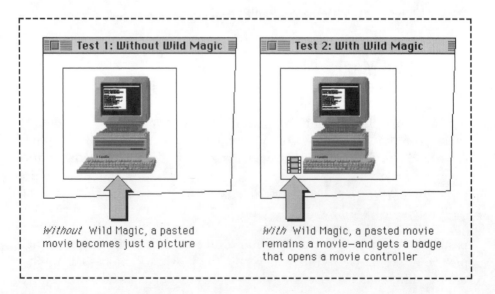

FIGURE 3.21

Wild Magic Adds Movie-Handling to Older Applications

Wild Magic works with just about any program that allows you to paste a picture into its documents. That's because Wild Magic stores information about the movie in the area that normally holds information about a PICT, or picture.

Here are the steps to getting a movie into the document of a program that doesn't support QuickTime movies.

1. Make sure Wild Magic is on by checking the Wild Magic control panel.

2. Run the MovieViewer program included with this book, or any other program that allows you to view and edit a movie.

3. Open a movie.

4. Select the frames you want to copy—any or all of them.

5. Select **Copy** from the Edit menu.

6. Run the application that is to receive the movie.

7. In the document that is to receive the movie, move the cursor to the area where the movie is to be pasted.

8. Select **Paste** from the Edit menu.

 Wild Magic must be on *before* you copy part or all of a movie that is to be pasted into a document. Pasting a movie that was copied *without* Wild Magic turned on will not be recognized by Wild Magic, and will appear in documents as just a picture—not a movie.

We tested Wild Magic using Microsoft Word 4.0 and Claris' MacWrite II 1.1. Both versions of these programs are about four years old, and don't normally support QuickTime movies. Normally, when you paste a movie into a document from either of these word processors, only a picture is pasted—not a movie.

To test Wild Magic, we made sure the Wild Magic control panel was set to On, then ran our MovieViewer program. We opened a movie and copied part of it. We then ran Microsoft Word 4.0 and selected **Paste** from the Edit menu. The movie, complete with badge, was pasted into the document. Clicking on the badge opened a movie controller. Success! We then ran MacWrite II 1.1 and pasted the same movie into a document. Again, the result was a fully functional movie being pasted into the document.

As always, if you plan on sending an electronic document to someone else, and it contains a movie, don't forget to send the movie file also. Wild Magic doesn't actually paste the entire movie into a document—only a reference to it. The movie must exist on disk.

Providing Others with Wild Magic

If you create documents using an application that doesn't support QuickTime movies, like version 4.0 of Microsoft Word, and you send electronic versions to others, you now know that you can include movies in them. If the person you send the document to has QuickTime and Wild Magic, that person can view the document as you created it—complete with movies that can be played and replayed.

If you regularly correspond with someone, send them a copy of Wild Magic. Apple allows, and encourages, users to freely distribute copies of Wild Magic—provided you also send the documentation that comes with the program. Therein lies the key word: *freely*. You may not sell Wild Magic, or include a copy of it in any product you sell. That explains why we didn't include a copy with this book!

Programs Written for QuickTime

With the advent of QuickTime, a host of companies released new versions of existing software products—versions that would support QuickTime movies. We have discussed several of these programs in this chapter. But QuickTime also spawned a line of entirely new programs that didn't exist, and couldn't exist, before QuickTime. Here we'll look at two of the most popular ones.

Morph

Morphing, from the word metamorphosis, is the gradual transition of one image to another. Until a few years ago, morphing was impractical on a home computer, since it requires a good deal of microprocessor power and speed. But now, with Macs that have more memory and more horsepower, morphing on a home computer is a reality. With a Macintosh and Gryphon Software's Morph program, anyone can do it.

The Morph program is simple and intuitive to use. When you start it up, you'll see what Gryphon Software calls a Storyboard. You double-click on the left side of it to open a dialog box that lets you select a picture—a PICT file. This becomes the starting image. You do the same for the right side to select an ending image. Figure 3.22 shows a Morph Storyboard with a starting and ending image in it.

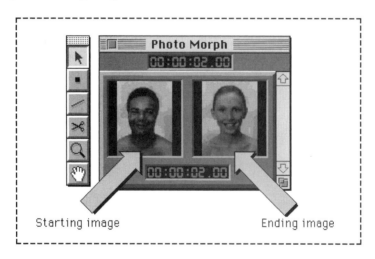

FIGURE 3.22

The Morph Storyboard with Starting and Ending Images

You supply the two images. They can be any size, but they should be equal in size to one another. In the next chapter we describe how you can turn a video clip into a QuickTime movie. We also describe how to turn an individual frame from a video clip into a PICT file. VCR tapes or home movies are ideal for obtaining images to morph.

The only images you need are the starting and ending pictures—Morph creates all the intermediary images. How does Morph know how to determine that an eye in the starting image should be transformed into an eye in the ending image? It can't. Morph doesn't know *what* the images are. That's where you come in. Before starting the morphing process, you provide pairs of points on the two images that help Morph in its calculations.

Once you have two images loaded, you select **Start Image** from the Windows menu, then **End Image** from the same menu. You'll then see two windows like those shown in Figure 3.23. Alongside the windows is the Tool palette. Click on the **Key Point** tool (the second tool from the top of the palette). Then move to the start image and click the mouse on an identifiable part of the picture, such as an eye. When you then click the mouse button, you'll notice two things happen. A small square will appear where you clicked the mouse, and another one will appear in the end image, at approximately the same spot. This is shown in Figure 3.23.

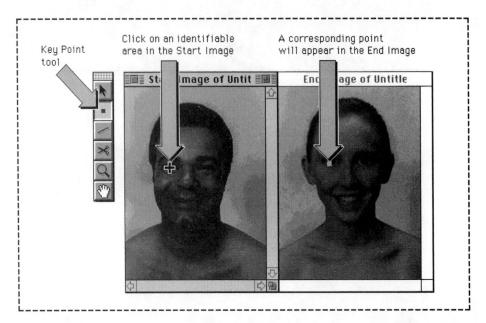

FIGURE 3.23

The Start Image and End Image Windows

Morph won't place the square in the end image in the exact spot you want it. To do that, select the top tool in the Tool palette—the **Adjusting tool.** Move to the end image, select the square, and move it to the location in the end image that corresponds to the same location in the start image. What you are doing is giving Morph common points in the two images. You're providing Morph with the basis for the transition between images. The secret to a smooth morphing? Provide lots of reference points for Morph to work with—the more the better. For points that form an outline of a part of a picture, you can provide Morph with even more information by connecting these points with the Line tool. Figure 3.24 shows how many point pairs it might take to create a smooth transition.

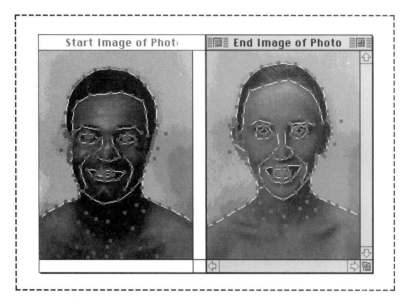

FIGURE 3.24
Several Point Pairs in the Image Windows

It might seem like a lot of work, but it's not. And remember, this is a one-time process for a morph. Morph is going to create all the images from just these two images. With the point pairs completed, it's time to let Morph do its work. Select **Morph Image** from the Windows menu. An empty window will open. Along the top of the window is a slider. Here you indicate to Morph at what point in the transition you'd like to make a single image. In Figure 3.25 we've moved the slider until the percentage reads 50. That will create an image at the midpoint of the transition. Next, select the **Morph** command from the Sequence menu. After a few seconds, an image will appear in the window. In Figure 3.25 we've shown the actual midpoint image for our sample morph. Notice that it looks like neither the starting image nor the ending image, but rather something in between—just as it should.

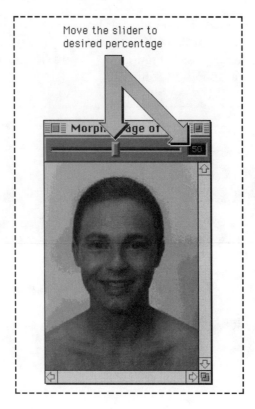

FIGURE 3.25

A Morphed Image in the Morph Image Window

Move the slider to a new location and again select **Morph** from the Sequence menu. The more images you create, the smoother the transition will look when it runs. Try making an image at every 10 percent increment.

Once you've created all the images, select **Save Movie** from the File menu. Morph can run movies, but you won't need Morph to run the movie that results from selecting this menu option. The morph movie will be a QuickTime movie that can be run from any movie-player.

Using Morph can be addictive. You might not have a practical use for movies of this type, but having the power to easily create such stunning effects will give you a real appreciation for the power of your Macintosh. And, just maybe, you might think of a morph movie that fits well into a presentation you're creating.

TheaterMaker

If you create a QuickTime movie that you really enjoy, you might want to share it with other people. But unless each person has a movie-playing utility on their computer, there is no way you can guarantee that each person will be able to play it, unless you use a program like TheaterMaker to make stand-alone QuickTime movies.

TheaterMaker takes a QuickTime movie and makes it self-contained. In a sense, it adds a simple movie player to the movie itself. But more than that, TheaterMaker adds a twist to viewing movies by filling your screen with a distinct background, and then playing the movie against it. TheaterMaker has just two options: Create Theater and Create Frame. They're shown in Figure 3.26.

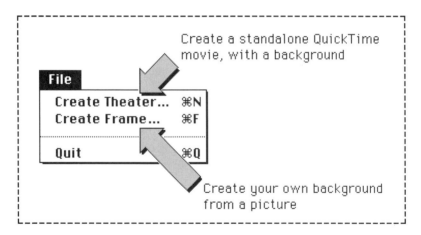

FIGURE 3.26
TheaterMaker Menu Items

TheaterMaker calls a self-contained movie a *Theater*. When you select **Create Theater** from the File menu, you'll see a dialog box like the one in Figure 3.27. From here you select a movie and a background for it to play against.

Click on the **Movie** button to open a dialog box that lets you select any QuickTime movie on your drive. We selected the morph movie that we created in the previous section of this chapter. After the movie is selected, click on the **Frame** button to select a background. You'll see a dialog box similar to the one shown in Figure 3.28.

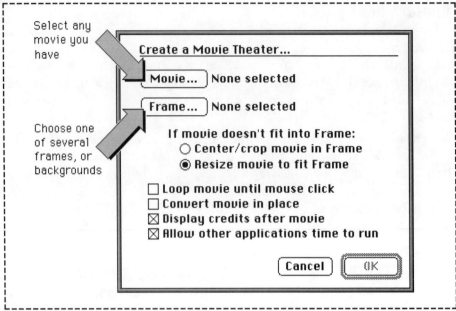

Select any movie you have

Choose one of several frames, or backgrounds

Create a Movie Theater...

[Movie...] None selected

[Frame...] None selected

If movie doesn't fit into Frame:
○ Center/crop movie in Frame
● Resize movie to fit Frame

☐ Loop movie until mouse click
☐ Convert movie in place
☒ Display credits after movie
☒ Allow other applications time to run

[Cancel] [OK]

FIGURE 3.27

Select a Movie and a Background Frame to Make a Theater

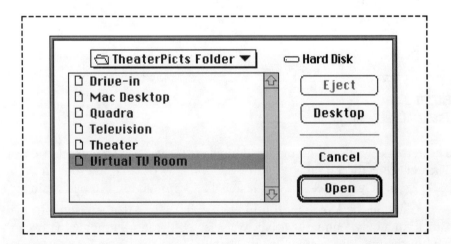

📁 **TheaterPicts Folder** ▼   💾 **Hard Disk**

🗋 **Drive-in**
🗋 **Mac Desktop**
🗋 **Quadra**
🗋 **Television**
🗋 **Theater**
🗋 **Virtual TV Room**

[Eject]

[Desktop]

[Cancel]

[Open]

FIGURE 3.28

The Select Frame Dialog Box

TheaterMaker comes with a half dozen backgrounds for you to use. We selected the one titled Virtual TV Room. With both the movie and the background selected, a click on the **OK** button gave us the opportunity to name the Theater. After that, TheaterMaker took just seconds to create the Theater. Double-clicking on the movie icon will turn your screen black, and then fill it with the background. Each background has an opening in which the movie plays. For the Virtual TV Room background, the movie plays, of course, in the TV. Figure 3.29 shows what our screen looked like as it played our morph movie.

FIGURE 3.29
A Theater in Action

Once a Theater is created, you can send it to anyone you'd like, without including a copy of the movie that will play in it. Remember, TheaterMaker makes self-contained, or stand-alone, movies.

To make things even more interesting—and to sidetrack you for several more hours—TheaterMaker provides a menu option that lets you make your own backgrounds. Before you do, first draw or find a large piece of clip art that you think will make a fun backdrop for a movie. Figure 3.30 shows how we modified a piece of clip art of Frankenstein's monster. We added a white rectangle to his forehead—that's where we're going to have the movie play.

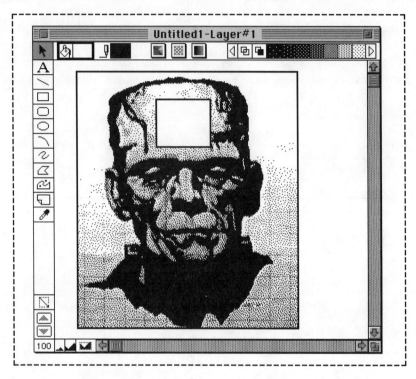

FIGURE 3.30
Creating a PICT for Our Own Background Frame

With a picture created, save it in a PICT or PICT2 format, as many drawing programs allow you to do. Then, back in TheaterMaker, select **Create Frame** from the File menu. You'll see a dialog box, like that shown in Figure 3.31, that lets you select a PICT file.

Once selected, your picture will be displayed on screen. Click the mouse and drag out a rectangle where you'll want your movie to play. We selected a rectangle in Frankenstein's forehead, using the white area we had added when we edited the picture. When done, hit the **Return** key. That will give you an opportunity to select a compression method for the background (your choices are shown in Figure 3.32). If you've used a video clip, compression will be good idea. We used a small black-and-white graphic PICT, so we simply chose **Normal**.

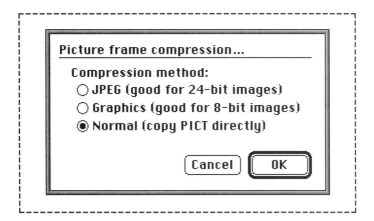

FIGURE 3.31

Selecting Our PICT File to Make a Frame

FIGURE 3.32

Compressing the Frame

Once you click the **OK** button, TheaterMaker converts your picture to a background. We tested out our new background by selecting **Create Theater** from the File menu. When we clicked the **Frame** button, our new background was now one of the backgrounds to select. When we did so, we created a Theater that looked like the one in Figure 3.33.

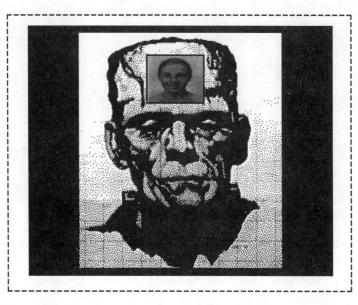

FIGURE 3.33

Playing a Theater Using Our Own Frame

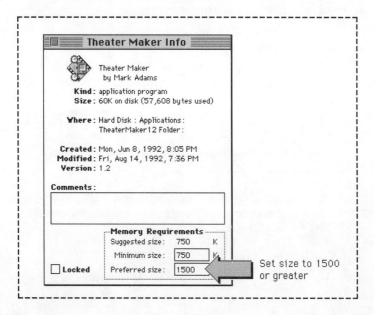

FIGURE 3.34

Giving TheaterMaker More Memory

If you run into memory problems while compressing the background, try increasing the amount of memory allocated to TheaterMaker. To do this, quit the program. Select **Get Info** from the File menu in the Finder. Increase the Preferred size by typing in a new value; 1500 should be sufficient. That's what we've done in Figure 3.34. Close the Get Info dialog box and rerun TheaterMaker. If this doesn't work, select the **Normal** option when you get to the compression dialog. Your background will occupy more disk space, but it will work just fine.

TheaterMaker is a shareware product from Mark Adams. You can download it from services like America Online and try it out. If you like it, you're requested to send a $10 registration fee to Mr. Adams.

Chapter Summary

Many new versions of existing applications support QuickTime movies. Just as you can paste text or a pictures in a document, you can now paste a movie. Word processors, graphics programs, and presentation software all allow you to embed a QuickTime movie within a document.

Owners of older versions of programs—applications that don't recognize movies—can now force these products to accept a movie. Wild Magic, distributed by Apple, allows you to paste movies in documents produced by these older programs. The pasted movie will act just as if it were in a new, updated version of the program; the user can open a movie controller and play and replay any movie.

Until recently, morphing, the special effect of transforming one image into another, was too advanced a technology to be used on a home computer. That's changed. Morph is a software program that allows you to easily create a QuickTime movie that morphs one image to another.

QuickTime movies normally require a movie player to run. But with TheaterMaker, you can turn any movie into a standalone program. Double-clicking on a file made by TheaterMaker plays a movie without a movie-playing utility. What's more, it will play the movie against one of several catchy backgrounds—or any background you design.

Capturing Video

hapter 2 showed you how to make movies using clip art or pictures that you drew in a graphics program. This form of movie will fill many of your needs. But there's nothing quite like looking at your screen and seeing the action of a QuickTime movie that contains actual video footage. In this chapter we'll look at some products that make this possible.

The process of transferring video film from a VCR or camcorder to your computer is called digitizing. This chapter will explain why digitizing is necessary. You'll also learn about two products you can buy that will do the digitizing for you.

Capturing video means reproducing each frame of a movie clip so that it can be made into a QuickTime movie. You can also capture a single frame of a video. You can use this captured image as a picture in a word processor or graphics program, or insert it into a QuickTime movie. This chapter discusses both video capture and single still-image capture.

Digitizing Video

Though a television and a computer monitor seem similar, they are quite different. To capture the images in a video signal and convert them to a form recognizable by your Macintosh requires *digitizing*.

Why Digitize?

Video, as viewed on a television set, comes from an *analog* video signal. An analog signal is a stream of electricity with a wave-like shape. This wave of electricity can be understood and translated into a picture by the hardware components in your television. A signal of this type cannot, however, be understood by your computer. Computers are *digital* devices that work with incremental values, not continuous waves.

Anyone who wants to view video on their computer will require a piece of hardware called a *video digitizer*, which can receive an analog signal and convert it into a digital signal form recognizable by your Macintosh. If you have a Macintosh, a VCR or camcorder, and a video digitizer, you can easily transfer video from a tape to a QuickTime movie.

Capture Rates

Every second that a video plays, 30 frames are displayed on a television screen. Each of these images has to be captured and digitized. Although digitizing hardware is capable of performing this feat, you aren't assured of actually viewing the full 30 frames per second on your computer monitor. That's because the transfer of a single image from the digitizer to the Mac's display takes longer than 1/30th of a second. Although you can preview a video on your computer screen before recording, the preview may seem a little jerky.

Viewing a QuickTime movie after capturing it from video may also seem less than perfectly smooth. The reason? Digitizers compress and pass each captured image to your hard drive. No matter which compression scheme a manufacturer uses, some frames are sacrificed in the process. How many frames you lose depends on the speed of your computer. The faster your computer model, the higher the resulting capture rate. Macintosh Quadras, currently the fastest Macs on the market, allow you to create movies with little or no loss of frames—their capture rate is about 30 frames per second. If making and displaying QuickTime movies will be an important application for you, get the fastest model you can afford.

Digitizers

In the remainder of this chapter we'll look at two popular Macintosh video digitizers—Digital Vision's ComputerEyes/RT and SuperMac's VideoSpigot—and the software used by each.

The ComputerEyes/RT digitizer is an *external device*. You don't need to open the case of your Macintosh to hook it up; you simply attach it to the SCSI port on the back of the machine. If you already have a device hooked up to this port, such as an external hard drive, don't worry. SCSI devices can be *daisy-chained*—that is, you can hook up two or more devices to one another, then connect just one of them to the SCSI port.

The VideoSpigot digitizer is an *internal device*—you open your Macintosh and insert the card that holds the digitizing hardware. Like an internal hard drive, once an internal device is connected you won't have to open your Mac to use it.

ComputerEyes/RT comes with two software programs. The first, ComputerEyes/RT, lets you control the capture of a still image (a single frame of a video movie). The second, Apple's Movie Recorder utility, lets you control the capture of clips of movies.

VideoSpigot comes with one software program, ScreenPlay, that allows you to perform both still-image captures and the capture of clips of movies.

Capturing Video with a Digitizer

No matter which video digitizer you choose, you'll need a video source from which the digitizer receives the video signal. For examples, we'll use a VCR, but a camcorder or any device that plays a video tape and has video output jacks on it will work just as well.

Using ComputerEyes/RT to Capture Video

Because it's an external device, the ComputerEyes/RT digitizer is simple to hook up. If you're afraid to open up your Macintosh (and there's really no need to be), you might consider this a plus. The software used to control the making of the movie is Apple's own Movie Recorder program.

Hooking Up the ComputerEyes/RT Hardware

Figure 4.1 shows how the ComputerEyes/RT video digitizer is connected to your computer through its SCSI port. You'll use a Macintosh SCSI cable that has a male connector on each end. The other side of the digitizer gets connected to the video output jack of your video source. A cable with a single RCA connector on each end will work here.

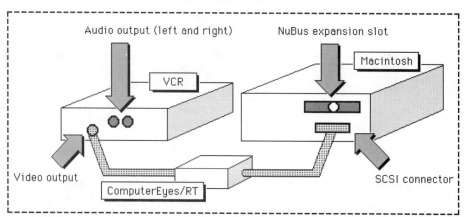

FIGURE 4.1
Connections for the ComputerEyes/RT Digitizer and a VCR

Making a Movie Using the ComputerEyes/RT Software

With the digitizer connected, run the Movie Recorder program that came with the hardware. You'll now see a Monitor window like the one shown in Figure 4.2. If you don't have a tape playing in your video source, the Monitor window will appear blank, as in Figure 4.2. Insert a videotape into your VCR (use one that has recorded material on it).

FIGURE 4.2
The Monitor Window in Movie Recorder

To preview your videotape, press the **Play** button on your VCR. You'll see live action as the tape plays (illustrated in Figure 4.3).

FIGURE 4.3
The Monitor Window Previewing Video Input

To start recording the video, click on the **Record** button in the Monitor window. The text of the Record button will change to Stop. After a few seconds, press the **Stop** button. Movie Recorder takes a few seconds to apply compression to the recorder images, which greatly reduces the amount of disk space the movie will take up. A new window will then open, and in it will be the section of the videotape you just recorded. The window will look like that shown in Figure 4.4—it will have the standard movie controller that allows you to play the movie. To save the movie that's in the window, select **Save** from the File menu. Give the movie a name and click the **Save** button. Congratulate yourself—you've just made your first QuickTime movie containing live action video!

FIGURE 4.4

A QuickTime Movie, Made Using the ComputerEyes/RT Digitizer

A QuickTime movie made using a digitizer can be opened and played with any movie-playing utility. Apple's Movie Player, or the program included with this book, MovieViewer, will both work. To open your newly-created movie, run one of these utilities and select **Open** from its File menu.

Earlier in this chapter we discussed frame rate and how compression affects it. If you look at the Settings menu, shown in Figure 4.5, you'll notice that the first two menu items deal with compression. If you check **Use Simple Compression**, no compression takes place as the video is captured. Instead, Movie Recorder waits until you stop recording. Only then does it perform the compression using the Apple Video compressor. By not compressing during the capture of the video, the processor can spend all its time on the capture. This improves the recording frame rate.

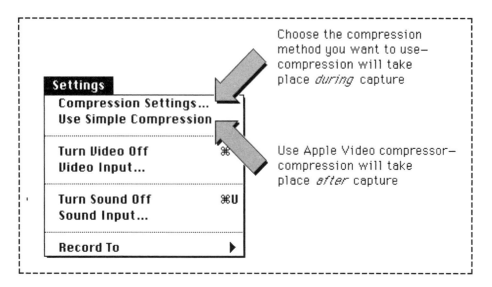

FIGURE 4.5
The Settings Menu of Movie Recorder

Figure 4.6 shows the Compression Settings dialog box you'll see if you decide to perform compression during the capture of the movie. This is the same dialog box used in Apple's Movie Converter utility. We covered the settings in detail in Chapter 2. For a review, refer back to the *Using Standard Compression Settings* section of that chapter.

The quality of video you record from may not always be superb. The lighting in home movies can vary dramatically, depending on the conditions when the movie was recorded. If you've ever been criticized for the quality of your camcorder movies, here's your chance to redeem yourself! Before capturing a movie to the Mac, load it into your video source and start to play it. But don't click the Record button in the Monitor window just yet. Instead, choose **Video Input** from the Settings menu. You'll see a dialog box, like the one shown in Figure 4.7, which allows you to adjust the color and brightness of the video. You can leave the settings as Movie Recorder has them, or you can move the sliders to vary different traits of the input signal. As you do, the changes will be reflected in the sample frame shown in the top left corner of the dialog box.

FIGURE 4.6

Compression Settings Dialog Box in Movie Recorder

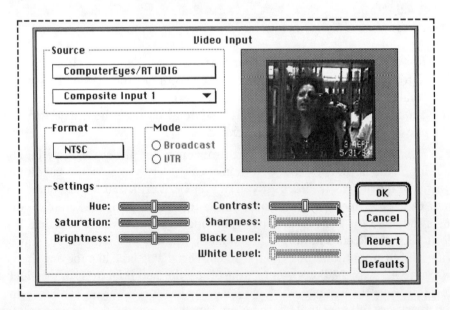

FIGURE 4.7

Video Input Dialog Box in Movie Recorder

Movie Recorder creates a QuickTime movie that is 160 pixels across and 120 pixels high. This is called *standard size*, and it's the size most QuickTime movies are played at. You can use the Resize menu, shown in Figure 4.8, to change the size of the movie.

FIGURE 4.8
The Resize Menu in Movie Recorder

Your first thought may be that bigger is better, but you should consider the drawback—and it's a big one—of recording a movie at a larger size. Doing so decreases the frame rate. Your Mac has to do a lot more work to capture and compress these oversized images; the result is a movie that won't play smoothly. Figure 4.9 compares a quarter-size movie and a half-size one.

FIGURE 4.9
A Quarter-size and Half-size QuickTime Movie

Using VideoSpigot to Capture Video

The VideoSpigot digitizer is an internal device. It comes on a board that plugs into your Macintosh. While the idea of opening the Mac's case and plugging something into it may intimidate some people, it really shouldn't. It's an easy process and you only have to do it once. After the board is plugged in you'll use VideoSpigot's own ScreenPlay software to control the recording of a video movie.

Hooking Up the VideoSpigot Hardware

Figure 4.10 shows how the VideoSpigot digitizer is connected to your computer. You plug the VideoSpigot board into a slot inside your Mac. Plugging a board into a slot inside a Macintosh isn't much different than plugging a cable into a port on the back of one. With VideoSpigot there are no wires to connect and no switches to set.

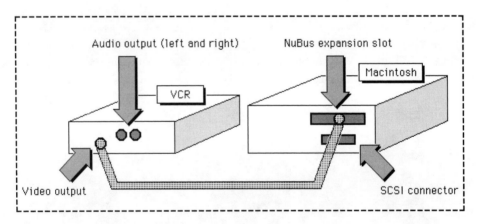

FIGURE 4.10
Connections for VideoSpigot Digitizer and a VCR

The VideoSpigot is not a SCSI device, as the ComputerEyes/RT digitizer is. So you won't be using the SCSI port for VideoSpigot. Instead, you'll connect your video source, such as the VCR shown in Figure 4.10, directly to the VideoSpigot card. Your VCR has an RCA jack labeled "Video output," and the VideoSpigot card has its own RCA jack built into it. To connect a video source to VideoSpigot you'll use a standard cable that has an RCA connector on each end. The RCA jack on the VideoSpigot card sticks out of an opening in the back of your Macintosh, so you don't have to open the Mac case to connect a video source.

Making a Movie Using the VideoSpigot Software

VideoSpigot comes with its own ScreenPlay software. When you run ScreenPlay, you'll see a window like the one shown in Figure 4.11. If you have a tape in your VCR and you press the VCR's **Play** button, you'll see the live-action in this window.

FIGURE 4.11
The Preview Window in ScreenPlay

To start recording, click the mouse on the **Record** button (the second button from the left). When done, click on the **Stop** button (the third button from the left). A new window will open, and in it will be your captured video. That's all there is to it. Select **Save** from the File menu to give your new movie a name and save it to disk.

You'll notice that when you create a QuickTime movie in ScreenPlay it is displayed in a window with a nonstandard controller. It will have a controller like the one in the ScreenPlay window in Figure 4.11. The controller for a movie is added by the program that plays the movie. So when you run a program such as Movie Player or MovieViewer, a movie created by ScreenPlay will be displayed in a window with a standard controller, like the movie shown in Figure 4.12. Although it was created in ScreenPlay, it looks like any other type of movie when viewed in Movie Player.

FIGURE 4.12
A Movie with a Standard Movie Controller

If you aren't satisfied with the color of a movie, select **Settings** from the Spigot menu, shown in Figure 4.13, to display a dialog box that lets you vary the color of the video input image.

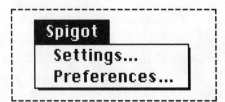

FIGURE 4.13
The Spigot Menu in ScreenPlay

You can see from Figure 4.14 that ScreenPlay allows you to vary the color of the input signal, but doesn't give you sliders to control brightness and contrast, as Apple's Movie Recorder software does. If you're recording from a videotape that is too dark or too light, this can be a big problem. The settings in this dialog box apply to the signal *before* you record it. They don't affect the images in a QuickTime movie after it's created. In the next chapter we'll present a way to alter ScreenPlay's shortcoming—we'll edit a movie to add or remove brightness *after* it's been created using a digitizer.

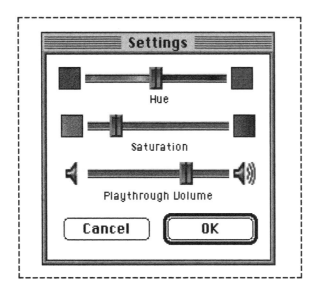

FIGURE 4.14
The Settings Dialog Box in ScreenPlay

The other menu item in the Settings menu is Preferences. The settings in the Preferences dialog box, shown in Figure 4.15, are most useful when you are capturing a still image (an image to be saved as a picture). Still images are covered later in this chapter.

Like Movie Recorder, ScreenPlay provides a range of compression options. Select **Compression** from the File menu to see the dialog box shown in Figure 4.16. In this dialog box you can select a compression method and the number of colors to use from the pop-up menus. You can also vary the quality of the compression by using the slider. The higher the quality, the sharper the images in the movie will look—and the more disk space the movie will occupy.

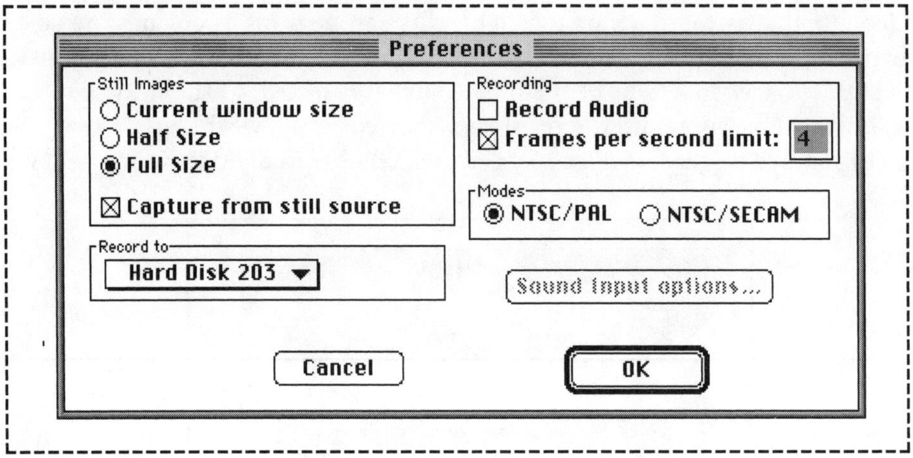

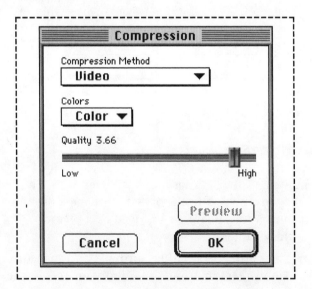

FIGURE 4.15

The Preference Dialog Box in ScreenPlay

FIGURE 4.16

The Compression Dialog Box in ScreenPlay

Capturing Still Images

QuickTime movies involve action—several images played in succession to form a live-action movie. You might think you won't have a use for capturing a single image, but there are instances when you might want to do so.

In Chapter 2 you saw how to string together a series of PICT files to create a movie. There we suggested that you might want to select a single background for use in each PICT that will make up a movie. You'll then place an object, such as a person or car, on top of the background at different locations. When the PICTs are shown together as a movie, the illusion of movement will be created. Capturing a single image, and saving it as a PICT file, is one way to obtain good backgrounds. It's also something both ComputerEyes/RT and VideoSpigot can do.

After creating a QuickTime movie you may want to edit it. You may want to create a single still image and paste it into a movie. For example, you might want to have a close-up of a person in the movie. You can capture a single still image from a videotape and paste it into an existing movie. The more times you paste that one image into the movie, the longer the close-up will be held during playback. Video digitizers allow you to capture a high-quality single still image at the same size as the movies you create. That means the picture size will be the same size as frames of a movie—and that makes it convenient to paste a single image into a movie.

Since you've paid hard-earned money for a digitizer, it's good to know it can be used for more than just movie-making. When you capture a single image, you can save the image as a file that can be imported into other types of applications, such as word processors or graphics programs.

Using ComputerEyes/RT to Capture an Image

ComputerEyes can capture single full-screen images in color, grayscale, or black and white. The image you capture will always be 640 x 480 pixels, but the ComputerEyes software allows you to scale the captured image down to any size.

ComputerEyes, in conjunction with Movie Recorder, lets you create QuickTime movies from a video source. ComputerEyes, using Digital Visions' own software, lets you capture a single high-quality frame of a

video. At the full-screen size of 640 x 480 pixels (something that not all digitizers can do). So ComputerEyes allows you to provide a large, high-quality
image, in addition to being able to create QuickTime movies.

When you start up the ComputerEyes/RT software by double-clicking
on it, one empty window will open. Because you must have a window open
before an image can be captured, ComputerEyes automatically starts with
one open. To capture an image, start by selecting the **Stills** item from the
Capture menu, shown in Figure 4.17.

FIGURE 4.17
The Capture Menu in ComputerEyes/RT

After selecting **Stills**, the Preview window shown in Figure 4.18 will appear.
If you don't have your video source running, the center of the window will
be blank.

Once your video source is running, the Preview window will display
the action. We hit the **Play** button on the VCR connected to our
ComputerEyes/RT hardware, and the image appears in the center of the
Preview window, shown in Figure 4.19. You'll see a live-action view as the
video plays-the Preview window is constantly being updated as a videotape
plays.

To enlarge the preview image, click on the pop-up menu at the bottom
of the Preview window. Figure 4.20 shows the preview size being changed
from small to large. Note that the image now fills the Preview window.

Set the preview size to whichever size you prefer. A smaller image will
be updated faster, so the playing of the video looks smoother. The larger
image plays slower, or more jerkily, but allows you to see more detail.
Preview size is a matter of personal preference. Regardless of the size at
which you preview a running video, capture performance is the same.

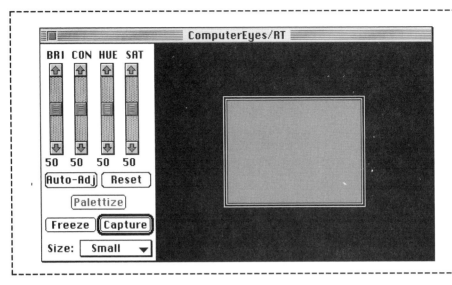

FIGURE 4.18

The Preview Window in ComputerEyes/RT

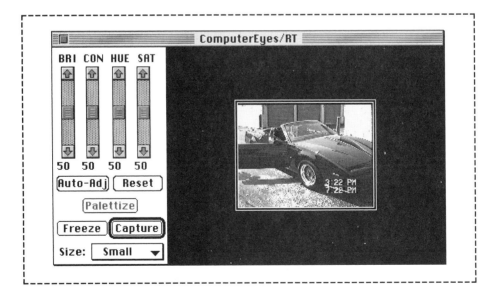

FIGURE 4.19

ComputerEyes/RT Preview Window with Live-Action Video

FIGURE 4.20
Changing the Preview Size in ComputerEyes/RT

 Remember, you're just capturing a single image here, not a movie. You shouldn't care how smooth the video appears to be playing, because you're just going to capture a single frame. The speed at which frames are displayed in the Preview window does not affect ComputerEyes' performance in capturing a single frame.

Another point to remember: the captured frame will always be 640 x 480 pixels in size, regardless of the size at which you preview the frames. If you want a smaller image, ComputerEyes gives you the option of reducing the image size, via a menu selection, *after* the capture is made.

Your video source may not have been filmed under optimum conditions. If you want to adjust the brightness, contrast, or colors, you can do so as you preview the video, or after the capture is made. To make adjustments before the capture, use the sliders in the Preview window. Figure 4.21 describes their effect on the image. As you vary the positions of the sliders, the changes will be reflected in the images displayed in the Preview window. When you capture an image (and we'll do that soon), the image will be captured with the values of these settings.

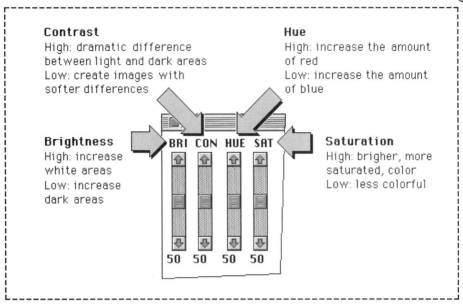

FIGURE 4.21
ComputerEyes/RT Preview Color Adjustments

While your video is running, try experimenting by varying the settings of the sliders. You can return to the original settings at any time by clicking on the **Reset** button in the Preview window. ComputerEyes has an automatic adjustment button, labeled Auto-Adj, that tells the software to calculate and adjust all settings to levels it feels are best for the displayed image. Again, if you aren't satisfied with the results, click the **Reset** button to return the settings to their original, or default, values. Figure 4.22 shows the Auto-Adj and Reset buttons in the Preview window.

ComputerEyes always grabs a 24-bit image—over 16 million colors. You can set ComputerEyes so that it reduces the number of colors to 256—an 8-bit capture. You can capture a 24-bit image even if you don't have a 24-bit display, and a 24-bit image has much better quality than an 8-bit image. But you may still consider using 8-bit capture for the following reasons:

- A 24-bit image occupies three times the disk space of an 8-bit image.
- Some programs import 8-bit images, but not 24-bit images.

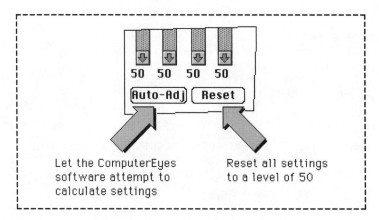

FIGURE 4.22
Allowing ComputerEyes/RT to Set the Color Levels

To set the capture to 8-bit or 24-bit, use the Image menu, shown in Figure 4.23. If you use 8-bit, you'll also have to make a few other choices in the Image menu. If you choose an 8-bit capture, ComputerEyes has to be told which 256 of the over 16 million available colors to use. Colors are grouped in *palettes*, with each palette holding 256 colors. There are separate settings for the image that's previewed and the image that's captured. Digital Vision recommends using the Standard Preview Palette and Best Capture Palette.

When displaying moving video images in the Preview window, no calculations will take place if you select the Standard Preview Palette. That won't have any effect on the captured image. For the capture itself, use Best Capture Palette to force ComputerEyes to spend a moment just before the capture to calculate the best 256 colors to use for the image about to be captured.

Now, the preliminaries are over. Don't worry, once you understand what the settings mean and become familiar with them, capturing a frame is fast and easy. You don't have to alter settings between captures if you don't want to.

With your video source running, you can capture an image in several ways. To capture a frame *on the fly*, that is, as the video is still running, click on the **Capture** button in the Preview window. ComputerEyes will capture the current frame, and display it in the open, empty window. If the **Capture** button is dim, you probably don't have a window open. ComputerEyes needs an open window as a destination for the captured image. If this is the case, select **New** from the File menu, as shown in Figure 4.24. The **Capture** button will then become enabled.

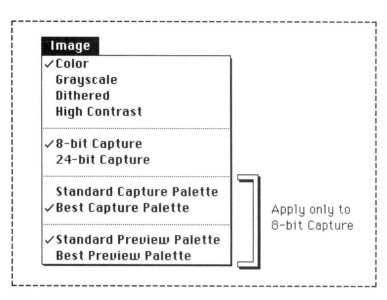

FIGURE 4.23
Palette Selections Apply to 8-bit Captures

FIGURE 4.24
The File Menu in ComputerEyes/RT

Instead of capturing an image on the fly, you can click on the **Freeze** button in the Preview window. Your video source, such as a VCR, will keep running, but a single frame will be held in the Preview window. Before clicking the **Capture** button, you can vary any of the sliders to fine-tune the image. Figure 4.25 shows both the **Freeze** and **Capture** buttons of the Preview window.

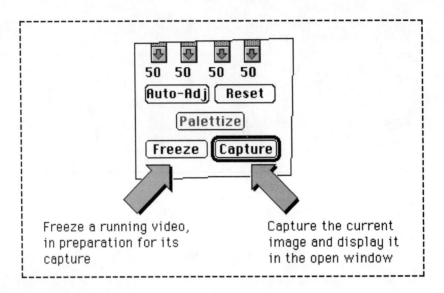

FIGURE 4.25

Stopping and Capturing a Still Image in ComputerEyes/RT

If your video source is a VCR, you can also use its Pause button to stop the action. The frame you pause on will appear in the Preview window. Click the **Capture** button in the Preview window to capture the image.

 Digital Vision doesn't recommend this method. We tried it, and though it does work, the captured images do seem less stable.

After capture, the image is shown in a window. The size of both the window and the displayed image depends on which menu choice you make from the Windows menu. This menu is shown in Figure 4.26.

You can change the size of the window that displays the image either before or after the image is captured. Remember, ComputerEyes always captures an image at 640 x 480 pixels, regardless of what window size you select. ComputerEyes allows you to scale the image to a different size after the capture. We'll cover this topic a little later.

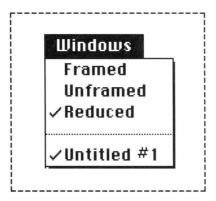

FIGURE 4.26
The Windows Menu in ComputerEyes/RT

The **Framed** menu item displays the image at its full-screen captured size of 640 x 480 pixels, in a resizable window with scroll bars. Resizing the window doesn't resize the image; it just changes the area of the image you view in the window. This is illustrated in Figure 4.27, which shows a window both before and after it's been resized using the window's grow box in its lower-right corner.

The **Unframed** menu item also displays the image at its full-screen captured size of 640 x 480 pixels, but not in a window. The image will cover your screen, and no further action can be taken until you change the Window option. You'll use this option to see the entire image, without scroll bars obscuring any of it.

The **Reduced** menu item displays the captured image at 50 percent of its captured size. The image will be in a nonresizable window. Again, this smaller view does not affect the size of the saved image—it will still be saved at its full-screen capture size.

Before capturing an image, while video film is running or in freeze mode, you can adjust the colors and contrast in the Preview window. You can also make these same adjustments after you capture an image. Select **Adjust Palette** from the Options menu, as shown in Figure 4.28.

FIGURE 4.27

Changing a Window's Size Doesn't Affect the Size of the Image

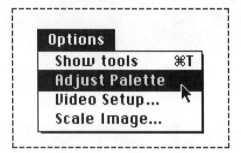

FIGURE 4.28

The Options Menu in ComputerEyes/RT

The **Adjust Palette** menu item brings up the dialog box shown in Figure 4.29. Changes made to the sliders in this window affect the captured image. Notice that there are three individual sliders for adjusting the color, whereas the Preview window uses a single Hue slider for the color.

As mentioned, all images are captured at a size of 640 x 480 pixels. After an image is captured you can change its size by selecting **Scale Image** from the Options menu, as shown in Figure 4.30. When you do, you'll see the dialog box shown in Figure 4.31. When you scale an image, the original will be preserved in one window, while the new, scaled image will appear in a separate window.

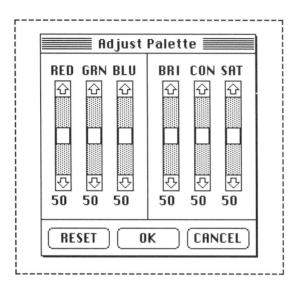

FIGURE 4.29
Adjusting Image Color After an Image is Captured

FIGURE 4.30
Selecting the Scale Image Option in ComputerEyes/RT

After capturing an image and making any adjustments to it, save it to a file by selecting **Save** from the File menu. ComputerEyes lets you save the image in one of three popular formats: MacPaint, PICT, or TIFF. The Save dialog box is shown in Figure 4.32.

FIGURE 4.31
The Scale Image Dialog Box in ComputerEyes/RT

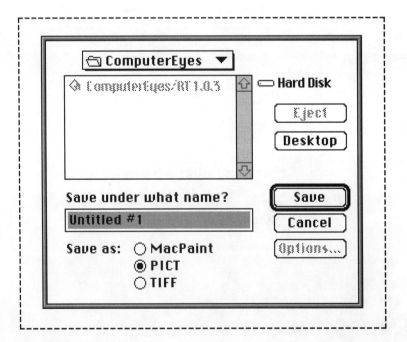

FIGURE 4.32
Saving an Image in ComputerEyes/RT

Using VideoSpigot to Capture an Image

Unlike ComputerEyes/RT, with VideoSpigot you use the same software to capture a still image as you do to capture a movie. Before making the capture, do a little preliminary work to make sure the image is captured just as you want it. If the colors aren't to your liking, select **Settings** from the Spigot menu to adjust the hue and saturation. Then, select **Preferences** from the same menu to establish the size of the captured image. ComputerEyes/RT always captures a full-screen image, then adjusts the size later. With VideoSpigot, the captured size is set before the capture takes place. Figure 4.33 shows the Preferences dialog box.

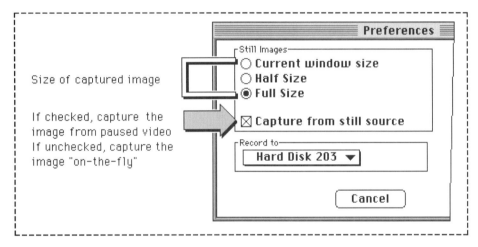

FIGURE 4.33
Specifying Still-Image Size in ScreenPlay

VideoSpigot allows you to capture images on the fly or with your video source set to Pause. If you're going to capture a paused image, let ScreenPlay know by checking the **Capture From Still Source** check box in the Preferences dialog box. To capture an image on the fly—that is, as the movie is playing—click the mouse in the ScreenPlay window at the moment you want to capture the image. While holding the mouse down, drag the cursor outside the boundaries of the ScreenPlay window. Then release the mouse. A still image will be captured and displayed in its own window; see Figure 4.34.

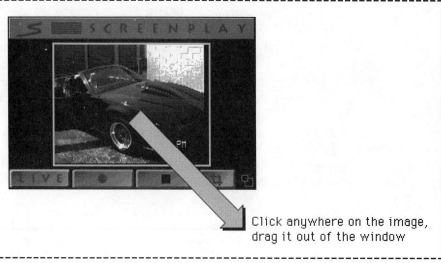

Click anywhere on the image,
drag it out of the window

FIGURE 4.34
Capturing a Still Image on the fly in ScreenPlay

Chapter Summary

Though the images on a television and on a computer monitor look quite similar, they are very different. The technique of digitizing is used to transfer the analog video images that a television understands to the digital images that a computer recognizes. The smoothness that a QuickTime movie plays back at—that is, the number of frames per second it displays—depends on the speed of the microprocessor in the Macintosh on which the movie was made and on which the movie plays.

The hardware component that digitizes video is called a video digitizer. Two popular models are Digital Vision's ComputerEyes/RT and SuperMac's VideoSpigot. Both can capture color or grayscale video and turn them into QuickTime movies. Both digitizers can also capture a single image and save it as a PICT file. ComputerEyes/RT can also save a single image in TIFF format. The ComputerEyes/RT digitizer is a SCSI device—it's an external device that connects to the SCSI port on the back of your Macintosh. The VideoSpigot digitizer is an internal device—a card that can be inserted into a slot inside your Mac.

Adding Sound

 uickTime is a breakthrough technology in that it brings multimedia movies to the screens of home computers inexpensively and easily. When people discuss QuickTime movies, they talk about video, movement, frames, and animation. But QuickTime is multimedia—it embodies both sight and sound. This chapter is about sound.

In the previous chapter you learned how to capture video using a video digitizer. In this chapter you'll see how to capture sound using a sound digitizer. You'll learn how to capture sound while you capture video from a camcorder or VCR. You'll also learn how to capture sound without video, and to save the sound in a separate file. You'll be able to record and save your voice, music, or anything else you can think of.

The audio contained in a sound file can be added to a QuickTime movie that doesn't have sound, or has sound you don't like. In this chapter you'll see how to create and save sound. In the next chapter you'll learn how to create new QuickTime movies by using movie-editing software to add sounds to movie clips.

Movie Tracks

A filmstrip—the type of movie you see in a movie theater—contains both an image track and a sound track. QuickTime movies also have multiple *tracks*. A single track carries either images or sound. The tracks of a movie are *synchronized*—they always match. This prevents one track from running ahead or lagging behind the other. To help conceptualize this, we've shown a single source moving across, and playing back, both the video and audio tracks of a movie in Figure 5.1.

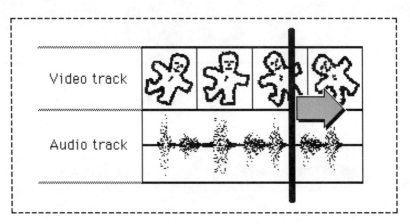

FIGURE 5.1

A QuickTime Movie Synchronizes the Video and Audio Tracks

Not only does a movie have both a video and audio track, it can have more than one of each. So our movie in Figure 5.1 could have two soundtracks— perhaps one for background music and a second for a narration. We lay the groundwork for multiple audio tracks in this chapter, and actually implement them in a movie in the next chapter.

So far, each movie we have worked with appears to have had only a video track. In fact, they had a soundtrack as well. For movies created from PICT files, like those made in Chapter 2 using Movie Converter or MovieMaker, the audio track wasn't *enabled*. A movie created from these utilities displays its movie controller with a dim Speaker button.

In Chapter 4 we created QuickTime movies from a video source. Because we did not connect the audio output of our source, such as a VCR, to our Macintosh, there was no sound in the QuickTime movie. But a movie created from a video source can have its soundtrack enabled. Figure 5.2 shows the Settings menu from Apple's Movie Recorder utility (we used this program with the ComputerEyes/RT digitizer in the previous chapter). Figure 5.2 shows that you can toggle the soundtrack on and off.

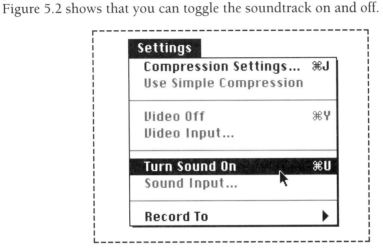

FIGURE 5.2
Turning Recording Sound On in Movie Recorder

Including sound in a movie created from a video source is easy. That topic is covered in the next two sections. Including sound in a movie made from PICT files requires a little more effort…but not an exceptional amount. Later in this chapter we'll discuss the recording of isolated sounds—sounds not part of any movie. In the next chapter we'll add sound to movies that were created without an enabled soundtrack.

Capturing Sound through a Built-in Sound Port

Most video digitizers don't have sound recording capabilities. If you're using a video digitizer and you want to create a movie that contains both the video track and soundtrack of the source, you can use a sound digitizer. That piece of hardware is discussed in the next section. If you own a Macintosh with a built-in sound port, you can use the Mac's hardware to capture the audio portion of your camcorder or VCR tapes.

Making the Connection

Many Macintosh models, such as the IIsi, LC, and Quadra, have a built-in sound port. You can plug the microphone provided with your Macintosh into it. Alternatively, you can run a cable from your video source to the jack. For a VCR, you'll need a cable with one or two RCA connectors on one end and a 1/8" miniplug on the other. For a video source playing a mono tape, do the following:

■ Use a cable with a single RCA connector on one end and a 1/8" miniplug on the other end.

■ Plug the RCA connector into the jack marked "Audio out R" on the back of your VCR.

■ Plug the 1/8" miniplug into the sound input jack (also called the microphone input) on the back of your Macintosh.

For a video source playing a stereo tape, follow the steps listed next. Refer to Figure 5.3 for a typical configuration.

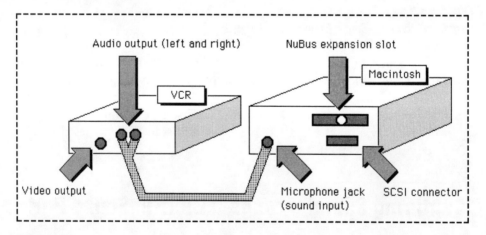

FIGURE 5.3
Connections for the Built-in Sound Port and a VCR

■ Use a cable with two RCA connectors on one end and a 1/8" miniplug on the other end.

■ Plug the two RCA connectors into the jacks marked "Audio out R" and "Audio out L" on back of your VCR.

■ Plug the 1/8" miniplug into the sound input jack (the microphone input) located on the back of your Macintosh.

If you're using a camcorder as your video source, your cable will have a single connector on each end. One end will have the 1/8" miniplug. Refer to your camcorder instructions for a description of the connector that goes into the camcorder's audio output jack.

In Chapter 4 we discussed connecting your Macintosh to a video source, such as VideoSpigot or ComputerEyes/RT. Those connections still apply; refer to Figures 4.1 and 4.10 of the previous chapter. The audio connections are in addition to your video connections.

Making the Movie

Whether you're using Movie Recorder or VideoSpigot's software, ScreenPlay, you'll need to do very little to add sound to your QuickTime movies.

Movie Recorder and Sound

When running Apple's Movie Recorder utility, as we've done when using the ComputerEyes/RT video digitizer, you can control some of the sound recording parameters. First, make sure that the software is set to record sound. The Settings menu contains an item that toggles sound recording on and off. When it's on, the menu item will read "Turn Sound Off." The menu item just below it, **Sound Input**, will then be enabled. Figure 5.4 shows **Sound Input** being selected.

When you select **Sound Input**, you'll see the dialog box pictured in Figure 5.5. We'll cover the options within this dialog box next.

The pop-up menu in the Source section of the dialog box lists all available sound input sources. If your Macintosh has a built-in sound input port, it will always be listed here. If you have additional audio input sources attached to your computer, such as the MacRecorder sound digitizer discussed later in this chapter, it too will be included in this menu. Figure 5.6 shows this part of the dialog box.

FIGURE 5.4
Selecting the Sound Input Menu Item in Movie Recorder

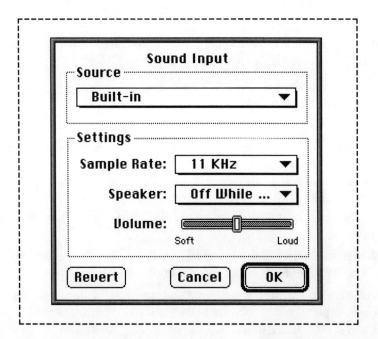

FIGURE 5.5
The Sound Input Dialog Box in Movie Recorder

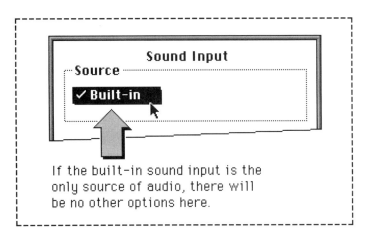

FIGURE 5.6
Selecting a Sound Input Source In Movie Recorder

The Settings section of the Sound Input dialog box allows you to vary the *sampling rate*—the number of sound samples made per second. The Mac's built-in sound input port offers a choice of 11 KHz or 22 KHz (11,000 or 22,000 samples per second). The more samples made, the higher the quality. For recording voice conversations, 11 KHz is usually adequate. If music is involved, use 22 KHz. Why not always use the higher, better-quality rate? The more samples made, the more disk space the resulting soundtrack will occupy. Figure 5.7 shows the two sampling rate options provided by the built-in port.

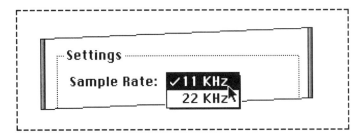

FIGURE 5.7
Selecting a Sound Sampling Rate in Movie Recorder

With your audio source plugged into your Mac's built-in sound port, and the sound turned on in the Settings menu, audio will always be recorded to the movie. But you can choose to send the audio to the speaker during preview, while both previewing and recording, or not at all. This is merely a convenience for you. As stated, whether you can hear the sound or not, it will be saved to the movie's soundtrack. Figure 5.8 shows the speaker menu options.

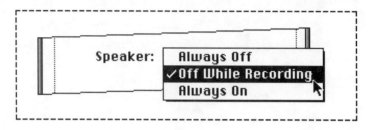

FIGURE 5.8

Specifying When to Send Sound to the Mac Speaker in Movie Recorder

The volume setting sets the input sound level for recording. This level is the volume which will be saved to the movie—so preview your tape and vary the volume setting here. Don't record the tape until you've found a suitable setting. Figure 5.9 shows the slider that sets the input volume.

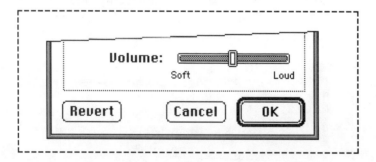

FIGURE 5.9

Setting the Recording Volume in Movie Recorder

Earlier we said that you might consider buying a sound digitizer for sound input—even if your Mac has a built-in sound input port. Volume control and sound quality are two reasons we suggested this. The slider shown in Figure

5.9 provides only limited control of the volume. You'll find that rather than providing a smooth range of volume settings, it is limited to only a few discrete settings. Regardless of the volume setting, the sound recorded using an audio digitizer is superior.

VideoSpigot ScreenPlay and Sound

When it comes to recording sound, ScreenPlay, the software that accompanies the VideoSpigot digitizer, doesn't offer the flexibility of Apple's Movie Recorder utility. ScreenPlay gives you just one option: to record sound or not. You'll make that choice from within the Preference dialog box, as shown in Figure 5.10.

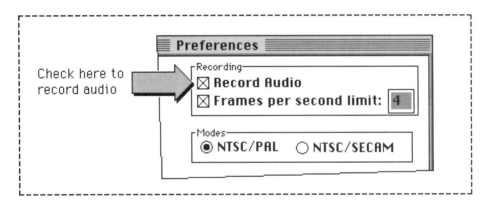

FIGURE 5.10
Setting ScreenPlay to Recorder Audio

Those of you with Macs that have a built-in sound port may still consider buying a sound digitizer. The next section explains why.

Capturing Sound with MacRecorder

If your Macintosh doesn't have a built-in sound input port, don't feel cheated. Using a sound digitizer to capture the soundtrack of a tape has several advantages over using the built-in port. This section discusses MacRecorder, Macromind's inexpensive and popular sound digitizer. Some things we liked about it: it has an adjustment knob that makes volume control precise, sound quality itself is very good, and it comes packaged with powerful sound editing software that allows you to edit and add special effects to sounds.

Making the Connection

The MacRecorder sound digitizer is an external device; you don't have to open your Macintosh to install it. It gets connected between your tape source and your Macintosh, as shown in Figure 5.11.

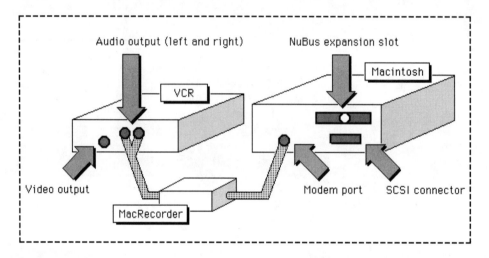

FIGURE 5.11

Connections for the MacRecorder Sound Digitizer and a VCR

MacRecorder comes with both cables pictured in Figure 5.11. You can plug the cable with the single connector to either the modem port or printer port of your Macintosh.

After hooking up MacRecorder, select the Sound control panel. Click on the **MacRecorder** icon in the Microphones window. That's shown in Figure 5.12. If your Macintosh doesn't have a built-in sound port, the icon labeled "Built-in" won't appear in the Microphones window.

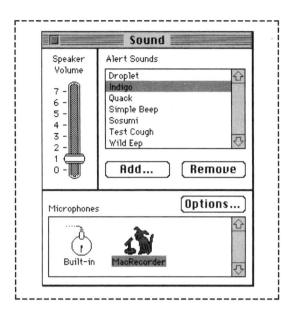

FIGURE 5.12
The MacRecorder Microphone Icon in the Sound Control Panel

While still in the Sound control panel, click the **Options** button. You'll see the dialog box shown in Figure 5.13. Make sure the Port Status is correct. We connected MacRecorder to the printer port, and the dialog box in Figure 5.13 reflects that by printing "MacRecorder connected" next to the printer icon.

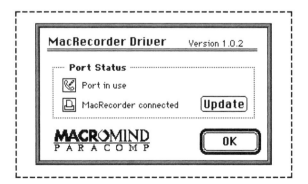

FIGURE 5.13
Verifying Port Setup in the Sound Control Panel

Making the Movie

Using MacRecorder, like using the built-in sound port of some Macs, requires little intervention on your part. Adding quality sound to your QuickTime movies is a straightforward process.

Movie Recorder and Sound

All the Sound Input settings that are adjusted using Movie Recorder's Settings menu work with MacRecorder. They were discussed in the previous section, *Capturing Sound with the Built-in Sound Port*. If you skipped that section, go back and read it now.

If your computer has a built-in sound port, both the MacRecorder and the built-in port will now appear in the Source section of the Sound Input dialog box, shown in Figure 5.14. If your Mac doesn't have the built-in port, only the MacRecorder will show up as the source.

```
                    Sound Input
  ┌ Source ─────────────────────────────────
  │  Built-in
  │ ✓MacRecorder
  │                    ꜛ
  ─────────────────────────────────────────

     Sample Rate:  ✓22 KHz
                     11 KHz ꜛ
        Speaker:     7 KHz        ···  ▼
                     5 KHz
         Volume:
                    Soft              Loud

   ( Revert )       ( Cancel )   ▢ OK ▢
```

FIGURE 5.14
Sound Input Options in Movie Recorder

MacRecorder gives you four sampling rates to choose from—two more than the built-in sound port. The 7-KHz and 5-KHz settings create sounds that occupy a much smaller amount of disk space than those recorded at 11 KHz or 22 KHz. The trade-off is that sound quality is lower. Although not acceptable for recording music, the 7-KHz rate may suit you for recording voices. MacRecorder's pop-up sampling rate menu is shown in Figure 5.14.

MacRecorder has an external volume adjustment knob that allows you to control the volume level as you preview a tape, or even as you record it. We found it best to set the volume to its maximum setting in Movie Recorder, then make adjustments using MacRecorder. That way you only have to access the Sound Input menu item one time—for the initial setting. After that, you can adjust the input volume from quiet to loud using MacRecorder—easily and as often as you like. Figure 5.15 shows the volume scale in Movie Recorder.

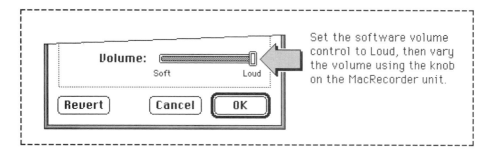

FIGURE 5.15
Setting the Recording Volume in Movie Recorder

VideoSpigot ScreenPlay and Sound

As with a built-in sound input port, VideoSpigot's ScreenPlay software provides just one audio setting. Click the **Record Audio** check box in the Preferences dialog box to record audio along with video, or uncheck to create a movie that consists of just the video track.

Using SoundEdit to Create and Edit Sounds

You've seen how you can record both video and audio at the same time to create a QuickTime movie that has both a video track and soundtrack. You can also record the video track and audio track separately in two passes through the same section of a tape. The first time you'll use your video digitizer to capture the video. The second time you'll capture just the audio part of the tape by recording from within SoundEdit Pro, the software that comes with MacRecorder. Then, using movie editing software such as Adobe Premiere, you can combine the video and audio into one QuickTime movie.

Why go through the extra work of recording something twice? If you're satisfied with the content and quality of the tape you're making a QuickTime movie from, you won't want to. But if you want to make changes or additions to the audio portion, you need to capture the audio as a separate sound file. Then, using SoundEdit Pro, you can add, delete, or edit the sound.

You can also use SoundEdit Pro to create sounds that can be added to a QuickTime movie that doesn't contain audio. Sounds don't have to be from a tape. You can use MacRecorder's built-in microphone, or plug in a better one, to record a dialog or narration. You'll save this recording as a sound file, then add it to a QuickTime movie using movie-editing software. You can also record music. The cable included with MacRecorder can easily be connected to an amplifier, receiver, tape deck, or compact disk player. With the MacRecorder connected to your Macintosh modem or printer port, you can create sound files that contain music. Again, you can use a movie editor to add the music to a QuickTime movie…any movie.

Using SoundEdit Pro—The Basics

When you start SoundEdit Pro you'll see two windows on your screen (shown in Figure 5.16). The Control Palette allows you to record and play back sounds. The document window—empty when you first run the program—displays the waveform of a sound.

Connect the MacRecorder hardware to your Macintosh. You don't need to connect any audio source, such as a VCR, to it. For our simple test we'll use the MacRecorder's built-in microphone. The meter icon in the top left corner of the Control Palette allows you to turn input sound monitoring on and off. Click once on the icon. The Input Level Meter will show a horizontal bar that varies in length—it reflects the input sound. Figure 5.17 shows these items. Try talking in the direction of the MacRecorder to move the bar. You can vary the strength of the input sound by adjusting the volume control knob on the MacRecorder unit.

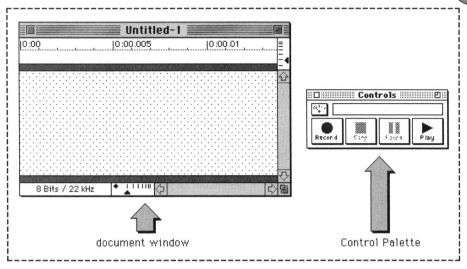

FIGURE 5.16
The Windows of SoundEdit Pro

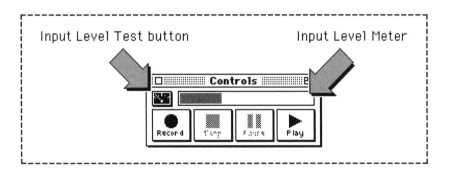

FIGURE 5.17
Previewing Sound Input in SoundEdit Pro

At this point you're just previewing the input sound. To record, click once on the **Record** button of the Control Palette. The **Stop** and **Pause** buttons will become enabled (shown in Figure 5.18). Say a few words, such as "Testing one, two, three," then click the **Stop** button.

After you click the **Stop** button, a waveform representing your words will appear in the document window. Figure 5.19 shows an example.

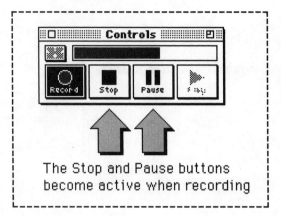

FIGURE 5.18

Recording a Sound in SoundEdit Pro

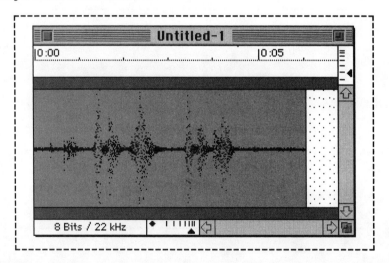

FIGURE 5.19

A Soundwave in the Document Window of SoundPlay Pro

To play back the sound, click the **Play** button. You'll hear your recorded words played back on the speaker of your Macintosh. Save your test sound by selecting **Save** from the File menu. You'll see a dialog box like the one in Figure 5.20. Type in a descriptive name for the sound, then select a sound format. In Figure 5.20 we've dropped down the menu that displays your sound format options.

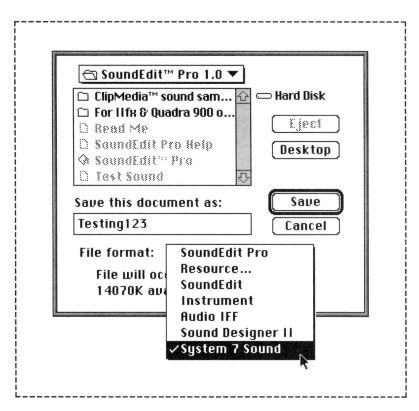

FIGURE 5.20
Selecting a Sound Format for a Sound in SoundEdit Pro

SoundEdit Pro lets you save a sound in several formats. Figure 5.20 shows the System 7 Sound format being selected. Saving a sound in the System 7 Sound format allows the sound to be opened and edited in Premiere, the movie editing software discussed in the next chapter. We recommend you save your sounds this way.

If you'll be using a program that doesn't recognize System 7 Sounds, the Audio IFF format might be the one to use. Audio IFF (audio interchange file format) is a standard sound format. Figure 5.21 shows how SoundEdit Pro gives sounds saved in different formats different identifying icons. Whatever format a sound is saved in, SoundEdit Pro is capable of reopening it later on.

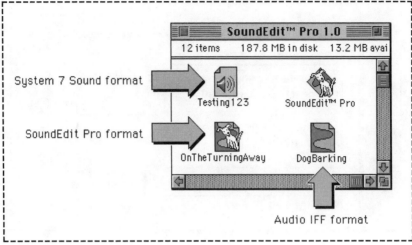

FIGURE 5.21

The Different Icons of SoundEdit Pro Sound Files

 Being recognized by the movie-editing program Premiere is one advantage to saving a sound in the System 7 Sound format. Here's a second advantage unrelated to QuickTime movies: you can easily add the sound to the list of alert sounds in the Sound control panel. Select it, and every time your Mac should beep, it will instead play the sound you added, whether it's your voice or a clip of music. Simply drag the sound file or a copy of it to your System Folder. Then open the Sound control panel and click on the sound name, as we've done with our Testing123 sound in Figure 5.22.

You've now successfully recorded and saved a sound to its own sound file. In the next section we'll open this file and edit the sound.

Using SoundEdit Pro to Edit Sounds

Once you've created a sound, you can use SoundEdit Pro to edit it. Select **Open** from the File menu, then click on the sound file to edit. Click the **Open** button and the sound's waveform will be displayed in a document window.

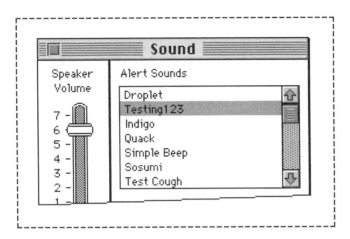

FIGURE 5.22
Adding a System 7 Sound to the Sound Control Panel

As with any Macintosh element that you edit, you first have to make a selection. To select an entire sound, double-click on it. To select part of a sound, click the mouse at a starting point and, with the mouse button held down, drag to the point that will end your selection. You can then perform standard editing commands on the selection, such as cut and copy. Move to a different point in the sound and click once to create an insertion point. Then paste in the copied or cut selection.

SoundEdit Pro allows you to have more than one sound file open at a time. That enables you to easily copy parts of one sound file and then paste them into a different sound file. In Figure 5.23 we combine part of a sound that has a dog barking with a sound that has a cat meowing.

Having standard editing commands such as copy and paste makes SoundEdit Pro a very useful tool. But its special effects menu is where SoundEdit Pro really shines. Figure 5.24 shows that menu.

After creating a sound or opening a sound file, select the entire sound or a portion of it. To apply a special effect to the selection, make a menu selection from the Effects menu. When you do, you'll encounter a dialog box that lets you specify details of how you want to implement the effect. Figure 5.25 shows the dialog box for the Amplify effect.

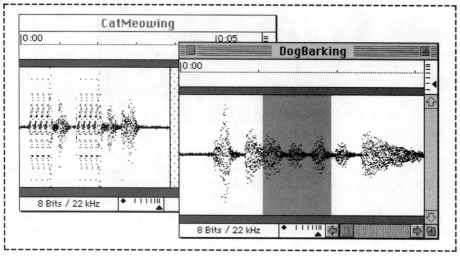

FIGURE 5.23

Editing Two Sound Files in SoundEdit Pro

FIGURE 5.24

The Effects Menu in SoundEdit Pro

Amplify

Amplitude: 50 %

Cancel   OK

FIGURE 5.25
The Amplify Dialog Box in SoundEdit Pro

We set the amplitude of a test sound to 50%. Figure 5.26 shows "before" and "after" windows for the test sound. You can see from the waveforms that the waveform has been reduced in height—we've quieted it down.

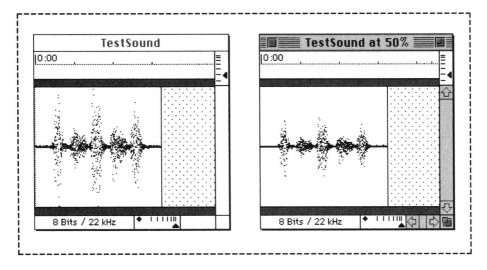

FIGURE 5.26
A Soundwave Before and After 50% Amplification

SoundEdit Pro lets you smooth out a sound, play it backwards, and achieve other effects. Figure 5.27 shows the dialog box for the Reverb menu item. When you add reverb to a section of sound, you get the echo effect of a sound in an empty room.

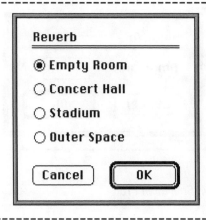

FIGURE 5.27

The Reverb Dialog Box in SoundEdit Pro

Using SoundEdit Pro to Mix Multiple Soundtracks

With SoundEdit Pro, you can create or open more than one sound, then mix them together to form a single sound. One soundtrack could be music or a background noise, such as the sound of a running stream, while the other soundtrack could be a narrative. Figure 5.28 shows the menu you'll use to add a second track to a sound.

With one sound file open, select **Add Track** from the Sound menu. You'll get a new, empty track, but not in a new document window. Instead, the new track will be added below the existing one. Click the **Record** button on the Control Panel and make a recording. Figure 5.29 shows what the document window will look like when it has two tracks in it.

If you want the second track to be from an existing sound file, select **Import File** from the File menu. After you select a sound file, a second track will be added to the document window.

You can have more than two tracks in a single document window, but we can't tell you exactly what the limit is—it depends on the size of each sound and the amount of memory your Macintosh has.

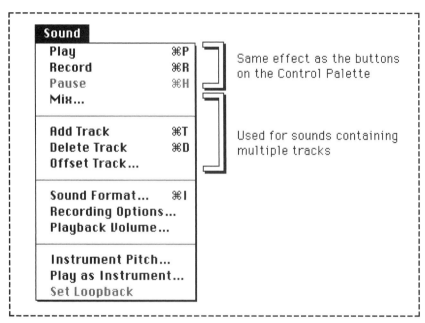

FIGURE 5.28
The Sound Menu in SoundEdit Pro

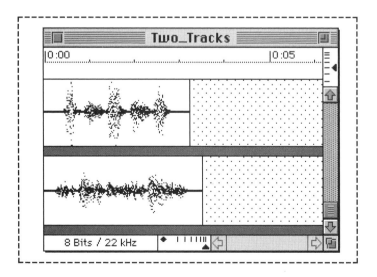

FIGURE 5.29
Two SoundTracks in One Document in SoundEdit Pro

To listen to more than one track, click the mouse at the start of a track and drag across it. Move downward to include the second track as well. That selects both tracks. Then click the **Play** button on the Control Palette. When you're satisfied with results, select **Mix** from the Sound menu. The two tracks will be combined into one.

Using SoundEdit Pro to Capture Music

Up to this point we've demonstrated SoundEdit's powers on sounds recorded with MacRecorder's built-in microphone. You don't have to capture sounds from the microphone, though. You've already seen that you can connect one end of a cable to the left and right audio outputs of a VCR, and the other end to the MacRecorder line input to capture the soundtrack of a VCR tape. You can do the same to capture music from your stereo.

MacRecorder comes with a cable. Connect the end of the cable that has two leads to the left and right audio outputs of an amplifier, receiver, boom box, tape deck, or compact disk player. Connect the other end of the lead to MacRecorder's line input jack. With SoundEdit Pro running, and music playing, follow these steps to record a music clip:

1. Click on the **Input Level Test** button of the SoundEdit Pro Control Palette to preview the music on the Input Level Meter.

2. Vary the volume control knob on the MacRecorder unit until the level of the meter approaches the right end of the Input Level Meter.

3. Click the **Record** button on the Control Palette.

4. Click the **Stop** button when done.

To save the sound to a file, select **Save** from the File menu, just as you've done before. That's all there is to it. Now you've got a great piece of music saved on disk, ready to be added to a QuickTime movie that is without sound. (That will come in the next chapter.)

Using SoundEdit Pro to Capture and Edit the Soundtrack of a Tape

Now that you know all about SoundEdit Pro's ability to edit and enhance sounds, you might want to try making changes to the sound track of a videotape you have. Because SoundEdit Pro edits sound files, not QuickTime movies, this feat will require a little extra effort on your part.

Begin by creating a QuickTime movie from your videotape, using any video digitizer you want. Don't be concerned with connecting MacRecorder to the VCR—you aren't concerned with the soundtrack at this point. When done, rewind the videotape to the point at which you started capturing the video.

Next, run SoundEdit Pro. Now is the time to connect the VCR audio outputs to the MacRecorder. Your video is already *queued*, or properly positioned, at the point at which taping should begin. Click **Record** on SoundEdit's Control Panel and select **Play** on your VCR. After capturing sound for at least as long as you did video, click the **Stop** button on both SoundEdit's Control Panel and your VCR. The result? You now have the soundtrack of your video, ready for editing and special effects enhancement. When completed, select **Save** from the File menu. Now, you have a QuickTime movie that contains a video track and a sound file that contains an audio track. The only step left is to add the soundtrack to the QuickTime movie. For that, you need movie-editing software like Adobe's Premiere. All the more reason to read Chapter 6!

Other Sources of Sounds

If you are making a QuickTime movie from a video source, such as a camcorder or VCR tape, sound may already be present on the tape you're using. In those cases, you can use the techniques described earlier in this chapter to make a QuickTime movie that includes the soundtrack along with the video track of the tape. But if your movie is made from a series of graphics, or made from a video that has a poor soundtrack, or none at all, you'll want to add a sound track. In this section we discuss a couple of sources of sounds—sound you can use as part of your own movies. In the next chapter we'll describe how to add these sounds to a QuickTime movie.

Obtaining Sounds from Information Services

Electronic telecommunications services, or *information services*, have libraries of shareware and free public domain software. Some of these libraries consist of sound files that members can download. You join a service by paying a small membership fee. You then pay an hourly fee for the time you are connected (the time you spend accessing the service using your modem).

Many members of information services, such as CompuServe and America Online, make sound files available to you. These members use audio digitizing equipment and techniques like those described in this chapter to create sound clips and then upload them to the information service.

As you navigate through the screens of an information service you'll find sound clips from topics such as part of a Pink Floyd song, a few seconds of Spock talking in a Star Trek film, or animal sounds. The variety is great. When you come across a sound that seems like it might fit in with a video you have, you can download it. Movie-editing software will then allow you to merge the sound, or sounds, with the video of a QuickTime movie.

Both the video and audio soundtracks of movies and other works, such as cartoons, are copyrighted material. So is the music on CDs. How then can these clips of sound be available for your use? Short sequences of copyrighted works are generally considered legal under the fair use provision. If you download a few seconds of a song and play it in your home, you have not deprived the artist of any income.

The situation changes when you include copyrighted video or audio in a QuickTime movie that you intend to sell or otherwise profit from. Commercial use of copyrighted material is illegal unless you first obtain permission from the holder of the copyright, or purchase the right to do so in the form of a licensed agreement from the copyright holder.

Most sound files you download, no matter what the source, are in a compressed format. A compressed file is smaller than its uncompressed counterpart, and thus downloads more quickly. If a file's name ends with the extension "sit," it was compressed with Aladdin Systems' StuffIt compression utility. To decompress a compressed file, run Aladdin's StuffIt or StuffIt Expander program. The StuffIt Expander program, like sound files, can be found in the libraries of information services. Download it one time and you can use it on all the sound files you ever download. Figure 5.30 shows the icon of StuffIt Expander, along with the icon of a compressed (stuffed) file, and the icon of the same file after expanding.

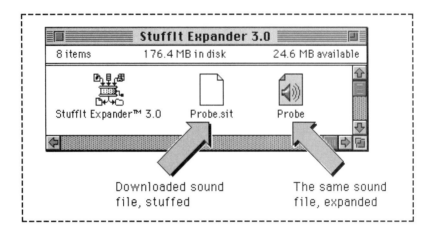

FIGURE 5.30
A Downloaded Sound File—Stuffed and Unstuffed

Notice that the icon of the Probe file in Figure 5.30 is the same as the icon of a sound file in System 7 Sound format (as shown back in Figure 5.21). Downloaded sound files—after being decompressed—can be used just like a sound file you create in SoundEdit Pro. That means you can open them from within SoundEdit Pro and edit or add special effects to them. And, as you'll see in the next chapter, they can be used as a soundtrack for a QuickTime movie.

CompuServe

CompuServe is a well-established information service with over 1.5 million members. With that many subscribers, it makes sense that CompuServe has large libraries of sound files. To move to a particular area in CompuServe, you first type in keywords, such as "GO MACFUN," to go to the Macintosh Entertainment Forum. Once there, you enter a library of sound files by making a menu selection. Figure 5.31 shows part of a typical CompuServe session.

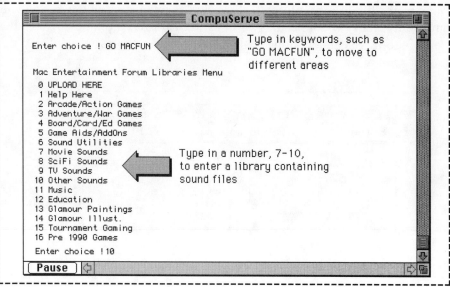

FIGURE 5.31

A Typical Session in CompuServe

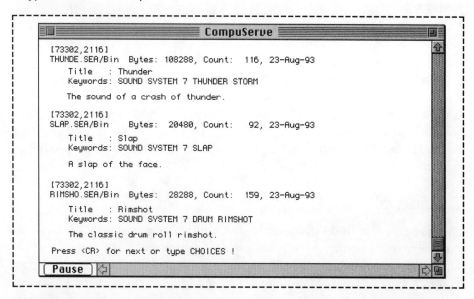

FIGURE 5.32

A Description of a Few Sound Files in CompuServe

Within a library you can browse through the sound files, getting a description of each one. When you find a file of interest, type "CHOICES" to get a list of downloading options. Figure 5.32 shows a few of the sound files we scrolled through.

America Online

America Online hasn't been around as long as CompuServe, but in the past year it had a surge in membership that made it the fastest growing online service in the country. Its half million members appreciate that America Online comes with *navigational software* that makes traversing the screens of information easy. The menus, windows, and icons of America Online are simple and intuitive, making it a good choice for anyone new to information services. Double-clicking on words and icons moves you to different libraries of software and information. Figure 5.33 shows a scrollable list of one sound sample library.

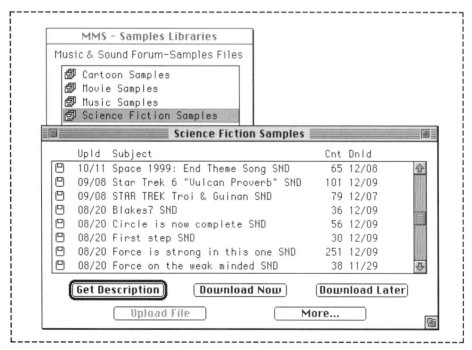

FIGURE 5.33
A Typical Session in America Online

When you come across a sound file name that seems intriguing, click on the name of the file, then click the **Get Description** button for some information about it. To download a sound file in America Online, click on the file name and then click the **Download Now** button. You'll see a dialog box like the one shown in Figure 5.34.

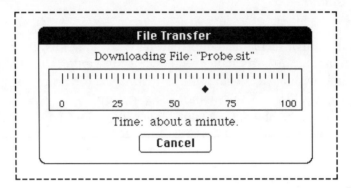

FIGURE 5.34
Downloading a File from America Online

Purchasing Sounds

Online services such as CompuServe and America Online are great ways to get sound files. But if you don't have a modem and a subscription to an information service, you aren't out of luck. Many companies now sell both video and audio files that you can incorporate into your own QuickTime movies. Packages are usually grouped and sold by subject. There are videos of rocket blastoffs, great baseball moments, travel highlights, and clips you can use as backgrounds. Audio files include jazz, ragtime, and rock sound clips, and noises and sound effects such as animal sounds and thunderstorms.

Many companies that distribute video and audio collections claim that the clips they contain are royalty-free. That means you can alter the clips and use them in your own productions, without paying a fee. If you do intend to sell your QuickTime movies, though, carefully read the fine print of the documentation that accompanies the movies and sounds. You might be required to include information about the copyright in your final movies.

The Appendix of QuickTime products lists several companies and their clip products.

Chapter Summary

A QuickTime movie is composed of both a video track and an audio track. The latter is usually referred to as a soundtrack. Though these tracks are independent of one another, they are synchronized so that they always match up, regardless of how fast or slow a movie plays.

Some Macintoshes have a built-in sound input port—the port on the back that a microphone plugs into. If your computer has this port, you can use it to capture the soundtrack of a movie as you capture the video track with a digitizer. You can also capture music by connecting the audio outputs of an amplifier, receiver, tape deck, or compact disk player to the sound port.

If your Macintosh doesn't have this port, you can buy a sound digitizer to capture sound. You can use the same audio sources mentioned for the sound port. A sound digitizer, such as the popular MacRecorder by MacroMind, has the advantage of providing an external volume control that lets you adjust the input volume before or during recording of a sound. It also comes with a fascinating sound-editing program that lets you view waveforms; cut, copy, and paste parts of a sound; add special effects to sounds; and save sounds to files. You can use movie-editing software to combine sound files with movie clips to create and enhance QuickTime movies.

In addition to recording your own sounds, you can obtain sounds captured by others. CompuServe and America Online, two popular online services, have libraries of sound files that you can download for your own use. If you don't have access to one of these services, you can purchase sound files from several companies.

Editing Movies

uickTime movies are easy to make. You can use simple animation techniques, or turn video, such as home movies, into QuickTime movies. But you might not always be satisfied with the results. A movie might have poor quality sound, or none at all. You might wish you could insert a close-up picture of a person in the middle of a video. Or you might like to string several videos together to form a single movie—perhaps a short clip of someone you know, at different years of their life. With movie-editing software, all these ideas can become realities, with surprisingly little effort. In this chapter we'll examine the use of Premiere, one of the most popular QuickTime movie editors.

Editing Sounds—Advanced

Sound is an important part of many QuickTime movies. Fortunately, software tools exist that allow you to modify or add sound to any QuickTime movie you have or are going to create. In the previous chapter we introduced soundtracks and how to edit them using MacroMind's SoundEdit Pro software. Now that you're familiar with the basic concepts of sound, we'll delve a little deeper into editing sound files. You'll be using sound files later in this chapter as you edit a QuickTime movie, so in preparation for that moment, you'll want to get your sounds just right!

Cue Points

SoundEdit Pro's ability to mix two or more tracks of sound into one soundtrack is a powerful feature. It allows you to combine two, three, or ten different sounds into one track that you can add to a movie.

When you open two sounds into one document window, the sounds both start at time zero. You don't have to leave the sounds at this point, however. You can slide individual tracks of sound all about the time line by pressing the **Option** key, clicking and holding the mouse button on a sound, and then dragging the sound to a different point in time. When working with more than one track, there will be times when lining up the start of one sound with a particular spot in another sound becomes important. For instances such as these, SoundEdit Pro provides you with *cue points*.

We'll use a two-track document window as an example of working with cue points. Imagine that the first track, the top track in the window, consists of people talking and a doorbell ringing. The second track, the lower track, consists of a dog barking. We want to line up the bottom track—the bark—with the location of the upper track at which the doorbell rings. While some might not consider the timing of this situation as critical, we, perfectionists that we are, do. If we place the lower track to far to the left—too early in time—the dog will bark before the doorbell rings. Since this piece of sound doesn't deal with the paranormal, we don't want people thinking we own a psychic pooch. On the other hand, if we place the lower track too far to the right—too late in time—we'll be accused of owning a slow-minded animal.

To create the cue point, we first selected the top soundtrack by clicking on it. Then we pressed the **Play** button on the Control Palette. As the top sound plays, a line sweeps over the track. At the moment the doorbell plays, we press **Command-M**. That places a cue point—a small triangular marker—just below the time line. SoundEdit Pro will give this first cue point a name of "Cue 1." Figure 6.1 shows this cue point.

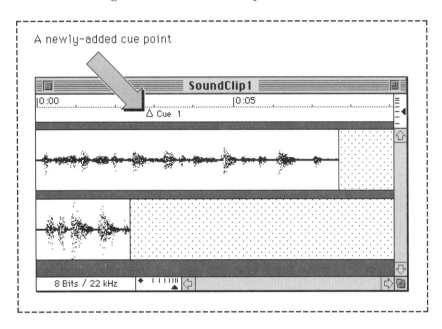

FIGURE 6.1

A Cue Point in SoundEdit Pro

A cue point is a mark in time. It isn't actually attached to any one soundtrack in the document window. It is simply a marker. We gave the marker a more descriptive title by clicking on its name. That placed a frame around the title. We then typed in a new name. As shown in Figure 6.2, we've renamed our cue point "Doorbell."

You can also make a cue point by selecting **Make Cue Point** from the Edit menu. But using the Command key combination is a far quicker and more accurate way of accomplishing this. An Edit menu item of note, however, is the **Cue Points** item. Figure 6.3 shows the Edit menu.

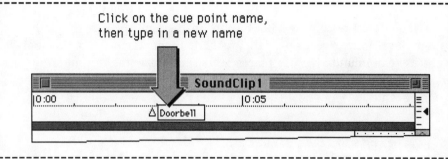

FIGURE 6.2

Renaming a SoundEdit Pro Cue Point

Edit	
Undo Change Cue Point Name	⌘Z
Cut	⌘X
Copy	⌘C
Paste	⌘V
Clear	
Select All	⌘A
Make Label	⌘L
Labels...	
Make Cue Point...	⌘M
Cue Points...	
Color	▶
Preferences...	
Show Clipboard	
Play Clipboard	

FIGURE 6.3

The Edit Menu in SoundEdit Pro

When you select the **Cue Points** menu item you'll see the dialog box pictured in Figure 6.4. It lists all the cue points in a document window. We have just the one: the Doorbell.

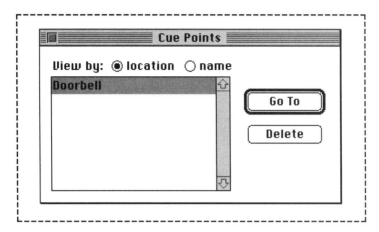

FIGURE 6.4
The Cue Dialog Box in SoundEdit Pro

You can move the document window insertion point to a cue point by first clicking on its name in the Cue Points dialog box. Then click the **Go To** button. The thin, vertical insertion point line will move directly under the cue point triangle, and will flash. If you don't have any one track selected, the insertion point will extend downward across all tracks (both tracks in our example). That's exactly what we want. We now know that the flashing insertion point marks the beginning of the doorbell sound. All we have to do now is drag the barking sound—the bottom track—to this insertion point. To move the track, we press the **Option** key and click the mouse on any part of the sound in the lower track. With the mouse button held down, we slide the sound until its left side lines up with the flashing insertion point, just as we've done in Figure 6.5.

The lower sound track will now start playing just as the doorbell chimes in the upper track. To check the alignment of the sounds, we clicked on the far left side of the top track and, with the mouse held down, swept down and across to the right to cover both tracks. That highlighted the entire window. Then a click of the **Play** button on the Control Palette played both sounds.

If you've added cue points to a sound, and you're done editing the sound, you might want to consider saving it twice. You can save it once using the System 7 Sound format; that way you can import it into Premiere and many other programs. You might also save it as in the SoundEdit Pro

Sound format. Why? Sounds saved in other formats lose their cue points. Cue points are only for your reference—they aren't needed as part of the sound file. If you aren't satisfied with the sound at a later point, and want to further edit it in SoundEdit Pro, you can then open the version saved as a SoundEdit Pro Sound—it retains all cue points.

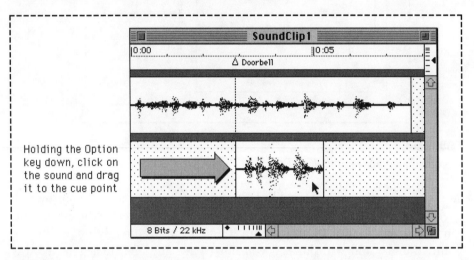

FIGURE 6.5
Lining Up Sound Clips in SoundEdit Pro

Labels

Cue points allow you to mark particular points in time in a soundtrack. Labels, too, are a means of marking a spot in a sound. But while cue points are precise markers used to align multiple soundtracks, *labels* are a more general mark used for locating and referring to larger sound sections.

As the number of sounds in your collection increases, you may want to keep track of certain words, sounds, or music clips that you might use again in a different movie. If a soundtrack is long and contains numerous different sound sections, you'll want to add labels to it. If you give each label a descriptive name for the sound section it is near, you'll be able to easily find particular sounds when you reopen a sound file later.

Recall that a cue point marked a point in time, and applied to all tracks in a document window. If you delete one track of a multiple-track document window, the cue points remain. A label marks a spot in one track of a document window. It applies only to that one track. If you delete the track, its labels will disappear along with the track.

To create a label, click the mouse at the location of a sound—that places the insertion point on the sound. Then select **Make Label** from the Edit menu. A label will appear underneath the sound, as shown in Figure 6.6.

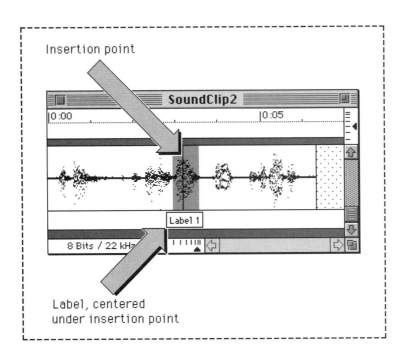

FIGURE 6.6
Adding a Label in SoundEdit Pro

To change the text of a label, click on it and type in a new name. You can add as many labels as you want to a soundtrack. Figure 6.7 shows two labels on a track—we've marked the location of the words "WOW!" and "Hey, you" that appear in the track.

The Edit menu also contains a **Label** command. Use this menu item to bring up the dialog box shown in Figure 6.8. Here you can move to a label by clicking on it and then clicking the **Go To** button.

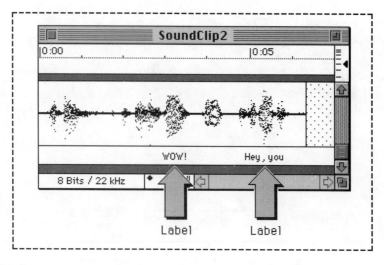

FIGURE 6.7
A SoundTrack with Two Labels in SoundEdit Pro

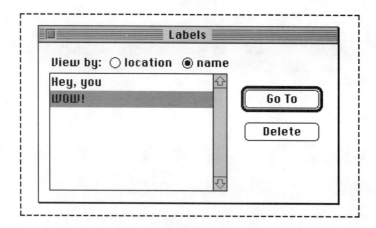

FIGURE 6.8
The Labels Dialog Box in SoundEdit Pro

Cue points and labels allow you to properly align sounds in multiple track document windows and keep track of the location of certain sounds in large sound files. With a firm knowledge of sound-editing techniques and movie-making, you're all set to create a polished QuickTime movie using movie-editing software such as Adobe Premiere.

Using Premiere to Edit Movies

Movie editors allow you to combine existing QuickTime movies, called video clips, with audio clips (sound files). You can combine more than one movie clip and more than one sound file into a new QuickTime movie. Additionally, movie editors allow you to add special effects, such as dissolves, to a movie. In this section we'll discuss movie editing using Adobe Premiere.

Premiere Basics

You use Premiere to piece together existing movie clips and sound files to make one QuickTime movie. Premiere provides two main windows to simplify constructing a movie. The first is the Project window. When you start the Premiere program, you'll face an empty Project window, like the one shown in Figure 6.9.

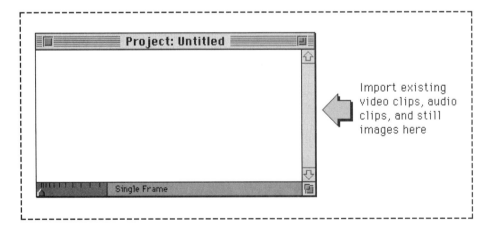

FIGURE 6.9
An Empty Project Window in Premiere

The Project window is used to hold a picture and description of each video, audio, and still image you're considering using in your movie. This is a holding bay from which you will pick and move clips to the second main type of window: the Construction window. Figure 6.10 shows an empty Construction window.

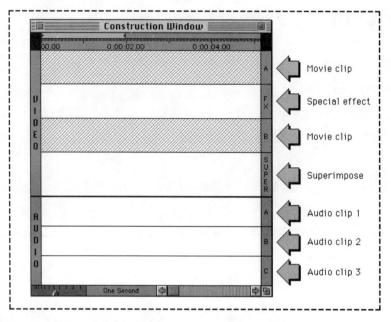

FIGURE 6.10

An Empty Construction Window in Premiere

The Construction window is where you piece together video clips, audio clips, and still images. This window also lets you add numerous special effects, like fade in or fade out. When satisfied with your efforts in the Construction window, you'll make one menu choice to combine all the individual elements in it into a single QuickTime movie.

To demonstrate the basics of Premiere, we'll assemble a simple movie. This example won't show off much of the power of Premiere, but it will let you quickly see just how a movie is made in this movie-editing environment.

You first import existing clips and images—the individual pieces that will make up your movie. Use the **Import** command in the File menu to do this. Figure 6.11 shows the **Import** command, and the rest of the File menu.

The **Import** command opens a standard Open dialog box that lets you select a QuickTime movie, a sound file, or a still image (a PICT file). Once you import a clip, it shows up in the Project window. If it's a video or still image, a *thumbnail*—a small, single image—shows up in the Project window. You'll also see additional information about the clip, such as the type of clip (movie or still). If the clip is audio, a small picture of a soundwave will appear in place of a thumbnail. Figure 6.12 shows the Project window after importing one video clip.

FIGURE 6.11
Premiere's File Menu

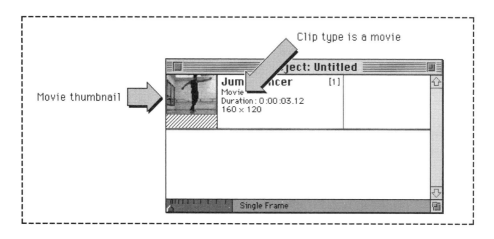

FIGURE 6.12
A Premiere Project Window with One Movie Clip Added to It

For our simple movie we'll use an existing QuickTime movie that has no soundtrack and give it one. In Figure 6.13 you can see that we've imported one movie and one sound file. Diagonal lines in a part of the thumbnail region tell you that the clip contains neither video nor audio. The QuickTime movie we imported doesn't have an audio track, and the sound file of course has no video with it.

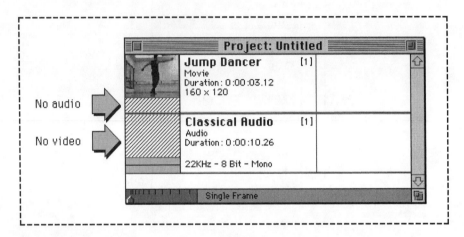

FIGURE 6.13

A Premiere Project Window with a Movie and Audio Clip

The Project window is where you preview and organize the clips you're going to use. The Construction window is where you actually set up the movie. To move a clip from the Project window to the Construction window, just click on it and, holding the mouse down, drag it over to the Construction window. If the clip is a video, drag it to the VIDEO A row. If it's an audio clip, drag it to the AUDIO A row. When you release the mouse, several frames of the video, or a horizontal line representing the audio, will appear. Figure 6.14 shows the Construction window after we dragged both the movie and audio clip to it.

Of our two clips, the audio is longer; you can see in Figure 6.14 that it extends past the right edge of the Construction window. To shorten a clip (audio or video), click the mouse on the right end of it and drag to the left. As you do, a vertical line will be present, running the entire height of the window. That makes it easy for you to align clips. In Figure 6.15 we're dragging the sound clip so that it lines up with the end of the video clip.

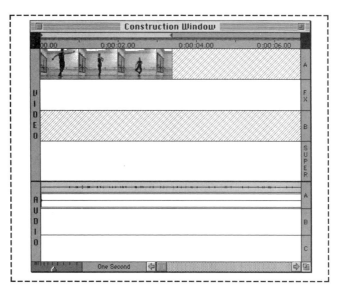

FIGURE 6.14

A Construction Window with a Movie and Audio Clip

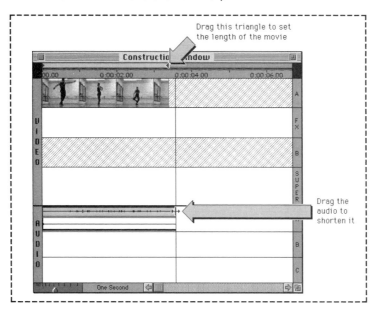

FIGURE 6.15

Editing the Length of an Audio Clip in Premiere

In Figure 6.15 you'll also notice a small triangle at the top of the Construction window. By sliding the triangle in either direction, you set the length of the QuickTime movie, not the length of the clip that appears below it. Why would you want to make the length of the QuickTime movie *longer* than the movie clip? You'll do that if you add a second movie clip after the first. In Premiere, you can drag as many movies as you want into the VIDEO A row. The final movie will play one after another.

With a video and audio track in the Construction window, we'll call our simple movie-editing session complete. To make a movie, we select **Make Movie** from the Project menu, shown in Figure 6.16.

```
┌─────────────────────────────────────┐
│  ┌──────────────────────────────┐   │
│  │ Project                      │   │
│  │ Make Movie...            ⌘K  │   │
│  │ Preview Work Area     [enter]│   │
│  │                              │   │
│  │ Add this clip            ⌘J  │   │
│  │ Add Matte...             ⌘-  │   │
│  │                              │   │
│  │ Construction Display      ▶  │   │
│  │                              │   │
│  │ Preview Options...       ⌘[  │   │
│  │ Output Options...        ⌘]  │   │
│  └──────────────────────────────┘   │
└─────────────────────────────────────┘
```

FIGURE 6.16
The Project Menu in Premiere

Once you select Make Movie, Premiere will compile, or add together, the different elements you've placed in the Construction movie. The result will be a QuickTime movie that you can run with any movie player.

Now that you're familiar with the basics of movie-editing, we'll devote a few pages to some of the interesting extras you can do with Premiere.

Editing

Premiere lets you cut off either or both ends of a movie if you think it's too long. Just double-click on the thumbnail of a movie clip in the Project window to move it into a Clip window. A Clip window is another Premiere window type; you can see in Figure 6.17 that it has buttons labeled In and Out. Set the movie to any frame, then click the **In** button. All the preceding frames will be omitted from the movie when you add it to the Construction window. The same applies to the Out button.

The Clip window also lets you preview a movie clip by playing part or all of the movie, or by stepping through it frame by frame.

FIGURE 6.17
Premiere's Clip Window

Special Effects

One of the most interesting features Premiere offers is special effects. Figure 6.18 shows a few of those available in the Special Effects Window.

Special effects allow you to make a smooth, or dramatic, transition from one movie clip to another. To add a special effect, simply click on it in the Special Effects window and drag it into the VIDEO FX row of the Construction window. The video clip directly above and below the special effect consists of videos that will be involved in the transition. We'll clarify this over the next few pages.

We wanted to add an opening screen to our movie, and have some kind of transition from it to the dancer clip. We first moved the dancer video clip in the VIDEO A row by clicking on it and dragging it to the right. We then selected Add Matte from the Project menu. That menu option lets you add a solid color or shade of grayscale to the Project window. We choose black, as shown in Figure 6.19.

FIGURE 6.18
Premiere's Special Effects Window

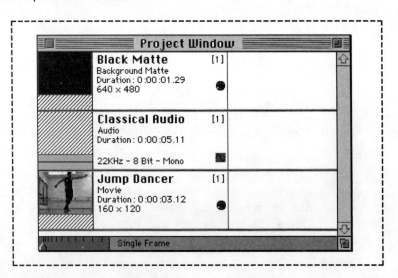

FIGURE 6.19
Adding a Matte to the Project Window

We then dragged the black matte to the Construction window and placed it before the dancer video clip, as shown in Figure 6.20. The size of the matte can be enlarged or reduced by clicking on its right side and dragging it in either direction.

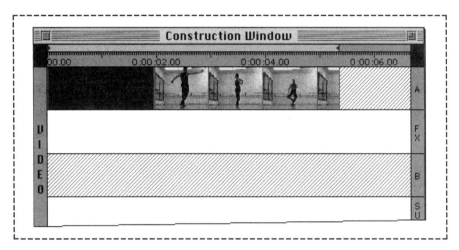

FIGURE 6.20
Adding the Matte to the Construction Window

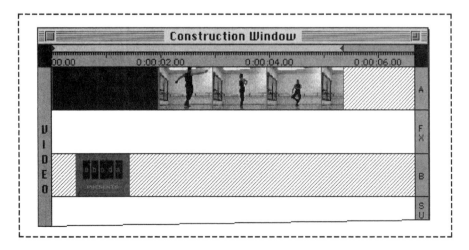

FIGURE 6.21
Adding a Still Image to the Construction Window

We chose a still image for our opening scene, imported it into the Project window and then dragged it into the VIDEO B row of the Construction window. You can enlarge a still image in the VIDEO B row by dragging its edge. Figure 6.21 shows what our Construction window looks like at this point.

Finally, we selected a special effect and dragged it from the Special Effects window to the VIDEO FX row of the Construction window. We enlarged the special effect to match the size of the image in the VIDEO B row. We're now at Figure 6.22.

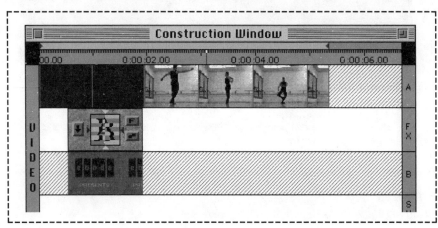

FIGURE 6.22
Adding a Special Effect to the Construction Window

We said that a special effect affected the video images directly above and below it. From Figure 6.22 you can see that the special effect will work on the black matte and the still image. The movie will open with a black screen that less than a second later will change into the still image. It won't be a sudden switch. Instead, it will be a band effect, as shown in Figure 6.23. Finally, the movie will abruptly change to the dancer.

Filters

Premiere offers a host of *filters* that can be applied to movie clips. Filters alter a movie by changing its tint, brightness, or other parameters. When we talked about making movies in Chapter 4, we noted that the ScreenPlay software that accompanies the VideoSpigot digitizer doesn't offer a brightness or contrast control—a big shortcoming. By placing a movie that is too dark or light in Premiere, then adding a brightness filter, you can create a new copy of your flawed movie.

FIGURE 6.23
The Band Special Effect in a Movie

To see the available filters, select **Filters** from the Clip menu. You'll see a dialog box like the one in Figure 6.24.

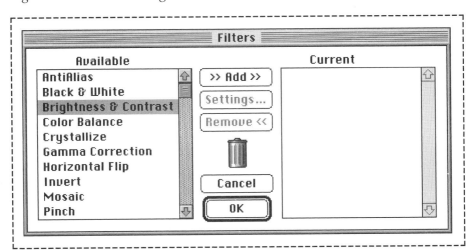

FIGURE 6.24
The Filters Dialog Box in Premiere

You can select one or more filters by dragging them to the right side of the dialog box. We dragged the Brightness & Contrast filter to the right side. When we did, we saw a Settings dialog box like that in Figure 6.25.

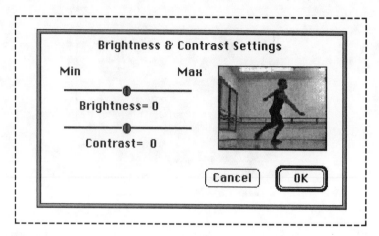

FIGURE 6.25

The Brightness & Contrast Filter Settings Dialog Box

Figure 6.26 shows a movie before and after the Brightness filter was applied to it. If you have a lot of home videos you'd like to clean up, the Brightness filter of Premiere may interest you.

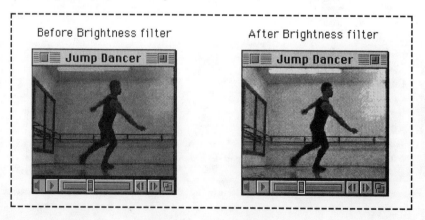

FIGURE 6.26

A Movie Without and With Brightness Filtering Applied

In this section on movie-editing, we've shown some powerful techniques for creating an entirely new movie from clips of other movies. But we've only touched the surface. Movie-editing software offers an incredible array of features that you can use to make very professional-looking videos for use in presentations, or just for fun. We showed how to apply a filter to a movie clip (Premiere, in fact, offers over 20 different filters). Movies, along with movie-editing software that's affordable and easy to use, are bound to play a significant role in home and business computing in the 1990s.

Using Files Other than PICTS in Movies

In this chapter you've seen that when you edit a movie, you can combine clips and single frames from several different movies into one new QuickTime movie. You've also seen that you can include the contents of a PICT file to serve as a frame in a movie. For PICT files, you can create your own pictures or use illustrations from public-domain clip art. You can also check online services such as CompuServe and America Online. Besides having libraries of sound files, they have libraries of Macintosh graphics files. Once you download one you can open it using the appropriate graphics program and view, modify, and save it to a PICT file.

There may come a time when you can't find a Macintosh graphics file that has just the right person, place, or thing in it, even after checking the online services. If you're already a member of an information service, don't log off just yet. There may be a picture that will serve your needs—in one of the PC libraries.

You're lucky enough to own or have access to a Macintosh. But millions of other computer users aren't. Over the years PC owners have created and uploaded thousands of graphic files to CompuServe and America Online. You now know you can easily convert a series of Macintosh PICT files into a QuickTime movie. You can do the same with a series of Macintosh graphics files that are in a format other than the Macintosh PICT file. You can even make a QuickTime movie from some PC graphics files.

Many PC owners, graphic artists, and others have created files for animation programs on PCs. If you can download some of these files you can use them to make movies on your Macintosh. First we'll tell you how to get the pictures. After that, we'll discuss using PC files to make Macintosh QuickTime movies.

Obtaining Pictures

In the previous chapter we discussed how you can download sound files from information services such as America Online and CompuServe. These services also have libraries of graphics files. Like sounds, these files are free—except for the time it takes to download them.

Getting Pictures from America Online

If you're looking for a series of Macintosh PICT files to make into a movie, or a single PICT file that you can edit and use as part of a movie (as a background, perhaps) try an online service such as America Online. But don't limit your search to just PICT files. Apple's Movie Converter program can make movies from several different file types. As you search the graphics libraries, keep an eye open for PICT, TIFF, GIF, and EPS formatted files. Movie Converter works with all of them. We explain just how later in this chapter.

After exhausting the Macintosh graphics libraries, try moving to the Windows forum. It too contains libraries of graphics files. Figure 6.27 shows the list of items in the Windows Forum.

```
┌──────────────────────────────────────────┐
│         ▤  Windows Forum  ▤▤              │
├──────────────────────────────────────────┤
│  ▯  About the Windows Forum               │
│  ✧  Weekly Forum Update                   │
│  🗀  Visual Basic                          │
│  🗂  Message Boards                        │
│  ▦  The Windows Meeting Room              │
│  ✧  Software Library                      │
│  🗀  Browse Individual Libraries           │
│  🗀  Company Support                       │
│  🗗  Free Uploading                        │
│                                           │
│            ┌─────────────────┐            │
│            │      Open       │            │
│            └─────────────────┘            │
└──────────────────────────────────────────┘
```

FIGURE 6.27

The Windows Area in America Online

Once in the Windows Forum, click on the **Search** icon to perform a file search. Enter the file type you're looking for. Bitmap drawings made by Windows graphics packages are often saved as BMP files. Do a search on BMP, as we do in Figure 6.28.

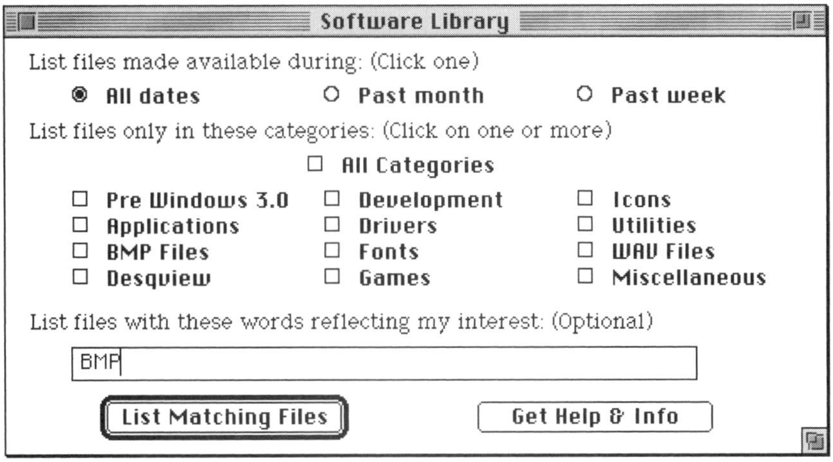

```
┌─────────────────── Software Library ───────────────────┐
  List files made available during: (Click one)
        ◉ All dates        ○ Past month        ○ Past week
  List files only in these categories: (Click on one or more)
                        ☐ All Categories
        ☐ Pre Windows 3.0   ☐ Development   ☐ Icons
        ☐ Applications      ☐ Drivers       ☐ Utilities
        ☐ BMP Files         ☐ Fonts         ☐ WAV Files
        ☐ Desqview          ☐ Games         ☐ Miscellaneous
  List files with these words reflecting my interest: (Optional)
   ┌────────────────────────────────────────────────────┐
   │ BMP                                                 │
   └────────────────────────────────────────────────────┘
      ┌─────────────────────┐      ┌─────────────────────┐
      │  List Matching Files │      │  Get Help & Info    │
      └─────────────────────┘      └─────────────────────┘
```

FIGURE 6.28

Searching for Bitmap Files in America Online

In response to your search, America Online will display a list of files that match your descriptive keyword. You can see in Figure 6.29 that over a thousand BMP, or bitmap files, are available for downloading. Not all of them should be downloaded, however. Files that use the PC form of compression called ZIP can't be read by your Macintosh. The Movie Converter program will not recognize them as BMP files. Instead of files that end in ".ZIP," look for ones that end in ".BMP," ".TIF," or ".GIF." All these types can be downloaded and converted by Movie Converter.

After downloading a BMP file, you'll notice that America Online has given it an icon that looks just like the icons it gives text files. This is shown in Figure 6.30. Don't become alarmed! Movie Converter will recognize it as a BMP file as long as the file name ends with the extension "BMP." If not, rename it by adding a period and the letters "BMP" to its name.

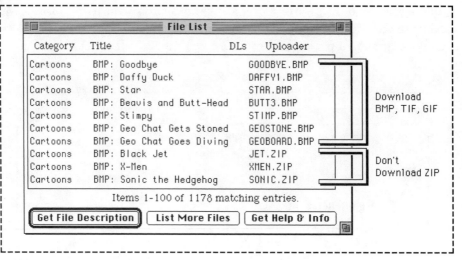

FIGURE 6.29
A Scrollable List of Files in America Online

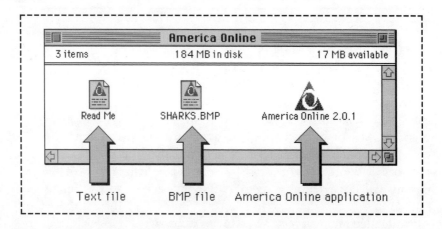

FIGURE 6.30
A Bitmap File Downloaded from America Online

Getting Pictures from CompuServe

In Chapter 5 we discussed downloading sound files from CompuServe. Finding and downloading picture files is done in a similar way. We type "GO

COMART" to get to the Computer Art Forum. Once there, we enter the software library to search for graphics files. Figure 6.31 shows a typical screen from a CompuServe session.

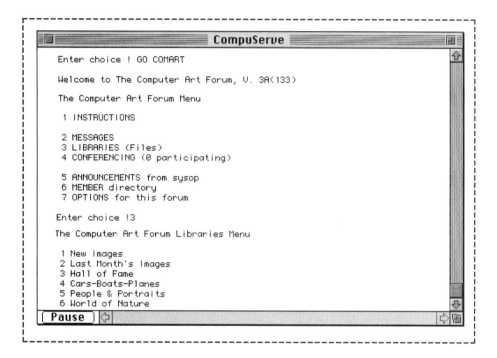

FIGURE 6.31
Entering a Computer Art Area in CompuServe

Like America Online, when a BMP, GIF, or TIFF file is downloaded from CompuServe, it appears in the Finder as a text file. This is shown in Figure 6.32. Again, don't worry. Movie Converter will figure out that this file is in GIF format, as long as you give it a name that ends in ".GIF." Note in Figure 6.32 that CompuServe doesn't come with its own navigational software, as America Online does. You can use any telecommunications software you have; we chose Software Venture's MicroPhone program.

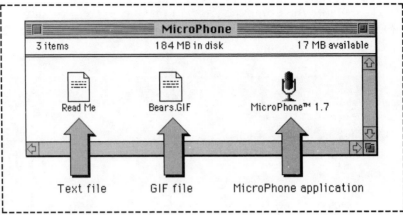

FIGURE 6.32
A Downloaded GIF File from CompuServe

Obtaining Pictures from Others

Still another way to obtain artwork is to solicit an artistic friend or coworker to draw up a series of pictures for you. Even if that person works on a PC rather than a Macintosh, you might still be in luck.

If the person you're receiving the files from has a CompuServe or America Online account, they can electronically mail you the files. Not just text files get mailed. When you log onto the online service, you can download your mail. This has the same effect as downloading a file from a library. It's a simple way to get graphics files on an IBM-formatted disk to your Macintosh hard drive. Once you have the files, you can use Movie S.B. Converter to turn them into a movie—with a little help from the Corel Converters extension files we are about to discuss.

Graphics to Movies: With the Help of Corel Converters

Apple's Movie Converter utility takes a series of PICT files and strings them together into a QuickTime movie. It's available as part of Apple's QuickTime Starter Kit and is described in more detail in Chapter 2.

The Corel Converters are a set of extensions that allow Apple's Movie Converter utility to recognize graphics files of a type other than PICT. The eight converters, shown in Figure 6.33, are also a part of Apple's QuickTime Starter Kit.

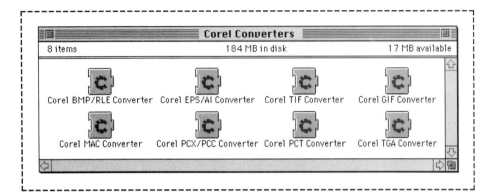

FIGURE 6.33
The Corel Converter Extensions

The File Formats

The Corel Converters work like any other extension; you drag them onto the System Folder of your System 7 Mac, and then restart your computer. From that point on, Apple's Movie Converter program will recognize several more types of files than it did without the Corel Converters present. The following is a summary of the types of files you can now use with Movie Converter.

- **BMP and RLE files**

  BMP and RLE are two types of bitmap files. Windows and OS/2 paint programs generate files of this type.

- **PCX and PCC files**

  Files of these types are created by ZSoft's PC Paintbrush program and by many software packages bundled with scanners.

- **TIFF files**

  TIFF is a file format common to both the PC and Macintosh. Several graphics programs generate files of this type.

■ GIF files

Many files that are compressed and available through online services are in GIF format.

■ EPS and AI files

Adobe Illustrator and other drawing packages produce files of this type. Many clip art libraries also contain files in this format.

Running Movie Converter

The steps involved in creating a QuickTime movie with Corel Converters in your System Folder are no different than for creating a movie without them. You open a single file from a series of files, then select **Convert** from the Conversions menu. What is different is the number of file types you have to choose from. Figure 6.34 shows what the pop-up menu in the Open dialog box looks like—with the Corel Converters installed and without them. To display all the file types that Movie Converter recognizes, leave the pop-up menu at the Any Available item.

```
With Corel Converters              Without Corel Converters

✓Any Available                      ✓Any Available
▶AIFF Sound File                    ▶AIFF Sound File
 BMP/RLE File Sequence               Movie File
 EPS/AI File Sequence                PICS Animation File
 GIF File Sequence                   PICT File Sequence
 MAC File Sequence                   Scrapbook File
 Movie File                          Snd Sound File
 PCT File Sequence
 PCX/PCC File Sequence
 PICS Animation File
 PICT File Sequence
 Scrapbook File
 Snd Sound File
 TGA File Sequence
 TIF File Sequence
```

FIGURE 6.34

The Movie Converter Pop-up After and Before Corel Converters

Back in Chapter 2, you saw Movie Converter open a single PICT file and place the PICT in a preview window. At that time, it wrote the words "PICT File Sequence" along the top left of the window (see Figure 6.35). Now that you know that Movie Converter can open and convert several different file types, you can understand why the program tells you the type of file it's working with.

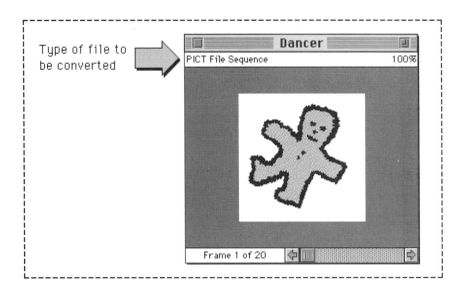

FIGURE 6.35
The Movie Recorder Preview Window with a PICT in It

We downloaded a BMP file from an online service, verified that the file name ended in ".BMP," and then ran Movie Converter. When we opened the file, the text in the window now read "BMP/RLE File Sequence," as shown in Figure 6.36.

We also downloaded a Macintosh graphics file—but not a PICT file. We downloaded a file in EPS format (the Illustrator graphics program is one Mac program that creates EPS files). Once again, the text in the preview window changed to reflect the type of file being worked with. Figure 6.37 shows the Movie Converter preview window.

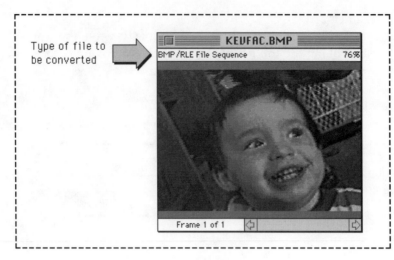

Type of file to be converted ➡

FIGURE 6.36
The Movie Recorder Preview Window with a BMP in It

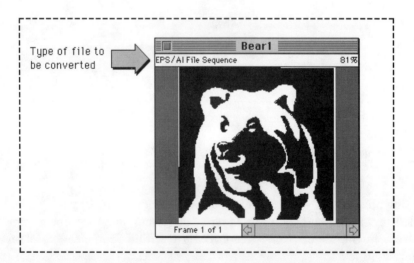

Type of file to be converted ➡

FIGURE 6.37
The Movie Recorder Preview Window with an EPS in It

All told, we downloaded GIF and BMP files from Windows libraries, and GIF, EPS, and TIFF files from Macintosh graphics libraries. We only selected Windows files that weren't compressed—no files whose names ended in

".ZIP" were downloaded. We didn't concern ourselves with compression issues when we selected files from the Macintosh libraries since we have the StuffIt Expander software that decompresses Macintosh files. All the files we downloaded were handled flawlessly by Movie Converter.

Using Graphics You Can't Read

In searches through online services you may find many graphics files you'd like to use, in Macintosh format or PC format. But you might find just a single file of interest—not an entire sequence that can be turned into a movie. If the file is in a format such as Macintosh EPS, and you don't have an EPS-compatible graphics program, are you out of luck? If the file is a Windows BMP file, and you want to view and edit it on your Macintosh, are you again out of luck? The answer to both questions is no. You can still turn this file into a file you can open with just about any Macintosh graphics program.

You've seen how you can turn a series of files—just about any type of file—into a movie by placing the Corel Converters in your System folder and using Movie Converter. Even if you only have a single graphics file—whether it be TIFF, GIF, BMP, or any other file that the Corel Converters recognize—you can make a movie from it. If you look back at the figures in the preceding section you'll notice that the preview window of Movie Converter says "Frame 1 of 1" in the bottom left corner. The QuickTime movies we made from the single graphics files are only one frame in length (not a very impressive use of QuickTime's power). But now that each figure is in a QuickTime movie format, we can import it into a movie-editing program like Premiere and add it to other movies. Or we can simply copy or cut the frame and paste it in to the Scrapbook. Then we can paste it into a movie at a later time.

A second trick you can do with a graphics file that is in a format unreadable by any of your applications is to run Movie Converter and open the file. It will appear in the Preview window. If it doesn't appear at 100% of its original size, select **Convert** from the Conversions menu to make a movie from it. The movie will open on your screen at 100% of its original size. Then, with the movie open on your screen, do a screen dump. A screen dump, or screen snapshot, is done by pressing the **Command**, **Shift**, and number **3** keys at the same time. You'll hear your Mac clicking for a second or two, and then a new file titled Picture 1 will appear in your Hard Drive folder.

This new file is a picture of the entire screen at the time you pressed the Command key combination, so it includes the single-frame QuickTime movie. Almost all graphics programs are capable of opening a PICT file; check the user's manual of yours. Open the screen dump file, and there will be the contents of the original graphics file. It may take a step or two to get there, but if the file was of interest to you, it will be worth it. This technique is especially useful for obtaining a background file that you'll make multiple copies of and use with a moving foreground object.

Chapter Summary

Sound is an important element of QuickTime movies. In the previous chapter we introduced SoundEdit Pro—software that allows you to edit sound files. In this chapter you saw how you can add cue points and labels to sounds. A cue point allows you to line up sounds in a multiple-track sound file. A label lets you mark and name a particular sound within a soundtrack—a useful tool for finding the location of a sound in a large file.

Movie-editing software allows you to make changes to an existing QuickTime movie or to create an entirely new movie. You combine video clips, audio clips, and still images to construct a movie that you have planned out. Software such as Adobe Premiere also lets you change the look of video clips by adding filtering to them. Finally, you can make slick-looking transitions between video clips by implementing one or several of the special effects supplied with Premiere.

As you make and edit movies, you'll be on the lookout for sources of graphics files that you can incorporate into your edited movies. Online services such as CompuServe and America Online offer libraries of graphic clips for you to download and use in movies. You don't have to settle for Macintosh PICT files. By using Corel Converter extensions, you can use Apple's Movie Converter utility to make single images or movies from files that aren't recognized by any application you own. That gives you the freedom to use graphic files created on PCs.

Introduction to QuickTime Programming

n this chapter you'll see how easy it is to write a Macintosh program capable of playing a QuickTime movie. You'll learn how the Macintosh Toolbox—routines supplied by Apple—take much of the effort out of QuickTime programming.

Movies are stored in movie files. In this chapter you'll learn the steps to open a movie file and load the movie into memory. After that, you'll open a standard Macintosh window in which to display the movie. With a movie loaded and displayed, there's nothing left to do except play it. This chapter will show you how.

Playing a Movie—Now!

At the start of this book we said that though you need some programming knowledge to write a QuickTime movie program, you don't require advanced programming skills. So perhaps, you're wondering why we are devoting three long chapters to QuickTime programming. We said you didn't *have* to have advanced skills. But, if you *do*, we've provided plenty of material for you.

To back up our claim that QuickTime programming can be easy, we now present the complete source code for a Macintosh program that will start up, play a movie, and then quit. There is no resource file, and you don't need any additional software to play the movie—just QuickTime. We won't describe the details of the source code just yet. Here, we're more interested in reassuring you that you can easily add movie-playing capabilities to any of your own programs. Hopefully this program will do just that.

The program, which we've named OneShot, is made up of less than 40 lines of code. Of those lines, 10 are used to declare variables and a half dozen are initialization calls that are common to every Mac program. That leaves less than 20 lines that actually do the work of opening an existing movie and playing it.

```
#include <Movies.h>

void  main( void )
{
    WindowPtr   the_window;
    Movie       the_movie;
    OSErr       error;
    short       movie_res_file;
    short       movie_res_ID = 0;
    Str255      movie_name;
    Boolean     was_changed;
    FSSpec      the_FSSpec;
    Rect        the_rect;
    Rect        movie_box;

    InitGraf( &thePort );
    InitFonts();
    InitWindows();
    InitMenus();
    TEInit();
    InitDialogs( nil );
```

```
    error = EnterMovies();
    error = FSMakeFSSpec( 0, 0L, "\pDancer", &the_FSSpec );
    error = OpenMovieFile( &the_FSSpec, &movie_res_file,
                    fsRdPerm );
    error = NewMovieFromFile( &the_movie, movie_res_file,
                    &movie_res_ID,movie_name,
                    newMovieActive, &was_changed );

    CloseMovieFile( movie_res_file );

    SetRect( &the_rect, 100, 100, 150, 150 );
    the_window = NewCWindow( nil, &the_rect, "\pMovie", false,
                    noGrowDocProc, (WindowPtr)-1L,
                    false, 0 );

    GetMovieBox( the_movie, &movie_box );
    OffsetRect( &movie_box, -movie_box.left, -movie_box.top );
    SetMovieBox( the_movie, &movie_box );

    SizeWindow( the_window, movie_box.right, movie_box.bottom,
                true );
    ShowWindow( the_window );

    SetMovieGWorld( the_movie, ( CGrafPtr )the_window, nil );
    StartMovie( the_movie );
    do
        MoviesTask( the_movie, 0 );
    while ( IsMovieDone( the_movie ) == false );
}
```

You'll find the source code and stand-alone program for the OneShot program in the OneShot folder of the For Programmers folder included with this book.

Everything that's done in the OneShot program is explained in this chapter. At the end of this chapter we provide, and explain, the source code for a program that incorporates all of the code used in OneShot. It's a children's game called QuickTrivia that plays a QuickTime movie every time the user guesses at a trivia question.

The Movie Toolbox

As we've mentioned, QuickTime is not an application that you run. It is an extension—code that extends the power of the Macintosh. Much of this code exists as precompiled functions that you can call from within programs you write. These functions, collectively called the *Movie Toolbox*, allow to open, play, and alter movies.

The original Macintosh Toolbox is a collection of thousands of routines that allow you to open windows, work with dialogs, draw shapes, and perform hundreds of other tasks. The Movie Toolbox is simply an additional set of routines to aid you in programming the Mac.

Initializing Movies

Before playing a movie in *any* program you write, you'll want to perform two preliminary tasks: verify that the Macintosh your program is running on has the QuickTime extension, and initialize the Movie Toolbox.

Checking for QuickTime

You have QuickTime on your Macintosh. But do you know for sure whether everyone else who may be using your program does? The first thing your program should do is verify that the QuickTime extension is present. You can do this with a call to the Toolbox routine *Gestalt()*.

The *Gestalt()* function gives your program information about the Macintosh it is running on. *Gestalt()* requires two parameters. The first one, called a *selector code*, tells *Gestalt()* what piece of information you're interested in. The second parameter is filled in, by the Toolbox, with the requested information. Figure 7.1 summarizes this. The selector codes are #defined constants which can be found in the header files *GestaltEqu.h*. One of these codes is *gestaltQuickTime*.

When you pass *Gestalt()* a value of *gestaltQuickTime*, *Gestalt()* returns the version number of the QuickTime extension that the user has. If QuickTime isn't present on the user's Mac, the *error* variable will be filled in with a nonzero value. Here's the call to *Gestalt()*:

```
#include <GestaltEqu.h>

OSErr   error;
long    result;
```

```
error = Gestalt( gestaltQuickTime, &result );

if ( error != noErr )
   ExitToShell();
```

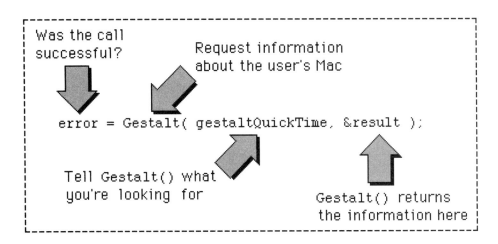

FIGURE 7.1

The Gestalt() Routine Provides Information about a Mac

By providing *Gestalt()* with a selector code of *gestaltQuickTime*, you make a request for the version number of the QuickTime extension installed in the user's Mac. Determining whether a Macintosh has QuickTime is just one use of *Gestalt()*. It can also be used to find information on many aspects of the user's Macintosh. If you know what selector code to use, you can find out what system the user has, how much RAM is in the user's computer, and so forth.

In most uses of *Gestalt()* you'll be interested in the value of *result*. It's filled in by the Toolbox and returned to your program. But when checking for the presence of QuickTime, you don't care what version the user has— you just care *if* the user has it. If it isn't present, *error* will be nonzero. So immediately after the call to *Gestalt()*, you'll compare the value of `error` to the value of *noErr*. The constant *noErr* is defined as zero. If QuickTime is not present, you'll call the Toolbox routine *ExitToShell()* to quit your program and return the user to the desktop.

Why is the function called Gestalt? In psychology, Gestalt psychotherapy aims to integrate the various aspects of the personality into a well-organized whole. The *Gestalt()* function gives you information about many of the individual aspects of the Macintosh that, together, make it such a powerful, capable computer. We won't even speculate on whether Apple is inferring that anyone who programs for a great length of time is a candidate for psychotherapy!

Initializing the Movie Toolbox

Once you know that QuickTime is available, you'll need to initialize the Movie Toolbox. First, perform the Toolbox initializations common to all Mac programs. Our *Initialize_Toolbox()* routine shown next does just that.

```
void  Initialize_Toolbox( void )
{
    InitGraf( &thePort );
    InitFonts();
    InitWindows();
    InitMenus();
    TEInit();
    InitDialogs( nil );
    InitCursor();
}
```

Notice that *Initialize_Toolbox()*, a function defined by one of our own applications, has an underscore in its name. That's intentional; each function we write for this book will have at least one underscore in its name. Toolbox routines and Movie Toolbox routines never contain underscores. Using this function-naming convention allows you to quickly determine if a routine we're discussing is one of our own or an Apple routine.

With the other Macintosh managers initialized, call *EnterMovies()*. This Movie Toolbox function sets aside an area of memory that the Movie Toolbox will use solely for your application. Like a call to *Gestalt()*, a call to *EnterMovies()* returns a value that lets you know if the call was successful.

```
#include <Movies.h>

OSErr  error;
```

```
error = EnterMovies();

if ( error != noErr )
   ExitToShell();
```

You'll need to include the Movies.h header file in your program listing. It contains the prototypes for each of the hundreds of movie-related functions at your disposal. If you're using the THINK C or Symantec C++ compiler, you may not have this header file. Check your Apple #includes folder to find out. If you don't have it, don't worry. We've included it on the disk that accompanies this book. Open the Header Files folder in the For Programmers folder. It contains several header files. Copy them all to your Apple #includes folder, as shown in Figure 7.2

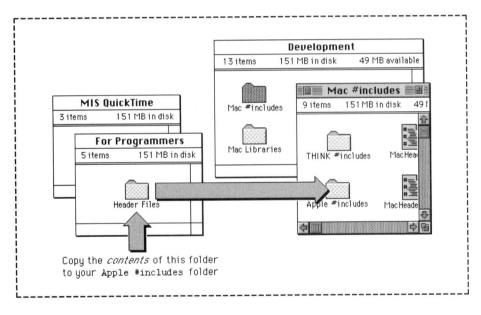

FIGURE 7.2

Copying Each of the Several Header Files to the Apple #includes File

Opening a Movie File

Movies exist in files on disk, like the three shown in Figure 7.3. Before your program can work with a movie, the file in which the movie resides must be opened. The Movie Toolbox routine *OpenMovieFile()* does this for you.

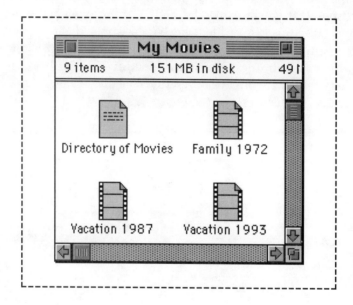

FIGURE 7.3
QuickTime Movies are Stored in Files on Disk

OpenMovieFile() can open any existing QuickTime movie file, so you have to tell the routine which movie you want opened. You specify the movie by telling *OpenMovieFile()* the name of the movie and where it is located. This information has to be in a format that the Movie Toolbox recognizes. So before covering *OpenMovieFile()*, we'll sidetrack a bit to discuss this format.

File Pathnames

The conventional method of letting a program know where to find a file is to provide the *pathname* to the file. The pathname gives the name of the *volume*, or drive that the file is on, and all of the directories, or folders, between the drive and the file. The pathname ends with the name of the file itself. A colon separates each directory. Figure 7.4 gives an example.

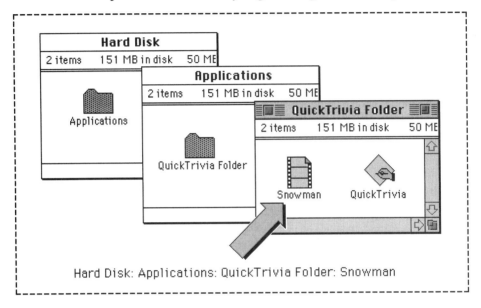

FIGURE 7.4
The Pathname of a File

With System 7, the format for specifying a file has changed. Now, a file is identified by a *file system specification*. There's now a data structure called an *FSSpec*, that holds this information for a file. *FSSpec* stands for file system specification. To take the work out of determining how a conventional pathname can be converted to an *FSSpec*, Apple provides a Toolbox routine that does the conversion for you: *FSMakeFSSpec()*.

When you provide *FSMakeFSSpec()* with three pieces of information, *FSMakeFSSpec()* turns this information into an *FSSpec* data structure. *FSMakeFSSpec()* then returns the *FSSpec*, in the last parameter, to your program. The three things *FSMakeFSSpec()* needs to create an *FSSpec* for a file are the volume reference number, the parent directory ID, and the name of a file. Let's look at each parameter.

The first parameter is the volume reference number. By passing a value of 0, you are telling *FSMakeFSSpec()* that the file resides on the default drive (the startup drive). This is usually the case.

The second parameter is the parent directory of the file. The parent directory contains the file in question. If you used a value of 0 for the volume reference number, and the file you're concerned with is in the same directory as the application that will use it, you can also use a value of 0 for the ID. A situation like this is shown back in Figure 7.4, where the Snowman file and the application that will use it, QuickTrivia, are in the same directory.

The third parameter is the name of the file. This parameter can be a string, such as \pSnowman, or a variable of type Str255 that has been assigned the name of the file.

The final parameter is a pointer to an FSSpec variable. Declare a variable of type FSSpec. Then use the name of this variable, preceded by the & operator, as the fourth parameter to FSMakeFSSpec(). After using the first three parameters to create the file specification, the routine will place the FSSpec information into the data structure pointed to by this parameter. You'll then be able to use this information later in your program.

Below is an example that creates an FSSpec for the Snowman file shown back in Figure 7.4. Notice that we use 0L as the second parameter. This parameter needs to be a long integer, and defining it as 0L rather than 0 forces it to occupy the space of a long. You do not need to do this if you use function prototypes.

```
#define      VOL_REF_NUM              0
#define      DIR_ID                  0L
#define      SNOWMAN_FILE    "\pSnowman"

OSErr   error;
FSSpec  the_FSSpec;

error = FSMakeFSSpec( VOL_REF_NUM, DIR_ID, SNOWMAN_FILE,
                      &the_FSSpec );
```

Here's a second example of creating the FSSpec for the Snowman file. This version is logically the same as the first. Here we've just dispensed with the #define directives to show that there's nothing complicated about a call to FSMakeFSSpec().

```
OSErr   error;
FSSpec  the_FSSpec;
```

```
error = FSMakeFSSpec( 0, 0L, "\pSnowman", &the_FSSpec );
```

Now that you know just how to specify a file, you're ready to actually open a movie file.

Opening the File

To work with a movie file you first have to open it. "Work with" means to play or edit the movie. In this chapter we'll write the code to play a movie. In Chapter 8 we'll demonstrate editing them.

To open a movie file, use the Movie Toolbox routine *OpenMovieFile()*. Here's a call to *OpenMovieFile()*. Notice that we precede the call to *OpenMovieFile()* with a call to *FSMakeFSSpec()*. That provides the *FSSpec* that is used as the first parameter to *OpenMovieFile()*.

```
short   movie_res_file;
FSSpec  the_FSSpec;

error = FSMakeFSSpec( 0, 0L, "\pSnowman", &the_FSSpec );
error = OpenMovieFile( &the_FSSpec, &movie_res_file, fsRdPerm );
```

OpenMovieFile() requires three parameters. The first is the file specification for the movie file to open. After opening the file, the Movie Toolbox fills the second parameter with a reference number. This number will be used in other Movie Toolbox functions. The third parameter is a *permission level* for the opened file. If your program simply plays a movie, set the level to "read" permission. If your program will alter the file, set the level to "write" permission. You should use one of the constants defined in the Movies.h file. In this chapter, where we simply play movies, we use *fsRdPerm*—read permission. You can also use *fsWrPerm* or *fsRdWrPerm*, as we do in Chapter 8.

Loading a Movie

After opening a movie file, you'll use the Movie Toolbox routine *NewMovieFromFile()* to load a movie into memory before it can be played. A movie in a file is in the form of a resource—a 'moov' resource. What *NewMovieFromFile()* does is create a movie from this resource and load it into memory. Below is a typical call to *NewMovieFromFile()*.

```
OSErr    error;
Movie    the_movie;
short    movie_res_file;
short    movie_res_ID = 0;
Str255   movie_name;
Boolean  was_changed;

error = NewMovieFromFile( &the_movie, movie_res_file, &movie_res_ID,
                          movie_name, newMovieActive, &was_changed);
```

After creating and loading the movie, the Movie Toolbox fills the first parameter: *the_movie*. This variable is of type *Movie*—a new Macintosh data type
used to identify QuickTime movies within programs. Because a program can
have more than one movie open at a time, you need a means of specifying
which movie you want to play.

The second parameter to *NewMovieFromFile()*, *movie_res_file*, is the
reference number that was obtained from *OpenMovieFile()*:

```
short   movie_res_file;

error = OpenMovieFile( &the_FSSpec, &movie_res_file, fsRdPerm );
```

You want to tell *NewMovieFromFile()* which file to create the movie from.
Movie_res_file does just that.

The third parameter to *NewMovieFromFile()* is *movie_res_ID*. You
wouldn't know it from looking at a movie file icon, but a movie file can contain more than one movie. If you open a movie file with ResEdit, you'll see a
list of 'moov' resources. If there's more than one, then that file contains more
than one movie. Figure 7.5 shows what one of the two 'moov' resources in a
movie file called BeforeAndAfter Movie looks like. The *movie_res_ID* parameter tells the Movie Toolbox which movie to use. If *movie_res_ID* is set to
0, as we've done, the first movie resource in the file is used. If there is only
one movie in the file, as is often the case, that movie will be used.

The Movie Toolbox fills in the value of the fourth parameter to
NewMovieFromFile()—the *movie_name* variable. The name of a movie is not
the name of the file it comes from. As just mentioned, a file can contain
more than one movie. The movie name is the name of the 'moov' resource
from which the movie is created. If the 'moov' resource hasn't been named,
movie_name will be *nil*, or empty. Figure 7.6 shows just where the movie
name comes from.

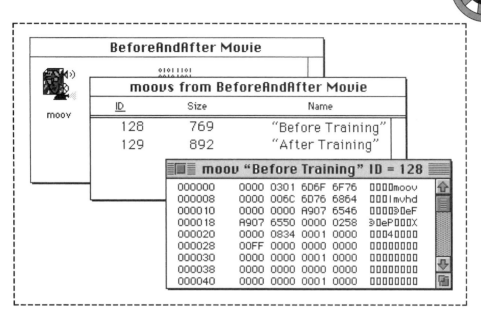

FIGURE 7.5

One of the 'moov' Resources from a File with Two Movies

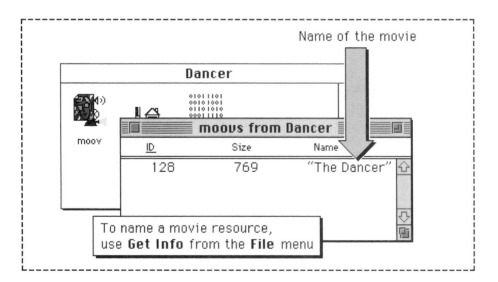

FIGURE 7.6

The Name of a Movie Is the Name of the moov Resource

You can use the fifth parameter to *NewMovieFromFile()* for different purposes. Typically, you'll pass a value of *newMovieActive*. This constant, defined in Movies.h, tells the Movie Toolbox to activate the new movie. A movie *must* be active in order to be played.

The last parameter to *NewMovieFromFile()* tells whether changes were made to the movie. The variable *was_changed* is filled in by the Movie Toolbox. We won't be concerned with the value given to this variable.

Closing a Movie File

You may be surprised to see a call to a routine that closes the movie file, since we haven't discussed playing the movie yet! Recall that *NewMovieFromFile()* used information in the movie file to create a movie and load it into memory. The file is now no longer needed by the program. Unless you're going to make changes to the movie, as we'll do in Chapter 10, close the file after calling *NewMovieFromFile()*.

To close a file, use the Movie Toolbox routine *CloseMovieFile()*. This routine requires a single parameter: the reference number of the movie to close. Use the reference number obtained from the call to *OpenMovieFile()*. Here's a call to *CloseMovieFile()*:

```
short   movie_res_file;

CloseMovieFile( movie_res_file );
```

Opening a Display Window for a Movie

At this point we've opened a movie file, created a movie from it, loaded that movie into memory, and closed the file that provided the movie information. The last step before playing the movie is to open a window in which to display the movie.

Creating a Display Window

A QuickTime movie is displayed in a window. There are two calls you can use to create a color window: *GetNewCWindow()* and *NewCWindow()*. The first call, *GetNewCWindow()*, uses descriptive information about a window from a 'WIND' resource. The second call, *NewCWindow()*, uses information you provide in the parameters when you call the function. In our examples we'll use *NewCWindow()*.

To open the window, first set a rectangle that will bound the window. Your concern will be the left and top coordinates of the window—they determine the placement of the window on the screen. QuickTime movies vary in size—you won't know the size of a movie until it's opened. For that reason, the size that you initially make the window is unimportant—you'll resize the window later so that it's the exact size of the movie. Here's the code to open a window:

```
WindowPtr   the_window;
Movie       the_movie;
Rect        the_rect;
Rect        movie_box;

SetRect( &the_rect, 100, 100, 150, 150 );
the_window = NewCWindow( nil, &the_rect, "\pMovie", false,
                         noGrowDocProc, (WindowPtr)-1L,
                         false, 0 );
```

Figure 7.7 summarizes the purpose of each parameter in the call to *NewCWindow()*.

Resizing the Display Window

Once the display window is created, you'll want to resize it to make it the same size as the movie. If you don't, some of the movie will get cut off, or will have extra white space around it. The Movie Toolbox has two routines designed for this. Call *GetMovieBox()* to determine the size of the movie. Pass this routine the *Movie* variable that was returned by *NewMovieFromFile()*. The second parameter is a pointer to a rectangle. The Movie Toolbox will set this variable to the exact size of the movie specified by *the_movie*.

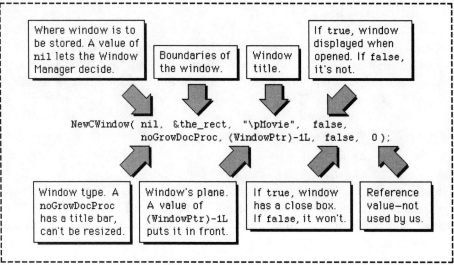

FIGURE 7.7

Definitions of the Parameters to NewCWindow()

```
Movie   the_movie;
Rect    movie_box;

GetMovieBox( the_movie, &movie_box );
```

After a call to *GetMovieBox()*, you'll have a rectangle the exact size of a frame in the movie. The left and top coordinates of box might not, however, each be set to zero. Figure 7.8 shows a frame of a movie that is 100 pixels high and 100 pixels wide. But notice that the coordinates don't start at (0, 0).

    GetMovieBox() returns the proper size of a movie frame, but doesn't guarantee that the left top coordinate will be (0, 0). This could present a problem later when you display the movie; you'll soon see why. The solution is to simply offset the rectangle, as we do in the next line of code.

```
OffsetRect( &movie_box, −movie_box.left, −movie_box.top );
```

A call to *OffsetRect()* moves a rectangle without altering its size. Figure 7.9 illustrates the purpose of this call.

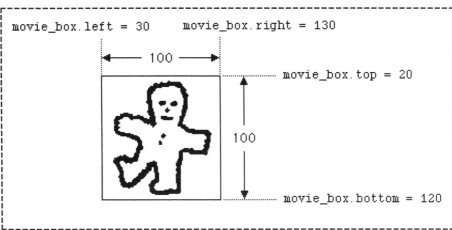

FIGURE 7.8
The Boundaries of a Movie Can Be Determined by GetMovieBox()

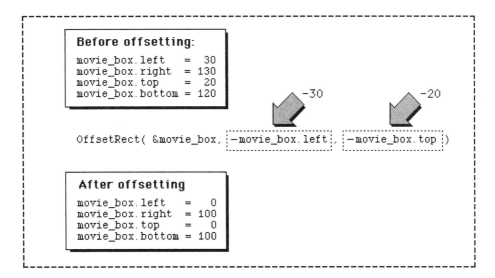

FIGURE 7.9
Using OffsetRect() to Change the Movie Box top left corner to (0, 0)

The coordinates of the movie box have been offset. Now call *SetMovieBox()* to apply these adjusted coordinates to the movie:

```
SetMovieBox( the_movie, &movie_box );
```

At this point the movie box is properly adjusted. But we haven't applied this sizing to the window. Remember, right before we called *NewCWindow()* we called *SetRect()* to establish the window boundaries. At that time we said only the top left corner of the window was important. A call to *SizeWindow()* will resize the window to the size of the movie, without moving the top left corner of the window. Here's the call:

```
SizeWindow(the_window, movie_box.right, movie_box.bottom, true);
```

Figure 7.10 shows the area the window would occupy after the call to *NewCWindow()*, and the area it would occupy after the adjustments and call to *SizeWindow()*. Note that the area changed, but the top left corner remains fixed. What is so significant about this? As the creator of a program, you know best where to put the movie window. It may depend on what other windows or dialog boxes you have on the screen, or you may just have an aesthetic preference. The method just used to size the movie window allows you to control the final placement of the window, regardless of its size.

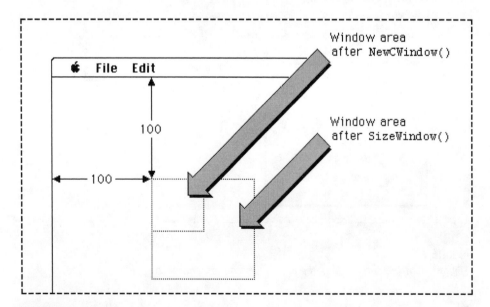

FIGURE 7.10
Window Area Before and After Resizing

Showing the Window

When the window was created with a call to *NewCWindow()*, the fourth parameter was set to *false*. This told the Window Manager not to make the window visible. That allowed the window resizing to go on behind the scenes (out of sight of the program user). Now it's time to display the perfectly sized window. A call to *ShowWindow()* does the trick:

```
ShowWindow( the_window );
```

Setting the Movie Graphics World

In the previous section we examined the method to open a window and to properly size it for a movie. But we didn't mention how the window and movie are related. As the movie plays, you'll want to make sure it's playing in the window you created for it.

A movie has its own *graphics world*—a drawing environment that pertains just to this one movie. Before playing a movie, you have to establish the display coordinates system for the movie by setting the graphics world. A call to *SetMovieGWorld()* does this.

```
Movie       the_movie;
WindowPtr   the_window;

SetMovieGWorld( the_movie, ( CGrafPtr )the_window, nil );
```

In the above call, *the_movie* is the movie created by *NewMovieFromFile()*. The variable *the_window* is the window that was opened by *NewCWindow()* and then carefully resized to match the size of *the_movie*. *SetMovieGWorld()* establishes a relationship between a movie and a window, ensuring that when you play the movie, the movie will play in the right window.

Let's gather the code for creating and displaying the movie window.

```
WindowPtr   the_window;
Movie       the_movie;
Rect        the_rect;
Rect        movie_box;

SetRect( &the_rect, 100, 100, 150, 150 );
```

```
the_window = NewCWindow( nil, &the_rect, "\pMovie", false,
                         noGrowDocProc, (WindowPtr)-1L,
                         false, 0 );

GetMovieBox( the_movie, &movie_box );
OffsetRect( &movie_box, -movie_box.left, -movie_box.top );
SetMovieBox( the_movie, &movie_box );

SizeWindow( the_window, movie_box.right, movie_box.bottom,
            true );
ShowWindow( the_window );

SetMovieGWorld( the_movie, ( CGrafPtr )the_window, nil );
```

Playing a Movie

With a window opened, sized, and displayed, you're ready to play the movie. All of the preliminary work is now done—honest! To begin playing a movie, call the Movie Toolbox routine *StartMovie()*. The only parameter it needs is the *Movie* variable of the movie to play.

```
StartMovie( the_movie );
```

StartMovie() readies a movie for playing by making the movie active and setting the movie playback rate. To get the movie going, and keep it going, you repeatedly call the Movie Toolbox routine *MoviesTask()*. A single call to *MoviesTask()* processes the movie you are playing by appropriately updating the display of it. Only during a call to *MoviesTask()* does the Movie Toolbox actually draw a frame of a movie. (This is obviously a crucial routine.) Here's a single call to *MoviesTask()*:

```
MoviesTask( the_movie, 0 );
```

The first parameter is the movie to service. A single call to *MoviesTask()* is capable of servicing more than one movie. If this first parameter is set to *nil*, every active movie on the screen will be serviced.

The second parameter is the number of milliseconds that the Movie Toolbox is allowed to spend servicing movies. If there is more than one active movie, *MoviesTask()* will service as many of them as it can in this allotted time. The usual value for this parameter is 0. That tells the *MoviesTask()* to service each active movie once.

You call *MoviesTask()* repeatedly until the movie specified by *the_movie* finishes playing. Use the Movie Toolbox routine *IsMovieDone()* to determine when a movie is finished. When called, *IsMovieDone()* returns a Boolean value: *true* if the movie is done, *false* if it isn't. Call this routine after each call to *MoviesTask()*. As long as *IsMovieDone()* returns *false*, you know the movie isn't finished and *MoviesTask()* needs to be called again. Here's the loop that actually plays the movie:

```
do
{
   MoviesTask( the_movie, 0 );
}
while ( IsMovieDone( the_movie ) == false );
```

In the previous section we talked about a movies graphics world. What would happen if you didn't include a call to *SetMovieGWorld()*? We commented out the call to this routine in the OneShot program presented at the start of this chapter. When we recompiled the program and ran it, the results were as expected (they're shown in Figure 7.11). What happened? Earlier, we made a call to *OffsetRect()* to establish the left top corner of the movie box at (0, 0). Our intention was to ready the movie to fit snugly in the window—the left top coordinate of a window is also (0, 0). But when we omit the call to *SetMovieGWorld()*, the movie doesn't know about the window, and instead uses screen coordinate (0, 0)—the left top corner of the screen.

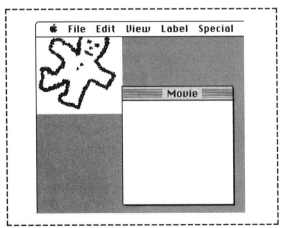

FIGURE 7.11

Result of Failing to Call SetMovieGWorld()

You have the source code for OneShot, so you can try this yourself. Simply comment out the one line of code, like so:

```
/* SetMovieGWorld(the_movie, (CGrafPtr)the_window, nil); */
```

and compile and run the program. You'll get results just like those in Figure 7.11.

When you're through playing a movie, clean things up by calling *DisposeMovie()* and *DisposeWindow()*. These two routines free any memory that was being used by the movie and the window.

```
DisposeMovie( the_Movie );
DisposeWindow( the_Window );
```

That covers the playing of a movie, from initialization to actually running it. Though we've spent quite a few pages explaining this, the actual amount of code necessary to perform these tasks is minimal. If you now look back to the OneShot program listing at the start of this chapter, you should understand each line in it.

Example Program: QuickTrivia

The OneShot program listed at the start of this chapter is a great way to learn how to write the code that will play a movie. But that's all it does: play a movie. A more practical use of the Movie Toolbox is to add movie-playing capabilities to a program that was designed to do other things. In this section we give a complete example of a program that does just that. It's called QuickTrivia, and the source code, resource file, and project file for the program are all included on the disk that came with this book. They're in the QuickTrivia folder in the For Programmers folder. QuickTrivia is a simple trivia game designed for children.

The QuickTrivia program opens a dialog box and displays a question in it. It also lists two possible answers. A user then chooses what they think is the right answer by clicking the mouse on one of two buttons. In the days before QuickTime movies, a program like this would probably write a line of text to congratulate the user on a correct choice, or admonish them for a wrong selection. Try holding a child's interest with that approach nowadays! QuickTrivia displays a QuickTime movie after every answer. Figure 7.12 shows what the game looks like.

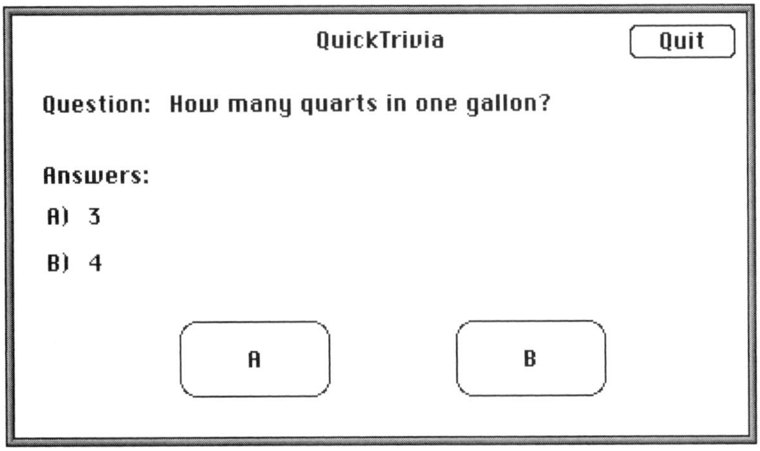

```
              QuickTrivia                    ( Quit )

  Question:  How many quarts in one gallon?

  Answers:

  A)  3

  B)  4


          (       A       )        (       B       )
```

FIGURE 7.12
The QuickTrivia Game

QuickTrivia displays the questions randomly from a set of questions you supply. It also displays movies randomly—again, from the movies you supply. It uses two separate lists for movie display. If the user makes a correct choice, the program randomly picks a movie from a list of correct movies. If the answer was wrong, the program looks to the other movie list. Through this method you can create a set of more "upbeat" movies to be played when the user picks correctly, and a set of more dark, or downbeat, movies when the user is wrong.

QuickTrivia comes with three questions and four movies: two "correct" movies and two "incorrect" movies. You can easily expand the program to any number of questions. You can add as many movies as you'd like, too. The section in this chapter titled *Adding to QuickTrivia—Without Programming!* tells you how to make these additions.

Program Project: QuickTrivia.π

This program, and the ones in Chapters 8 and 9, compile using the THINK C compiler. The source code, the resource file, and the program's THINK C project file for each program are included on the disk.

THINK C programs start as a *project*. A project names the source code files for a program. If you've written a Macintosh program using THINK C or Symantec C++, you should know how to create a project. If you don't, refer to the user's guide that came with your compiler.

A THINK C project has the same name that the final program will have, with a .π extension. Create the π character by holding the **Option** key while you type the letter **p**.

Program Resources: QuickTrivia.π.rsrc

When you compile the source code, THINK C will look for a resource file that has the project name with the extension *.rsrc*. Thus the QuickTrivia program has a resource file named *QuickTrivia.π.rsrc*.

The resource file for this program holds the definitions of the dialog box and several string lists. Figure 7.13 shows the resources, as viewed from Apple's resource editor ResEdit.

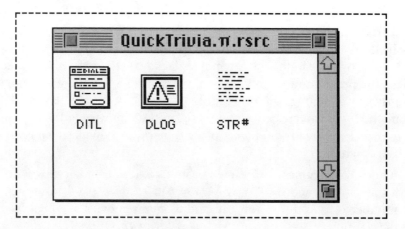

FIGURE 7.13
The QuickTrivia Resource File

The 'DLOG' resource holds the definition of the QuickTrivia dialog box. The 'DITL' resource holds the dialog items that appear in the dialog box. These two resources are shown in Figures 7.14 and 7.15, respectively.

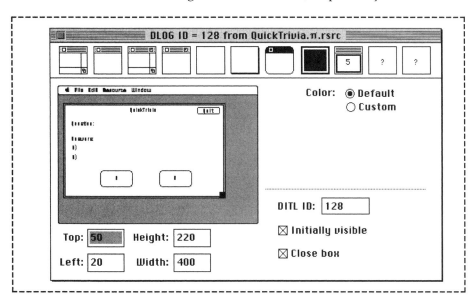

FIGURE 7.14
QuickTrivia's 'DLOG' Resource

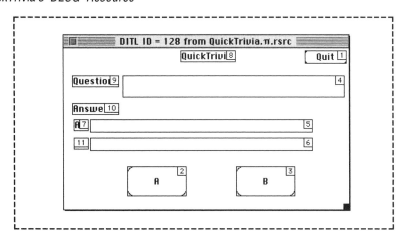

FIGURE 7.15
QuickTrivia's 'DITL' Resource

The 'STR#' resource type allows you to store any number of text strings in a resource file. You can retrieve one or more of these strings with a call to the Toolbox routine *GetIndString()*, and then use it in your program as you would any other string. Figure 7.16 shows the IDs and names of the six 'STR#' resources QuickTrivia uses.

ID	Size	Name
128	21	"Titles of "Right" Movies"
129	17	"Titles of "Wrong" Movies"
130	95	"Questions"
131	9	"Answers For "A" Button"
132	8	"Answers For "B" Button"
133	8	"Correct Answer List"

STR#s from QuickTrivia.π.rsrc

FIGURE 7.16
QuickTrivia's 'STR#' Resources

Each of the six 'STR#' resources contains more than one string. Figure 7.17 shows 'STR#' resource 128. It holds two strings. We'll describe each of the 'STR#' resources as we use them in the program.

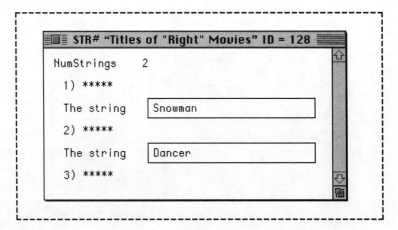

STR# "Titles of "Right" Movies" ID = 128

NumStrings   2

1) *****

The string   Snowman

2) *****

The string   Dancer

3) *****

FIGURE 7.17
Two Strings are Stored in this One 'STR#' Resource

Program Listing: QuickTrivia.c

Here, in its entirety, is the source code for QuickTrivia. After the source code, we'll provide details about the features of the listing.

```
/*++++++++++++++++++++++++++++++++++++++++++++++++++++++++++++++++++++*/

#include <GestaltEqu.h>
#include <Movies.h>

/*++++++++++++++++++++++++++++++++++++++++++++++++++++++++++++++++++++*/

int     abs( int );
void    Initialize_Toolbox( void );
void    Initialize_Movies( void );
void    Get_Movie_Info( void );
void    Draw_Comment( DialogPtr, Boolean );
void    Open_Dialog( void );
short   Generate_Random_Number( int );
void    Display_Question_And_Answers( DialogPtr );
void    Open_Play_Close_Movie( Boolean );
void    Determine_Movie_File( Boolean, Str255 * );
Movie   Get_A_Movie( Str255 );
void    Open_And_Size_Window( void );
void    Play_A_Movie( void );

/*++++++++++++++++++++++++++++++++++++++++++++++++++++++++++++++++++++*/

#define          RIGHT_MOVIES_STR_LIST          128
#define          WRONG_MOVIES_STR_LIST          129
#define          QUESTION_STR_LIST              130
#define          ANSWER_A_STR_LIST              131
#define          ANSWER_B_STR_LIST              132
#define          CORRECT_STR_LIST               133
#define          DIALOG_ID                      128
#define          DONE_BUTTON_ITEM                 1
#define          A_BUTTON_ITEM                    2
#define          B_BUTTON_ITEM                    3
#define          QUESTION_ITEM                    4
#define          ANSWER_A_ITEM                    5
#define          ANSWER_B_ITEM                    6

#define          VOL_REF_NUM                      0
#define          DIR_ID                          0L
#define          IN_FRONT            (WindowPtr)-1L

/*++++++++++++++++++++++++++++++++++++++++++++++++++++++++++++++++++++*/
```

```
WindowPtr      The_Window;
Movie          The_Movie;
Str255         Question_Str;
Str255         Answer_A_Str;
Str255         Answer_B_Str;
Boolean        Answer_A_Is_Correct;
short          Num_Questions;
short          Num_Right_Movies;
short          Num_Wrong_Movies;
Rect           White_Rect;

/*++++++++++++++++++++++++++++++++++++++++++++++++++++++++++++++++*/

void  main( void )
{
    Initialize_Toolbox();

    Initialize_Movies();

    Get_Movie_Info();

    SetRect( &White_Rect, 12, 3, 65, 20 );

    Open_Dialog();
}

/*++++++++++++++++++++++++++++++++++++++++++++++++++++++++++++++++*/

void  Initialize_Toolbox( void )
{
    InitGraf( &thePort );
    InitFonts();
    InitWindows();
    InitMenus();
    TEInit();
    InitDialogs( nil );
    InitCursor();
}

/*++++++++++++++++++++++++++++++++++++++++++++++++++++++++++++++++*/

void  Initialize_Movies( void )
{
    OSErr  error;
    long   result;

    error = Gestalt( gestaltQuickTime, &result );
    if ( error != noErr )
        ExitToShell();

    error = EnterMovies();
```

```
   if ( error != noErr )
      ExitToShell();
}

/*+++++++++++++++++++++++++++++++++++++++++++++++++++++++++++++++++*/

void  Get_Movie_Info( void )
{
   short   count;
   Str255  the_str;

   count = 0;
   do
   {
      count++;
      GetIndString( the_str, QUESTION_STR_LIST, count );
   } while ( the_str[0] != 0 );
   Num_Questions = --count;

   count = 0;
   do
   {
      count++;
      GetIndString( the_str, RIGHT_MOVIES_STR_LIST, count );
   } while ( the_str[0] != 0 );
   Num_Right_Movies = --count;

   count = 0;
   do
   {
      count++;
      GetIndString( the_str, WRONG_MOVIES_STR_LIST, count );
   } while ( the_str[0] != 0 );
   Num_Wrong_Movies = --count;
}

/*+++++++++++++++++++++++++++++++++++++++++++++++++++++++++++++++++*/

void  Draw_Comment( DialogPtr the_dialog, Boolean right_choice )
{
   SetPort( the_dialog );

   FillRect( &White_Rect, white );
   FrameRect( &White_Rect );

   MoveTo( White_Rect.left + 5, White_Rect.bottom - 4 );
   if ( right_choice == true )
      DrawString("\pRIGHT!");
   else
      DrawString("\pWRONG");
}
```

```
/*++++++++++++++++++++++++++++++++++++++++++++++++++++++++++++++++*/

void  Open_Dialog( void )
{
    DialogPtr    the_dialog;
    short        the_item;
    Boolean      done_with_dialog = false;
    Boolean      right_choice;

    the_dialog = GetNewDialog( DIALOG_ID, nil, IN_FRONT );
    ShowWindow( the_dialog );

    Display_Question_And_Answers( the_dialog );

    while ( done_with_dialog == false )
    {
        ModalDialog( nil, &the_item );

        switch ( the_item )
        {
            case DONE_BUTTON_ITEM:
                done_with_dialog = true;
                break;
            case A_BUTTON_ITEM:
                if ( Answer_A_Is_Correct == true )
                    right_choice = true;
                else
                    right_choice = false;
                Open_Play_Close_Movie( right_choice );
                Display_Question_And_Answers( the_dialog );
                break;
            case B_BUTTON_ITEM:
                if ( Answer_A_Is_Correct == true )
                    right_choice = false;
                else
                    right_choice = true;
                Open_Play_Close_Movie( right_choice );
                Display_Question_And_Answers( the_dialog );
                break;
        }
    }
    DisposDialog( the_dialog );
}

/*++++++++++++++++++++++++++++++++++++++++++++++++++++++++++++++++*/

short Generate_Random_Number( int max_number )
{
    long  raw_result;
    int   scaled;
```

```
    raw_result = abs( Random() );
    scaled = ( (raw_result * max_number)/ 32768 ) + 1;

    return ( scaled );
}

/*++++++++++++++++++++++++++++++++++++++++++++++++++++++++++++++++++++*/

void  Display_Question_And_Answers( DialogPtr the_dialog )
{
    int     str_index;
    short   item_type;
    Handle  item_handle;
    Rect    display_rect;
    Str255  correct_str;

    SetPort( the_dialog );

    str_index   = Generate_Random_Number( Num_Questions );

    GetIndString( Question_Str, QUESTION_STR_LIST, str_index );
    GetIndString( Answer_A_Str, ANSWER_A_STR_LIST, str_index );
    GetIndString( Answer_B_Str, ANSWER_B_STR_LIST, str_index );
    GetIndString( correct_str,  CORRECT_STR_LIST,  str_index );

    if ( correct_str[1] == 'A' )
       Answer_A_Is_Correct = true;
    else
       Answer_A_Is_Correct = false;

    GetDItem( the_dialog, QUESTION_ITEM, &item_type,
             &item_handle, &display_rect );
    SetIText( item_handle, Question_Str );

    GetDItem( the_dialog, ANSWER_A_ITEM, &item_type,
             &item_handle, &display_rect );
    SetIText( item_handle, Answer_A_Str );

    GetDItem( the_dialog, ANSWER_B_ITEM, &item_type,
             &item_handle, &display_rect );
    SetIText( item_handle, Answer_B_Str );
}

/*++++++++++++++++++++++++++++++++++++++++++++++++++++++++++++++++++++*/

void  Open_Play_Close_Movie( Boolean right_choice )
{
    Str255  movie_name;

    Determine_Movie_File( right_choice, &movie_name );
```

```
      The_Movie = Get_A_Movie( movie_name );
      if ( The_Movie == nil )
         ExitToShell();

      Open_And_Size_Window();

      Play_A_Movie();

      DisposeMovie( The_Movie );
      DisposeWindow( The_Window );
   }

/*+++++++++++++++++++++++++++++++++++++++++++++++++++++++++++++++++*/

void   Determine_Movie_File( Boolean right_choice, Str255
                             *file_name )
   {
      short   str_list_id;
      short   str_index;
      short   num_movies_in_list;

      if ( right_choice == true )
      {
         str_list_id = RIGHT_MOVIES_STR_LIST;
         num_movies_in_list = Num_Right_Movies;
      }
      else
      {
         str_list_id = WRONG_MOVIES_STR_LIST;
         num_movies_in_list = Num_Wrong_Movies;
      }

      str_index = Generate_Random_Number( num_movies_in_list );

      GetIndString( *file_name, str_list_id, str_index );
   }

/*+++++++++++++++++++++++++++++++++++++++++++++++++++++++++++++++++*/

Movie   Get_A_Movie( Str255 file_name )
   {
      OSErr     error;
      Movie     get_movie = nil;
      short     movie_res_file;
      short     movie_res_ID = 0;
      Str255    movie_name;
      Boolean   was_changed;
      FSSpec    the_FSSpec;

      error = FSMakeFSSpec( VOL_REF_NUM, DIR_ID, file_name,
                            &the_FSSpec);
```

```
   if ( error != noErr )
      ExitToShell();

   error = OpenMovieFile( &the_FSSpec, &movie_res_file,
                          fsRdPerm );
   if ( error == noErr )
   {
      error = NewMovieFromFile(&get_movie, movie_res_file,
                               &movie_res_ID,
                               movie_name, newMovieActive,
                               &was_changed );

      CloseMovieFile( movie_res_file );
   }
   return get_movie;
}

/*++++++++++++++++++++++++++++++++++++++++++++++++++++++++++++*/

void  Open_And_Size_Window( void )
{
   Rect  the_rect;
   Rect  movie_box;

   SetRect(&the_rect, 100, 100, 150, 150);
   The_Window = NewCWindow( nil, &the_rect, "\pMovie", false,
                            noGrowDocProc, IN_FRONT, false, 0 );

   GetMovieBox( The_Movie, &movie_box );
   OffsetRect( &movie_box, -movie_box.left, -movie_box.top );
   SetMovieBox( The_Movie, &movie_box );

   SizeWindow( The_Window, movie_box.right, movie_box.bottom,
               true );
   ShowWindow( The_Window);

   SetMovieGWorld( The_Movie, ( CGrafPtr )The_Window, nil );
}

/*++++++++++++++++++++++++++++++++++++++++++++++++++++++++++++*/

void  Play_A_Movie( void )
{
   short i;

   for (i = 1; i <= 2; i++)
   {
      GoToBeginningOfMovie( The_Movie );
      StartMovie( The_Movie );
      do
      {
```

```
        MoviesTask( The_Movie, 0 );
    }
    while ( IsMovieDone( The_Movie ) == false );
    }
}
```

Stepping Through the Code

The remainder of this section is a walkthrough of the QuickTrivia source code, starting with the #include files.

The #include File

QuickTrivia makes a call to the Toolbox routine *Gestalt()*, so you need to include the header file GestaltEqu.h. To make use of all the Movie Toolbox routines, you also need to include the Movies.h header file.

```
#include <GestaltEqu.h>
#include <Movies.h>
```

Function Prototypes

Function prototypes help the compiler do its job. They also help you catch bugs. Here are the prototype for each routine in QuickTrivia.

```
int     abs( int );
void    Handle_One_Event( void );
void    Initialize_Toolbox( void );
void    Initialize_Movies( void );
void    Get_Movie_Info( void );
void    Draw_Comment( DialogPtr, Boolean );
void    Open_Dialog( void );
short   Generate_Random_Number( int );
void    Display_Question_And_Answers( DialogPtr );
void    Open_Play_Close_Movie( Boolean );
void    Determine_Movie_File( Boolean, Str255 * );
Movie   Get_A_Movie( Str255 );
void    Open_And_Size_Window( void );
void    Play_A_Movie( void );
```

The #define Directives

We've kept numbers out of the source code by using several *#define* directives. All but three are resource IDs. The first six are the IDs of the 'STR#'

resources. The next, *DIALOG_ID*, is the ID of the 'DLOG' resource. The next six #*defines* are the item numbers of the enabled items in the dialog. You can refer back to Figure 7.15 to see where they came from.

The last three #*defines*, *VOL_REF_NUM*, *DIR_ID*, and *IN_FRONT*, are parameters to the Toolbox routines *FSMakeFSSpec()* and *NewCWindow()*.

```
#define     RIGHT_MOVIES_STR_LIST       128
#define     WRONG_MOVIES_STR_LIST       129
#define     QUESTION_STR_LIST           130
#define     ANSWER_A_STR_LIST           131
#define     ANSWER_B_STR_LIST           132
#define     CORRECT_STR_LIST            133
#define     DIALOG_ID                   128
#define     DONE_BUTTON_ITEM              1
#define     A_BUTTON_ITEM                 2
#define     B_BUTTON_ITEM                 3
#define     QUESTION_ITEM                 4
#define     ANSWER_A_ITEM                 5
#define     ANSWER_B_ITEM                 6

#define     VOL_REF_NUM                   0
#define     DIR_ID                       0L
#define     IN_FRONT          (WindowPtr)-1L
```

Global Variables

Next we come to the declaration of the program's global variables. *The_Window* will be the display window that holds the movie. Variable *The_Movie* is the movie itself. The questions and answers displayed in the dialog box will change as the program runs. *Question_Str*, *Answer_A_Str*, and *Answer_B_Str* are *Str255* variables that hold the text that make up these strings. The program needs to know how many questions it should randomly choose from; *Num_Questions* holds this value. The program also needs to know how many movies it should choose from; *Num_Right_Movies* and *Num_Wrong_Movies* provide this information. Finally, we use *White_Rect* to keep track of the coordinates of a rectangle that will display a "Right" or "Wrong" message.

```
WindowPtr   The_Window;
Movie       The_Movie;
Str255      Question_Str;
Str255      Answer_A_Str;
Str255      Answer_B_Str;
Boolean     Answer_A_Is_Correct;
```

```
short       Num_Questions;
short       Num_Right_Movies;
short       Num_Wrong_Movies;
Rect        White_Rect;
```

The main() Function

QuickTrivia begins by initializing the various managers of the Toolbox and the Movie Toolbox. It then gets some information about the number of questions and movies that are available. The program displays a small rectangle that contains the word "Right" or "Wrong" in response to the user's choice. We set the coordinates of that rectangle here—it will be used later in the program. After that, a dialog box is opened. From then on, all action is handled from within the dialog box.

```
void  main( void )
{
    Initialize_Toolbox();

    Initialize_Movies();

    Get_Movie_Info();

    SetRect( &White_Rect, 12, 3, 65, 20 );

    Open_Dialog();
}
```

Initializations

To initialize the various managers, all Macintosh programs should have a routine similar to our *Initialize_Toolbox()*. If your program uses QuickTime, it should also have a routine like our *Initialize_Movies()*. This routine combines the check for QuickTime that we covered in the *Checking For QuickTime* section of this chapter with a call to the Movie Toolbox initialization routine *EnterMovies()*, discussed in this chapter's *Initializing the Movie Toolbox* section.

```
void  Initialize_Toolbox( void )
{
    InitGraf( &thePort );
    InitFonts();
    InitWindows();
    InitMenus();
    TEInit();
```

```
   InitDialogs( nil );
   InitCursor();
}

void  Initialize_Movies( void )
{
   OSErr  error;
   long   result;

   error = Gestalt( gestaltQuickTime, &result );
   if ( error != noErr )
      ExitToShell();

   error = EnterMovies();
   if ( error != noErr )
      ExitToShell();
}
```

Getting Information about 'STR#' Resources

QuickTrivia stores the text of each trivia question as a string in a 'STR#' resource: resource ID 130. If you want to add more questions to the game, you can add more strings to this resource (covered later in this chapter). The point is, the number of questions can vary from one running of the program to the next. QuickTrivia uses a loop to count the number of strings in this one resource. That number is the number of questions it can display.

A *string* is an array of characters. But the very first character in a string isn't a letter—it's the length of the string. After calling *GetIndString()* to retrieve a string from the resource, we check its length. When we reach a string with a length of zero, we know we've passed the last string.

We keep a running count of the number of strings we retrieve. When the zero length string is reached, we subtract it out of the total, and assign this count to the global variable *Num_Questions*. We'll use *Num_Questions* later in the program. Here's the code:

```
#define   QUESTION_STR_LIST    130

short   count;
Str255  the_str;

count = 0;
do
{
   count++;
   GetIndString( the_str, QUESTION_STR_LIST, count );
```

```
} while ( the_str[0] != 0 );

Num_Questions = --count;
```

QuickTrivia can play any movie that you keep in the folder that houses the QuickTrivia program. But you have to let the program know the names of the movie files so it can find and open them. You'll store all the names in two separate 'STR#' resources. One lists the movies to play when the answer is correct, and one lists the movies to play when the user gets a question wrong.

To determine the number of QuickTime movies the program can potentially play, we employ the same trick we used to determine the number of questions. We've bundled these three checks into one routine called *Get_Movie_Info()*.

```
void  Get_Movie_Info( void )
{
    short   count;
    Str255  the_str;

    count = 0;
    do
    {
        count++;
        GetIndString( the_str, QUESTION_STR_LIST, count );
    } while ( the_str[0] != 0 );
    Num_Questions = --count;

    count = 0;
    do
    {
        count++;
        GetIndString( the_str, RIGHT_MOVIES_STR_LIST, count );
    } while ( the_str[0] != 0 );
    Num_Right_Movies = --count;

    count = 0;
    do
    {
        count++;
        GetIndString( the_str, WRONG_MOVIES_STR_LIST, count );
    } while ( the_str[0] != 0 );
    Num_Wrong_Movies = --count;
}
```

Opening the Dialog Box

QuickTrivia uses a modal dialog box to interact with the user. A modal dialog box "owns" the screen—as long as it's up, no action can take place outside it. That makes it good for a children's game, because menus can't be accessed during the running of the game.

Open_Dialog() uses a call to *GetNewDialog()* to open the dialog box defined by the 'DLOG' and 'DITL' resources. The routine then makes a call to *Display_Question_And_Answers()* to write a question and the two possible answers to the dialog. We'll cover this routine in a moment.

After displaying a question, *Open_Dialog()* enters a never-ending loop (at least, not until the program ends). When the user clicks on the small **Quit** button in the upper-right corner of the dialog, the loop will end and so will the program.

When the user clicks on the button labeled **A**, *Open_Dialog()* checks to see if that is the correct choice for the question displayed. Based on the current value of the global *Boolean* variable *Answer_A_Is_Correct*, the local *Boolean* variable *right_choice* is appropriately set to *true* or *false*. *Answer_A_Is_Correct* changes value with each question that is displayed—its value is set in the *Display_Question_And_Answers()* routine we're about to cover.

After setting the *right_choice* variable, *Draw_Comment()* is called to give the user some feedback. It simply frames a rectangle in the upper-left corner of the dialog and writes the word "Right" or "Wrong" in it. Remember, any time you write or draw to a dialog or window you should make a call to *SetPort()* to ensure that the drawing takes place in the dialog box or window you want it to.

Next, *Open_Play_Close_Movie()* is called. This routine does all the things its name says: it opens a window, plays a movie, and then closes the window. We'll cover this routine shortly.

After a movie is played, *Display_Question_And_Answers()* is again called to display a new question. This cycle of displaying a question, then playing a movie, is repeated until the user quits.

```
void  Draw_Comment( DialogPtr the_dialog, Boolean right_choice )
{
   SetPort( the_dialog );

   FillRect( &White_Rect, white );
```

```
        FrameRect( &White_Rect );

    MoveTo( White_Rect.left + 5, White_Rect.bottom - 4 );
    if ( right_choice == true )
        DrawString("\pRIGHT!");
    else
        DrawString("\pWRONG");
}

void  Open_Dialog( void )
{
    DialogPtr   the_dialog;
    short       the_item;
    Boolean     done_with_dialog = false;
    Boolean     right_choice;

    the_dialog = GetNewDialog( DIALOG_ID, nil, IN_FRONT );
    ShowWindow( the_dialog );

    Display_Question_And_Answers( the_dialog );

    while ( done_with_dialog == false )
    {
        ModalDialog( nil, &the_item );

        switch ( the_item )
        {
            case DONE_BUTTON_ITEM:
                done_with_dialog = true;
                break;
            case A_BUTTON_ITEM:
                if ( Answer_A_Is_Correct == true )
                    right_choice = true;
                else
                    right_choice = false;
                Draw_Comment( the_dialog, right_choice );
                Open_Play_Close_Movie( right_choice );
                SetPort( the_dialog );
                FillRect( &White_Rect, white );
                Display_Question_And_Answers( the_dialog );
                break;
            case B_BUTTON_ITEM:
                if ( Answer_A_Is_Correct == true )
                    right_choice = false;
                else
                    right_choice = true;
                Draw_Comment( the_dialog, right_choice );
                Open_Play_Close_Movie( right_choice );
                SetPort( the_dialog );
                FillRect( &White_Rect, white );
                Display_Question_And_Answers( the_dialog );
```

```
            break;
      }
   }
   DisposDialog( the_dialog );
}
```

Generating a Random Number

Before discussing *Display_Question_And_Answers()*, let's take a look at the one routine it calls: *Generate_Random_Number()*. This useful routine generates a random number in the range of 1 to any number you specify in the passed-in *max_number*.

Our random number generator makes use of a Toolbox function called *Random()*. This function returns a random number in the range of –32,768 to 32,767. Because we have no need for negative numbers in our program, we use the ANSI C function *abs()* to get the absolute value of the number returned by *Random()*.

Next, we take *raw_result*, which is in the range of 0 to 32,767, and multiply it by the maximum number in our own range. We then divide that value by the original range of 32,768. The result of this operation will be truncated—the fractional part will be dropped off. This will *always* give a value between 0 and one less than *max_number*. So we always add 1, to give a value in the desired range of 1 to *max_number*.

```
short Generate_Random_Number( int max_number )
{
   long   raw_result;
   int    scaled;

   raw_result = abs( Random() );
   scaled = ( (raw_result * max_number)/ 32768 ) + 1;

   return ( scaled );
}
```

Displaying a Question and Its Answers

QuickTrivia repeatedly, and randomly, displays a question and the two multiple choice answers that accompany it. The key word in that sentence is "randomly." To decide on a question to display, *Display_Question_And_Answers()* calls *Generate_Random_Number()*. The number it passes is *Num_Questions*—the number of possible questions to choose from. Here's the call:

```
str_index    = Generate_Random_Number( Num_Questions );
```

If there are three questions in the resource file, then *Num_Questions* will be three, and *string_index* will take on a value in the range of 1 to 3. This value will be used as an index into four of the 'STR#' resources. The Toolbox routine *GetIndString()* is called four times in a row. Each time, it retrieves a string from a different 'STR#' resource and assigns the result to a *Str255* variable. Following are the four calls to *GetIndString()*:

```
GetIndString( Question_Str, QUESTION_STR_LIST, str_index );
GetIndString( Answer_A_Str, ANSWER_A_STR_LIST, str_index );
GetIndString( Answer_B_Str, ANSWER_B_STR_LIST, str_index );
GetIndString( correct_str,  CORRECT_STR_LIST,  str_index );
```

When a question is added to 'STR#' resource ID 130, an answer is added to both 'STR#' resource 131 and 132. One answer represents the "A" choice, one the "B" choice. Only one answer is correct. 'STR#' resource 133 holds the letter, "A" or "B", of the correct answer. Figure 7.18 explains the relationship between these calls. Take note of the titles of each of the four windows in the figure.

The last call to *GetIndString()* sets local *Str255* variable *correct_str* to either "A" or "B". This letter represents the correct choice for this one question. We know this string is always just one character, so we'll look at only the first character to decide which way to set the global *Boolean* variable *Answer_A_Is_Correct*.

```
if ( correct_str[1] == 'A' )
   Answer_A_Is_Correct = true;
else
   Answer_A_Is_Correct = false;
```

The *Answer_A_Is_Correct* variable is used back in the *Open_Dialog()* routine. There we compare the value of *Answer_A_Is_Correct* to the button the user clicked on to determine if the user made the right choice.

The last task *Display_Question_And_Answers* performs is displaying the strings in the dialog box. To display the question string we first use *GetDItem()* to get a handle to the static text item that is to hold the string. We then call *SetDItem()* to set the text of this item to the question string. Figure 7.19 illustrates the effect of calling *GetDItem()* and *SetDItem()*.

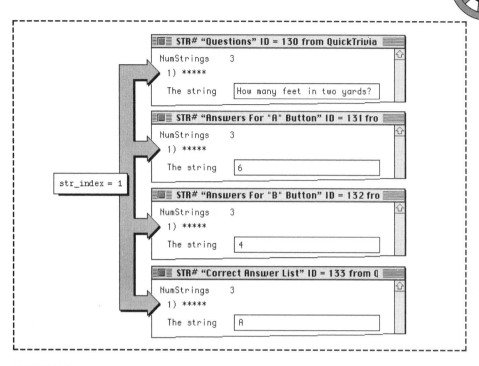

FIGURE 7.18
Relationship between Four of the 'STR#' Resources

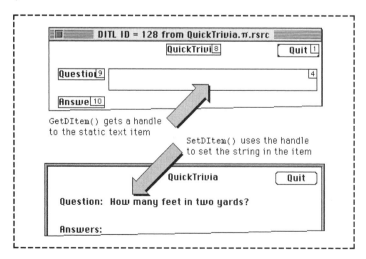

FIGURE 7.19
Effect of Calling GetDItem() and SetDItem()

```
#define     QUESTION_ITEM     4

short   item_type;
Handle  item_handle;
Rect    display_rect;

GetDItem( the_dialog, QUESTION_ITEM, &item_type,
          &item_handle, &display_rect );
SetIText( item_handle, Question_Str );
```

The text for the two multiple choice answers is displayed in the same manner as the text for the question.

```
void  Display_Question_And_Answers( DialogPtr the_dialog )
{
   int     str_index;
   short   item_type;
   Handle  item_handle;
   Rect    display_rect;
   Str255  correct_str;

   SetPort( the_dialog );

   str_index   = Generate_Random_Number( Num_Questions );

   GetIndString( Question_Str, QUESTION_STR_LIST, str_index );
   GetIndString( Answer_A_Str, ANSWER_A_STR_LIST, str_index );
   GetIndString( Answer_B_Str, ANSWER_B_STR_LIST, str_index );
   GetIndString( correct_str,  CORRECT_STR_LIST,  str_index );

   if ( correct_str[1] == 'A' )
      Answer_A_Is_Correct = true;
   else
      Answer_A_Is_Correct = false;

   GetDItem( the_dialog, QUESTION_ITEM, &item_type,
             &item_handle, &display_rect );
   SetIText( item_handle, Question_Str );

   GetDItem( the_dialog, ANSWER_A_ITEM, &item_type,
             &item_handle, &display_rect );
   SetIText( item_handle, Answer_A_Str );

   GetDItem( the_dialog, ANSWER_B_ITEM, &item_type,
             &item_handle, &display_rect );
   SetIText( item_handle, Answer_B_Str );
}
```

Playing a Movie

In response to a click on either of the multiple choice buttons, *Open_Dialog()* calls *Open_Play_Close_Movie()* to play a movie. This routine calls a series of functions that: determine which movie to play, open the movie file, open a display window, and play the movie. We'll cover each of these subordinate routines right after this:

```
void  Open_Play_Close_Movie( Boolean right_choice )
{
   Str255  movie_name;

   Determine_Movie_File( right_choice, &movie_name );

   The_Movie = Get_A_Movie( movie_name );
   if ( The_Movie == nil )
      ExitToShell();

   Open_And_Size_Window();

   Play_A_Movie();

   DisposeMovie( The_Movie );
   DisposeWindow( The_Window );
}
```

When a button was clicked on, *Open_Dialog()* determined if it was the button for the correct answer. The routine set a *Boolean* variable and passed it on to *Open_Play_Close_Movie()*. In determining which movie to play, *Open_Play_Close_Movie()* again passes this *Boolean* value to another function: *Determine_Movie_File()*. The second parameter to this routine is a pointer to a *Str255* variable. When *Determine_Movie_File()* is complete, this variable will contain the name of the movie file to use.

QuickTrivia divides the movies it will show into two sets: one for when the user makes a correct choice, the other for when the user is wrong. The titles of all the movie files for the "right" movies are kept in 'STR#' resource 128. The titles to the "wrong" movies are kept in 'STR#' resource 129. Figure 7.20 shows these two resources.

Determine_Movie_File() first determines which 'STR#' resource will be used. It bases this decision on the passed-in *right_choice* variable. Next, an index into the 'STR#' resource is randomly selected by calling our own *Generate_Random_Number()* function. Finally, a call to *GetIndString()* retrieves the string that is the title of a movie file.

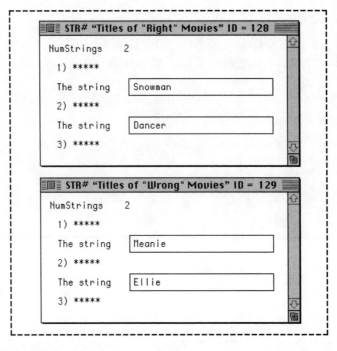

FIGURE 7.20

The 'STR#' Resources that Hold Movie File Names

```
void  Determine_Movie_File( Boolean right_choice, Str255
                            *file_name )
{
    short   str_list_id;
    short   str_index;
    short   num_movies_in_list;

    if ( right_choice == true )
    {
        str_list_id = RIGHT_MOVIES_STR_LIST;
        num_movies_in_list = Num_Right_Movies;
    }
    else
    {
        str_list_id = WRONG_MOVIES_STR_LIST;
        num_movies_in_list = Num_Wrong_Movies;
    }

    str_index = Generate_Random_Number( num_movies_in_list );

    GetIndString( *file_name, str_list_id, str_index );
}
```

From this chapter you know the sequence of events that precede the playing of a movie. A call to *FSMakeFSSpec()* establishes an *FSSpec*—a file system specification—for a movie. That helps the Movie Toolbox find the movie file on disk. Then a call to *OpenMovieFile()* opens the movie file. The routine *NewMovieFromFile()* creates a movie from the information in the movie file. After the movie is created, the file isn't needed by the program, so *CloseMovieFile()* is called. These are exactly the steps *Get_A_Movie()* performs. When the routine is done it returns the newly-created *Movie* to the calling routine, *Open_Play_Close_Movie()*.

```
Movie  Get_A_Movie( Str255 file_name )
{
   OSErr    error;
   Movie    get_movie = nil;
   short    movie_res_file;
   short    movie_res_ID = 0;
   Str255   movie_name;
   Boolean  was_changed;
   FSSpec   the_FSSpec;

   error = FSMakeFSSpec( VOL_REF_NUM, DIR_ID, file_name,
                       &the_FSSpec);
   if ( error != noErr )
      ExitToShell();

   error = OpenMovieFile( &the_FSSpec, &movie_res_file,
                        fsRdPerm );
   if ( error == noErr )
   {
      error = NewMovieFromFile(&get_movie, movie_res_file,
                            &movie_res_ID,
                            movie_name, newMovieActive,
                            &was_changed);

      CloseMovieFile( movie_res_file );
   }
   return get_movie;
}
```

This chapter's section, *Opening a Display Window for a Movie*, covered the steps necessary to open and resize a movie window. The *Open_And_Size_Window()* routine uses the same technique we covered earlier: open a window, adjust the movie box, set the size of the window to the size of the movie box, show the window, and then set the movie's graphics world.

```
void  Open_And_Size_Window( void )
{
    Rect  the_rect;
    Rect  movie_box;

    SetRect(&the_rect, 100, 100, 150, 150);
    The_Window = NewCWindow( nil, &the_rect, "\pMovie", false,
                             noGrowDocProc, IN_FRONT, false, 0 );

    GetMovieBox( The_Movie, &movie_box );
    OffsetRect( &movie_box, -movie_box.left, -movie_box.top );
    SetMovieBox( The_Movie, &movie_box );

    SizeWindow( The_Window, movie_box.right, movie_box.bottom,
                true );
    ShowWindow( The_Window);

    SetMovieGWorld( The_Movie, ( CGrafPtr )The_Window, nil );
}
```

When it's time to actually play the movie, *Play_A_Movie()* is called. We've added a little twist to playing a movie—we use a loop to play it twice. You can play a movie as many times as you want. Before playing the movie, though, call the Movie Toolbox routine *GoToBeginningOfMovie()* to set the movie to the beginning. Without this call the movie would run fine the first time. But the second time the movie would start playing from where it ended—at the end!

```
void  Play_A_Movie( void )
{
    short i;

    for (i = 1; i <= 2; i++)
    {
        GoToBeginningOfMovie( The_Movie );
        StartMovie( The_Movie );
        do
        {
            MoviesTask( The_Movie, 0 );
        }
        while ( IsMovieDone( The_Movie ) == false );
    }
}
```

Adding to QuickTrivia—Without Programming!

Apple emphasizes that you should store text in resources whenever possible. That makes adding and changing text easy to do. We've complied with Apple's suggestion in our QuickTrivia program. The result was worth the effort—you can make changes to QuickTrivia without changing any code and without recompiling the program.

Making Changes with ResEdit

You can add to the lists of movies that QuickTrivia will play, or add new multiple choice questions to the program. To do so, run ResEdit. When you're requested to select a file to open, select the QuickTrivia program itself, not the resource file. You'll be making the changes directly to the program. Figure 7.21 shows which file to select.

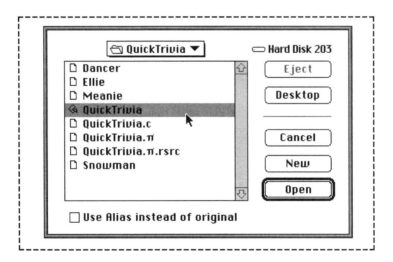

FIGURE 7.21
Opening the QuickTrivia Program Using ResEdit

After opening the QuickTrivia program with ResEdit, you'll see a window like the one shown in Figure 7.22. Notice that the 'STR#' resources are all there. That's where you'll be making all your changes.

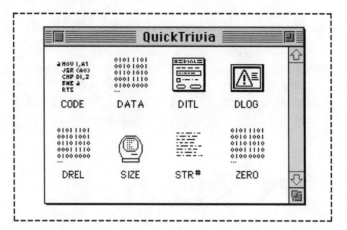

FIGURE 7.22
The QuickTrivia Resources

Adding to QuickTrivia's Lists of Movies

QuickTrivia will use any movies you keep in the QuickTrivia folder, provided it's aware that they're there. The more movies QuickTrivia knows about, the more it will randomly select from, and the more interesting the game will become.

Run ResEdit, selecting the QuickTrivia program as the file to open. Then open either 'STR#' resource 128 or 129. Go to the last movie listed and click on the number that appears after it. QuickTrivia comes with just two "right" movies listed, so you'll click on the number **3**, as shown in Figure 7.23. Then select **Insert New Field** from the Resource menu. A new edit text box will open, as pictured in Figure 7.24.

Simply type in the name of the movie file you've added to the QuickTrivia folder. Save the file and quit ResEdit. That's it! The next time you run the QuickTrivia program it will use your newly-added movie.

Adding to QuickTrivia's Questions

QuickTrivia comes with just three multiple choice questions—not nearly enough to hold anyone's interest. You can change these three questions, and add as many more questions as you'd like.

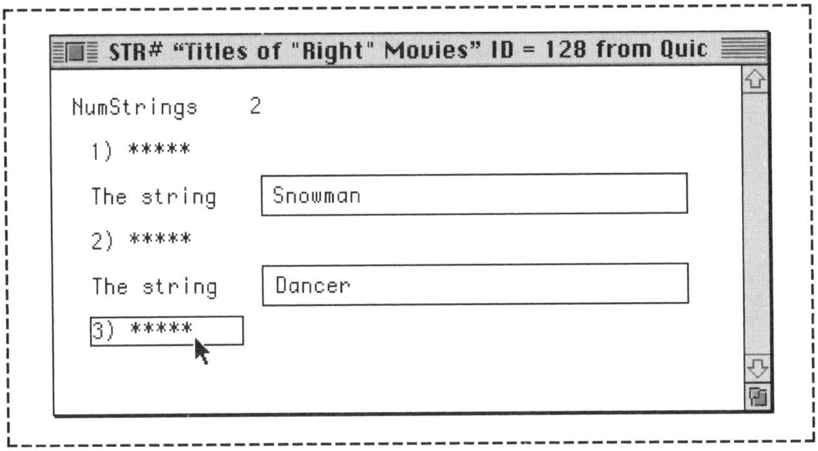

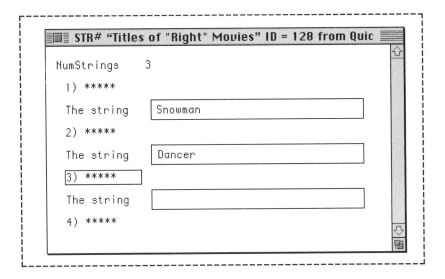

FIGURE 7.23
Adding a New Item to a 'STR#' Resource

FIGURE 7.24
Ready to Type in a New Movie File Name

Again, run ResEdit and select the QuickTrivia program. You'll be making changes to 'STR#' resources 130, 131, 132, and 133. Remember the relationship between these four resources? Figure 7.25 provides a recap.

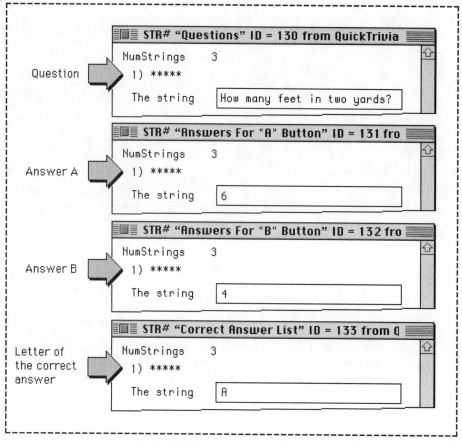

FIGURE 7.25

Relationship between Four of the 'STR#' Resources

Each question requires four entries: the question itself, the two multiple choice answers, and a single character string that tells which of the two answers is the correct one. To make these additions, first select 'STR#' resource with ID 130. Click on the last number in the resource. Select **Insert New Field** from the Resource menu. A new edit text box will open. Type in your new question. Make the necessary additions to the other three 'STR#' resources for this one question. Save your file and quit ResEdit. When you run QuickTrivia again, the new question will be used in the game.

NOTE You might want to rename the QuickTrivia program—perhaps as QuickTriviaPlus. Why? If you ever run THINK C and recompile the program, you'll risk overwriting the previous version of the program—the one with all your changes!

Chapter Summary

The Movie Toolbox is the collection of hundreds of Apple-supplied routines written expressly for working with QuickTime movies. Once you've used the *Gestalt()* routine to verify that QuickTime is installed, and you've initialized the Movie Toolbox with a call to *EnterMovies()*, you're free to make use of all the Toolbox routines.

Movies are stored in movie files. To use a file, you need to create a file system specification for it. That enables the system to find it. After using the *FSMakeFSSpec()* routine to create the specification, open the file by calling *OpenMovieFile()*.

Opening a movie file isn't enough to play a movie. You have to load the movie from the file into memory. The Movie Toolbox routine *NewMovieFromFile()* does that for you. Once loaded, this routine returns a variable of type *Movie* to your program. You'll use this *Movie* variable whenever you refer to the movie in other Toolbox calls.

A movie is displayed in a standard Macintosh window. Use the *GetNewCWindow()* routine to create a new color window. Once opened, resize the window to the size of the movie. Three routines will help you do that: *GetMovieBox()*, *OffsetRect()*, and *SetMovieBox()*. Finally, a call to *SizeWindow()* resizes the window, and a call to *ShowWindow()* shows the window. Call *SetMovieGWorld()* to tie the movie and the window together.

To play a movie you repeatedly call the MovieToolbox routine *MoviesTask()*. This routine services, or updates, the movie. Call this routine until the movie is done playing. You can get that information by calling *IsMovieDone()* after every call to *MoviesTask()*.

Programming with Movie Controllers

 n the previous chapter you saw how easy it is to play a QuickTime movie from within your own C language program. In this chapter you'll see how you can let users of your program select the movies they want to play. Once a user selects a movie, your program will display the movie with a *movie controller*. The controller is a narrow control panel at the bottom of the movie that allows the user to play or step through a movie.

Here you'll see how to let your application know when there is a QuickTime movie on the screen, and what it should do to handle that movie. You'll also learn how to let the user edit a movie with standard edit commands such as cut, copy, and paste. You will also see how to implement a save command that lets the user save any editing changes made to a movie.

QuickTime Components

The Macintosh Toolbox consists of thousands of routines. To organize this many routines, Apple grouped them into logically related sets called *managers*. For example, the routines that create, move, and resize a window are all part of the Window Manager. The Component Manager manages, of course, *components*. Apple has grouped the hundreds of routines that make up the new Movie Toolbox into related sets. Each group is called a component. A single component is a code resource that is dedicated to one feature of QuickTime.

One of the most commonly used features of QuickTime is its interface between a movie and its means of controlling that movie. *Movie controller components* allow programmers to easily implement *movie controllers* in their QuickTime programs. By attaching a movie controller to a movie, a programmer gives the program user a standardized means of working with the movie. A movie controller does much of the work of playing a movie. Figure 8.1 shows a movie controller attached to a movie.

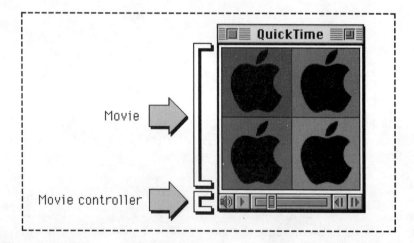

FIGURE 8.1

A Movie Controller is Attached to a Movie

This chapter focuses on movie controllers. Movie controllers are one of the most powerful and easy to implement programming tools you'll find—on a Macintosh or any other computer.

QuickTime movies use image-compression to reduce the size of a movie file to as little as 1/20 the size it would be without compression. Movie-making applications use image-compression, and usually provide a dialog box that allows the user to vary parameters that control compression. To help application developers implement a consistent interface, Apple provides the programmer with the *standard image-compression dialog components.*

Sequence grabber components are used by applications to obtain, or grab, digitized data from external sources. Apple's Movie Recorder program, discussed earlier in this book, uses sequence grabber components to capture images from your camcorder or VCR.

The Movie Controller Component

As you saw in the previous chapter, it's possible, and very easy, to play a movie without using a movie controller. But in that chapter's two programs, OneShot and QuickTrivia, the movies played themselves, with no intervention by the user. If you want the user to be able to work with a movie, you'll want to use a movie controller.

After loading a movie into memory, you can attach a movie controller to it. Then, by using routines from the Movie Toolbox, you can give the user the ability to work with the movie in a standardized way. With almost no effort on your part, the user can play the movie by clicking the movie controller's **Play** button, or step through the movie by clicking on either the **Step Forward** or **Step Backward** buttons. If a movie has a sound track, the Speaker, or volume control, button can be used to raise or lower the volume. These parts of the movie controller are shown in Figure 8.2.

Movie editing becomes easy with a movie controller. When the user holds down the **Shift** key and then moves the slider, or clicks one of the Step buttons, a part of the movie is selected. The movie controller gives visual feedback of this by turning to black the section of the play bar that represents the selected movie portion. This is shown in Figure 8.3.

Once again, you, the programmer, will not have to work hard to give the user this ability. Through the use of just a few Movie Toolbox routines, you'll allow the user to cut and copy the selected portion of a movie, and save it to be pasted into the same movie or another movie.

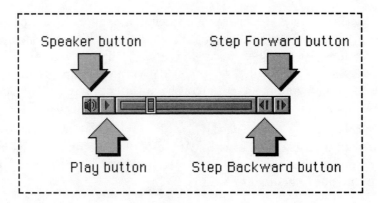

FIGURE 8.2

The Play, Step Backward, and Step Forward Buttons of the Movie Controller

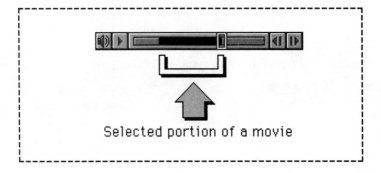

FIGURE 8.3

Selecting Part of a Movie

With a movie controller, you'll allow the user to resize a movie through menu commands. You can provide menu commands that allow the user to resize a movie by some exact ratio, such as doubling the size of the movie, or reducing it by half. See Figure 8.4.

The movie controller gives your QuickTime programs a slick, standardized look and feel. Before discussing how to create and use them, we'll cover one other topic that deals with the interface: the display of a standard "Open" dialog box that allows the user to open a QuickTime movie from a scrollable list.

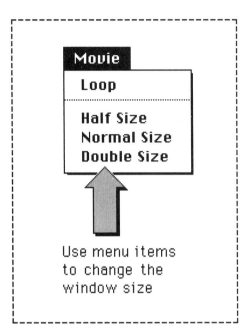

FIGURE 8.4
Resizing a Window Using Menu Commands

Opening a Movie File

Chapter 7 has a section with the same title as this one: *Opening a Movie File*. There, we discuss how a program uses a file system specification to find a file on disk. The data type that holds this information about a file is an *FSSpec*. In Chapter 7 we passed the name of a file to the Toolbox routine *FSMakeFSSpec()*, and the routine returned an *FSSpec*. We then passed this *FSSpec* to the Movie Toolbox routine *OpenMovieFile()* to open the movie file.

The above method of creating an *FSSpec* worked great for our QuickTrivia program, which opened and played movies without user intervention. Some of your programs may, however, let the user choose which movie to play. In these cases, you'll want a dialog box to let the user select which movie to open.

The Standard Get File Dialog Box

You've seen the standard dialog box that allows the user to select a file from a list of files—all Mac word processors use it. Figure 8.5 shows the dialog box you'll see if you select the **Open** command from the File menu of Apple's TeachText program.

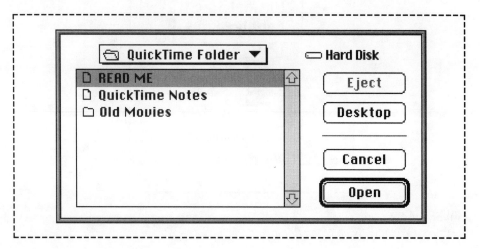

FIGURE 8.5

Standard Dialog for Selecting a File

Notice in Figure 8.5 that only folders and the files of the type the application uses—text files—are shown in the list. The dialog box filters out programs or files that TeachText can't open. To open a dialog box of this type, you would use the Toolbox routine *StandardGetFile()*.

You can use a similar dialog box to allow the user to open QuickTime movies. The Movie Toolbox routine *StandardGetFilePreview()* displays the dialog box shown in Figure 8.6. Except for the check box in the bottom left corner, it is identical to the dialog box displayed by the *StandardGetFile()* call.

Clicking on the check box expands the left side of the dialog box. In the expanded portion of the dialog box will be displayed one frame from the movie highlighted in the list. If the QuickTime movie is larger than the preview area, the displayed frame will be reduced to fit. Figure 8.7 illustrates this feature.

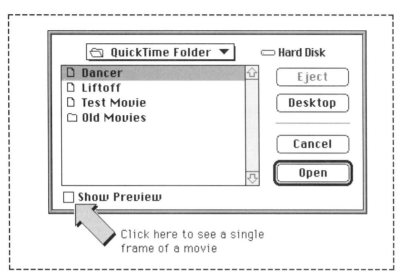

FIGURE 8.6
The Standard Get File Preview Dialog Box for Selecting a File

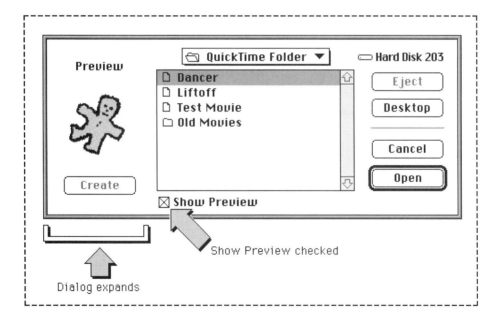

FIGURE 8.7
The Standard Get File Preview Dialog Box with Show Preview Checked

Displaying the Standard Get File Dialog Box

To display a list of movies to open, you'll have an Open menu item in the File menu of your application. In response to the user's selection of this item, call the Movie Toolbox routine *StandardGetFilePreview()*. This routine displays the standard Get File Preview dialog box shown in Figure 8.7. Once the dialog box is displayed, all activity in it is handled by this powerful routine. The user can change folders, scroll through the list of movies, check the Show Preview check box, or open a movie without any intervention on your behalf. Here's a call to *StandardGetFilePreview()*:

```
SFTypeList          type_list = { MovieFileType, 0, 0, 0 };
StandardFileReply   the_reply;

StandardGetFilePreview( nil, 1, type_list, &the_reply );
```

StandardGetFilePreview() requires four parameters. The first three tell the function which types of files to place in the dialog box's list. The dialog box will display only the type or types you specify, filtering out all other types of files.

You can list up to four file types. If you have more, you can use the first parameter to *StandardGetFilePreview()* as a pointer to an optional filter function that you write. If you don't need the filter function (and we won't), just pass *nil* as the first parameter.

The second parameter tells how many types to list. If your program is only opening movies, set this value to 1.

The third parameter gives the types of files to list. This parameter is of *SFTypeList* type, which is simply an array of four types. Each type is four characters surrounded by single quotes. Here's a definition that would set the type list to display applications and text files:

```
SFTypeList  type_list = { 'APPL', 'TEXT', 0, 0 };
```

Since you'll be displaying movies, your definition will look like this:

```
SFTypeList  type_list = { MovieFileType, 0, 0, 0 };
```

The *MovieFileType* is a constant defined in the Movies.h header file. It makes the above declaration the same as this one:

```
SFTypeList  type_list = { 'MooV', 0, 0, 0 };
```

The fourth parameter is a pointer to a reply structure. This *StandardFileReply* type has several members, all of which will be filled in for you after the user selects a file. Of these, only two will be of interest. The *sfGood* field is a *Boolean* value that tells you if the user opened a file (*true*) or canceled (*false*). The *sfFile* is of *FSSpec* type. Remember, the *FSSpec* is the file system specification, or path, to a file.

After the call to *StandardGetFilePreview()* you'll call *OpenMovieFile()* to open the file and *NewMovieFromFile()* to create the movie in memory—just as you did last chapter. Here's a function that displays the Get File dialog box, opens a file, creates a movie, and then returns the movie to the calling routine.

```
Movie Get_A_Movie( void )
{
   OSErr               error;
   Movie               get_movie = nil;
   SFTypeList          type_list = { MovieFileType, 0, 0, 0 };
   StandardFileReply   the_reply;
   Str255              movie_name;
   Boolean             was_changed;

   Movie_Res_ID = 0;

   StandardGetFilePreview( nil, 1, type_list, &the_reply );

   if ( the_reply.sfGood == true )
   {
      error = OpenMovieFile( &the_reply.sfFile, &Movie_Res_File,
                             fsRdWrPerm );
      if ( error == noErr )
         error = NewMovieFromFile( &get_movie, Movie_Res_File,
                                   &Movie_Res_ID,
                                   movie_name, newMovieActive,
                                   &was_changed );
   }
   return ( get_movie );
}
```

You may recall from Chapter 7 that after opening a movie file and creating the movie, we closed the file with a call to *CloseMovieFile()*. Here, we don't close the file. That's because we're going to be adding a movie controller to the opened movie. A movie controller makes it easy for the user to edit the movie, and then save the new version. Saving a movie involves writing the new information to a file, so we leave the movie file open. We'll close it when the user is done working with the movie.

NewMovieFromFile() fills in one of its parameters with the 'MooV' resource used to create the new movie. Last chapter we named that variable *movie_res_ID* and made it local to *Get_A_Movie()*. In this chapter we've made it global. It will be used later when we save the movie. The same holds true for the second parameter to *OpenMovieFile()*—it's now a global variable. We'll have more to say about these global variables in this chapter's *Saving a Movie* section, and in this chapter's sample program, MovieViewer.

In the last chapter we passed the constant *fsRdPerm* as the last parameter to *OpenMovieFile()*. Here, since we are allowing the user to edit the movie, we pass the constant *fsRdWrPerm*. That gives the user permission both to read (play) and write (save) the movie.

Figure 8.8 illustrates the similarities and differences between this version of *Get_A_Movie()* and last chapter's version of the same routine.

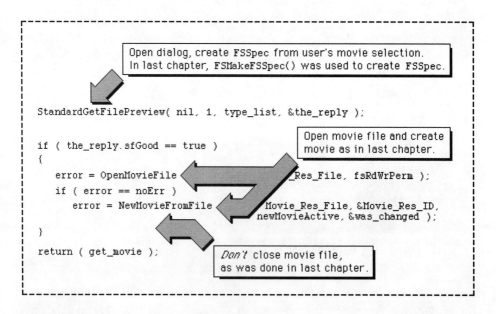

FIGURE 8.8

Similarities and Differences in Get_A_Movie()

Attaching a Controller to a Movie

After opening a movie file with *OpenMovieFile()* , and loading the movie into memory with *NewMovieFromFile()*, it's time to attach a movie controller to the movie. This is true whether the movie was selected using this chapter's *StandardGetFilePreview()* or last chapter's *FSMakeFSSpec()*.

Before adding the controller you'll want to open a window and associate it with the loaded movie, just as you did last chapter. *NewCWindow()* opens the window; *SetMovieGWorld()* pairs it with a movie.

```
WindowPtr   The_Window;
Movie       The_Movie;

Rect        the_rect;

SetRect(&the_rect, 100, 100, 150, 150);
The_Window = NewCWindow( nil, &the_rect, "\pMovie", false,
                         noGrowDocProc, IN_FRONT, true, 0 );

SetMovieGWorld( The_Movie, ( CGrafPtr )The_Window, nil );
```

In Chapter 7, after opening the window, we sized it to match the size of the movie. Here, we're going to add the controller to the movie before resizing the window. That's because both the movie and the controller will be placed in the window, as shown in Figure 8.9.

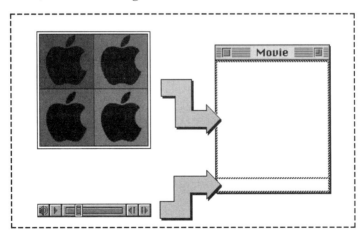

FIGURE 8.9
Both the Movie and Movie Controller Fit into a Window

Before creating the controller, call *GetMovieBox()* to get the size of the movie. The controller should have the same width as the movie, so this information is necessary. Then, create the controller and attach it to the movie with a call to the Movie Toolbox routine *NewMovieController()*.

```
MovieController   The_Controller;
Movie             The_Movie;

Rect   movie_rect;

GetMovieBox( The_Movie, &movie_box );

The_Controller = NewMovieController(The_Movie, &movie_box,
                   mcTopLeftMovie);
```

NewMovieController() requires three parameters. The first is the movie that the controller will attach itself to. The second is the rectangle that holds the size of the movie. The third parameter tells *NewMovieController()* where in the window to place the movie. You'll usually use the constant *mcTopLeftMovie* to place the movie in the window's top left corner. Figure 8.10 shows what a call to *NewMovieController()* accomplishes. Keep in mind that the window was set to an arbitrary size by *SetRect()* before the call to *NewCWindow()*.

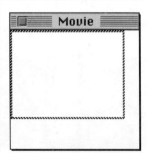
An invisible rectangle
movie_box in size is
placed in the top left
corner (mcTopLeftMovie)

The_Movie is placed in
the rectangle.

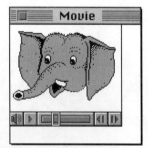
The_Controller is
added to the bottom
of the movie.

FIGURE 8.10
What a Call to NewMovieController() Accomplishes

With the window opened and the movie and controller in it, it's time to size the window. A call to *GetMovieBox()* won't do here—you need the size of the movie box together with the attached controller. The Movie Toolbox routine *MCGetControllerBoundsRect()* will give you this information. Pass it the controller (which is attached to a movie) and a pointer to a rectangle—any rectangle. The routine will fill the rectangle with the boundaries of the movie/controller pair. Use that rectangle in a call to *SizeWindow()* (see Figure 8.11). Finally, call *ShowWindow()*—the window has been invisible this whole time.

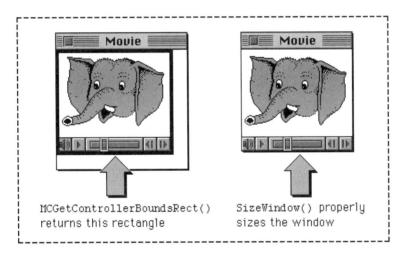

FIGURE 8.11
Sizing the Window to Fit the Movie and the Controller

To keep things organized, we'll now place all the code that created the window and controller, and sized the window, into a function called *Open_And_Size_Window()*.

```
void  Open_And_Size_Window( void )
{
   ComponentResult   comp_result;
   Rect              movie_box;
   Rect              the_rect;

   SetRect(&the_rect, 100, 100, 150, 150);
   The_Window = NewCWindow( nil, &the_rect, "\pMovie", false,
                            noGrowDocProc, IN_FRONT, true, 0 );
```

```
SetMovieGWorld( The_Movie, ( CGrafPtr )The_Window, nil );

GetMovieBox( The_Movie, &movie_box );

The_Controller = NewMovieController(The_Movie, &movie_box,
                                    mcTopLeftMovie);
if (The_Controller == nil)
    ExitToShell();

comp_result = MCGetControllerBoundsRect(The_Controller,
                                        &the_rect);

SizeWindow( The_Window, the_rect.right, the_rect.bottom,
            true );
ShowWindow(The_Window);
}
```

Movies and the Event Loop

At the start of this chapter we promised that allowing the user to work with
a movie controller would take very little programming effort on your part.
Here, we'll back up those words by showing you the few lines of code you'll
need to add to your program.

In last chapter's sample program, QuickTrivia, there was no main event
loop. That's because the program put up a modal dialog that controlled the
screen. When the modal dialog was dismissed, the program ended. There
was no menu bar and no other windows—nothing for the user to interact
with. Most Macintosh programs have a main event loop. Here's how we call
ours:

```
Boolean  All_Done = false;

void  main( void )
{
   [ initializations ]

   while ( All_Done == false )
      Handle_One_Event();
}
```

The *Handle_One_Event()* function, called repeatedly until the program ends,
has the following format:

```
void  Handle_One_Event( void )
{
   WaitNextEvent(everyEvent, &The_Event, 0, nil);

   switch (The_Event.what)
   {
      case mouseDown:
         [ handle mouse click ]

      case updateEvt:
         [ handle window update ]

      [ handle each event type ]
   }
}
```

With a movie controller present, you'll want to call the Movie Toolbox
routine *MCIsPlayerEvent()* at each pass through the main event loop. This
routine handles most movie-related tasks for you. If the user clicks on the
controller's Play button, on either of its Step buttons, or moves the slider
along the controller's slide bar, *MCIsPlayerEvent()* will take *all* the necessary
actions to work the controller. You'll write *no* additional code to handle any
of these events.

   You pass *MCIsPlayerEvent()* the *MovieController* variable for the open
movie, and the event that was retrieved by *WaitNextEvent()*. If your program
allows the user to open and close movies, you'll want to make sure that the
movie controller is actually present before calling *MCIsPlayerEvent()*—if a
movie isn't opened, the *MovieController* variable will be *nil*. Here's a look at
how the main event loop changes when you write a program that works
with QuickTime movies.

```
void  Handle_One_Event( void )
{
   long  movie_related_event;

   WaitNextEvent(everyEvent, &The_Event, 0, nil);

   if ( The_Controller == nil )
      movie_related_event = 0;
   else
      movie_related_event = MCIsPlayerEvent(The_Controller,
                                            &The_Event);

   if ( movie_related_event == 0 )
   {
```

```
    switch (The_Event.what)
    {
        [ handle events not involving movies ]
    }
  }
}
```

After calling *WaitNextEvent()*, check to see if *The_Controller* is *nil*. If there is no movie with a controller open, your controller variable will be *nil*. You'll then skip the call to *MCIsPlayerEvent()* and handle the event as a normal event. Figure 8.12 shows this case. If a movie is open, the controller variable won't be *nil*. You then know to call *MCIsPlayerEvent()*. *MCIsPlayerEvent()* will return a value of either 1 or 0. Here's the significance of these values:

■   If *MCIsPlayerEvent()* returns a 0, the event *did not* involve a movie. Now it's up to the event loop to handle the event as it normally does—by using a *switch* statement to determine the event type and then processing the event appropriately. Figure 8.13 illustrates this scenario.

■   If *MCIsPlayerEvent()* returns a 1, the event *did* involve a movie and *MCIsPlayerEvent()* handled the event for you. Since the event is handled, the rest of the event loop can be skipped. See Figure 8.14.

```
                                    If there is no controller,
                                    there is no movie

if ( The_Controller == nil )        Set to zero
    movie_related_event = 0;
else
    movie_related_event = MCIsPlayerEvent(The_Controller, &The_Event);

if ( movie_related_event == 0 )     Since there is no movie,
{                                   the event doesn't involve
    switch (The_Event.what)         a movie and is handled here
    {
        [ handle events not involving movies ]
    }
}
```

FIGURE 8.12
Handling an Event with No Open Controllers Present

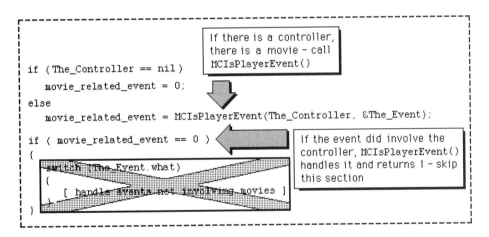

FIGURE 8.13

Handling a Non-movie Event with an Open Controller Present

```
if (The_Controller == nil)
   movie_related_event = 0;
else
   movie_related_event = MCIsPlayerEvent(The_Controller, &The_Event);

if ( movie_related_event == 0 )
{
   switch (The_Event.what)
   {
       [ handle events not involving movies ]
   }
}
```

> If there is a controller, there is a movie - call MCIsPlayerEvent()

> If the event did involve the controller, MCIsPlayerEvent() handles it and returns 1 - skip this section

FIGURE 8.14

Handling a Movie Event with an Open Controller Present

Changing Controller Features

In the previous section you saw how powerful the Movie Toolbox routine *MCIsPlayerEvent()* is—it does all the handling of events that take place in a movie controller. You can use another Movie Toolbox routine to change how *MCIsPlayerEvent()* handles a controller. That routine is *MCDoAction()*.

Movie Looping With MCDoAction()

MCDoAction() tells a specific controller to perform an action. *MCDoAction()* accepts three parameters. The first is the movie controller to be affected. The second parameter is the action to take. These are constants defined in the Movies.h header file. The last parameter is a pointer to additional information that pertains to the action. *MCDoAction()* returns a *ComponentResult*. This value is of most use when an error occurs (we'll usually be ignoring it).

Here's a call to *MCDoAction()* that tells a controller to repeatedly loop through a movie:

```
ComponentResult  comp_result;

comp_result = MCDoAction( The_Controller, mcActionSetLooping,
                          (Ptr)true );
```

The above call to *MCDoAction()* doesn't start a movie looping right away. Instead, it sets the controller of a movie to loop mode. The next time the user clicks the mouse on the **Play** button of the controller, the movie will loop until the user again clicks the mouse. Every time the user clicks the **Play** button, the movie will begin looping. To revert back to normal playing mode, again call *MCDoAction()*. This time set the third parameter to *false*.

```
comp_result = MCDoAction( The_Controller, mcActionSetLooping,
                          (Ptr)false );
```

Initiating movie looping is usually done by the user through a menu option. In this chapter's sample program we give an example of how you can let the user toggle looping on and off for a movie by checking or unchecking a menu item.

Enabling Keystrokes with MCDoAction()

When the user holds down the **Shift** key and moves the slider along the controller's slide bar, a part of the movie is selected. This is true only if the controller recognizes that the user is holding down the **Shift** key (that is, if keystrokes are enabled for that controller). When you create a controller, keystrokes are disabled. You'll most likely want to enable keystrokes for a movie's controller. *MCDoAction()* can do that. After creating the controller, use the *mcActionSetKeysEnabled* constant in a call to *MCDoAction()*:

```
comp_result = MCDoAction(The_Controller,
                      mcActionSetKeysEnabled,(Ptr)true );
```

You'll only have to make the above call once. As long as the controller exists, it will recognize when the user presses keys.

Movie Editing

Movie controllers and the Movie Toolbox make movie editing simple. After enabling movie editing for a movie, the user can use the standard Edit menu commands, or Command key equivalents, to cut, copy, and paste the frames of a movie.

Enabling Movie Editing

If you want to give users of your program the ability to edit movies, you'll have to enable movie editing. The *MCEnableEditing()* routine allows you to enable or disable editing for a movie. That gives you the ability to let the user edit some movies, or prevent them from tampering with a movie you don't want changed—perhaps a movie you'll play elsewhere in the program.

To enable editing, pass *MCEnableEditing()* the controller associated with the movie to edit. Then pass the routine a value of *true* to enable editing or *false* to disable editing. Here's a call to enable editing:

```
MovieController   The_Controller;
ComponentResult   comp_result;

comp_result = MCEnableEditing( The_Controller, true );
```

Using Movie Editing Routines

Once you have a movie opened, and a movie controller attached, editing the movie is simple—just one or two Movie Toolbox routines are all that are needed to perform an editing action.

All editing takes place on the selected portion of a movie. The user selects as few or as many movie frames as desired by holding the **Shift** key and moving the slider. If no selection is present, editing takes place at the current frame.

Implementing Cut

To copy the current selection of the movie associated with *The_Controller*, call *MCCut()*. Pass the controller as the parameter. The *MCCut()* routine will remove the selection and return it as a *Movie*.

```
MovieController   The_Controller;
Movie             temp_movie;

temp_movie = MCCut( The_Controller );
```

The Movie Toolbox does not automatically save the cut portion of the movie to the clipboard (also called the *scrap*). Use the Movie Toolbox routine *PutMovieOnScrap()* to do this. Pass this routine *temp_movie*—the cut portion of the movie that was returned by *MCCut()*. The second parameter to *PutMovieOnScrap()* is a constant that tells the routine whether to put just *temp_movie* on the scrap (*movieScrapOnlyPutMovie*), or to add *temp_movie* to whatever is currently on the scrap (*movieScrapDontZeroScrap*).

```
OSErr             error;

error = PutMovieOnScrap( temp_movie, movieScrapOnlyPutMovie );
```

With the cut and transfer to the scrap complete, call *DisposeMovie()* to dispose of the temporary movie. Here's the complete code to cut a section of a movie:

```
MovieController   The_Controller;
OSErr             error;
Movie             temp_movie;
```

```
temp_movie = MCCut( The_Controller );
error = PutMovieOnScrap( temp_movie, movieScrapOnlyPutMovie );
DisposeMovie( temp_movie )
```

Movies consist of graphics, and graphics can occupy a lot of memory. To free that memory, always use *DisposeMovie()* when you are through with a movie.

Implementing Copy

Copying a movie is done in the same manner as a cut. Use a call to *MCCopy()* to copy the selected portion of the movie. Then place it on the scrap, and dispose of it.

```
MovieController  The_Controller;
OSErr            error;
Movie            temp_movie;

temp_movie = MCCopy( The_Controller );
error = PutMovieOnScrap( temp_movie, movieScrapOnlyPutMovie );
DisposeMovie( temp_movie )
```

Implementing Paste

Pasting a copied portion of a movie requires just a single Movie Toolbox call. *MCPaste()* pastes the contents of the scrap into the movie specified by *The_Controller*. The second parameter specifies the movie to paste. You can pass a Movie variable, but you'll more likely pass a value of *nil*. That tells *MCPaste()* to retrieve the contents of the scrap and paste them into the current selection.

```
MovieController  The_Controller;
ComponentResult  comp_result;

comp_result = MCPaste( The_Controller, nil );
```

Implementing Clear

You can clear the current movie selection by calling *MCClear()*. *MCClear()* cuts out the selection, but doesn't return the cut portion to your program.

```
MovieController  The_Controller;
ComponentResult  comp_result;

comp_result = MCClear( The_Controller );
```

Implementing Undo

Everybody makes mistakes, and when users of your program do, they'll appreciate that they can undo their most recent edit operation by selecting an **Undo** command from the Edit menu. All you need to do is add a call to *MCUndo()*.

```
MovieController  The_Controller;
ComponentResult  comp_result;

comp_result = MCUndo( The_Controller );
```

The Application Editing Function

If your QuickTime program allows movie editing, you should implement the standard Edit menu, as shown in Figure 8.15.

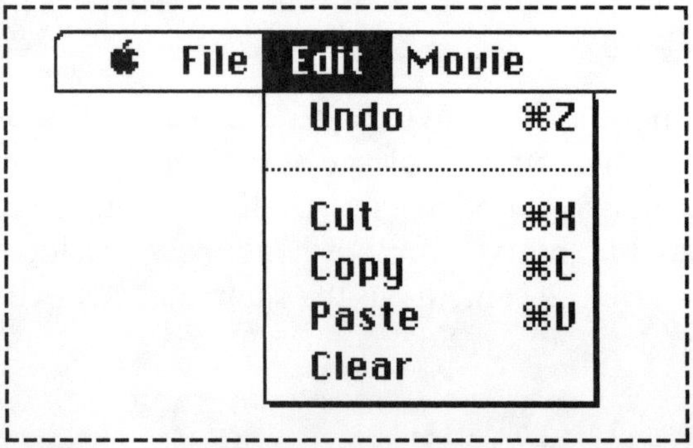

FIGURE 8.15
The Edit Menu Includes the Standard Editing Items

Your application should then have a function that handles each of these editing commands—whether made by a menu selection or a press of the Command key equivalent. Before looking at that function, let's see how your program would make its way to the edit-handling routine.

When your main event loop encounters a key press or a mouse click, it should branch off to a routine that appropriately handles each event. If the event was a mouse down event, and it occurred in the menu bar, the code should go to a menu-handling routine. If the event was a keystroke, and it is determined to be a Command key equivalent to a menu item, the code should again go to the menu-handling routine.

From the menu-handling routine the code should again branch to a routine written to handle selections made to a specific menu. A click in the Edit menu should result in a call to a *Handle_Edit_Menu()* routine (or one similarly named). Figure 8.16 shows the paths to the routine that handles an edit operation (your function names may, of course, differ from ours).

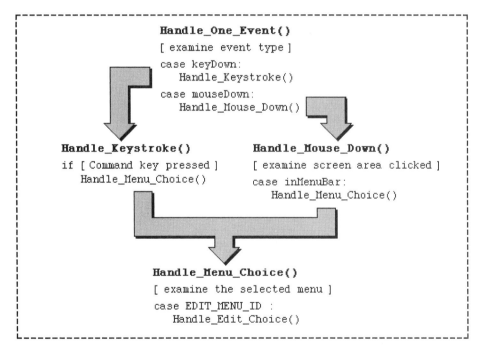

FIGURE 8.16
Program Code Branches to an Edit-Handling Routine

The sample program given at the end of this chapter uses the branching technique shown in Figure 8.16.

Now for a look at the edit-handling routine itself. You'll pass in the menu item selected, then call the appropriate Movie Toolbox routines to carry out the action.

```
void   Handle_Edit_Choice( short the_item )
{
    Movie              temp_movie;
    OSErr              error;
    ComponentResult    comp_result;

    switch ( the_item )
    {
        case UNDO_ITEM:
            comp_result = MCUndo( The_Controller );
            break;

        case CUT_ITEM:
            temp_movie = MCCut( The_Controller );
            error = PutMovieOnScrap( temp_movie,
                                        movieScrapOnlyPutMovie );
            DisposeMovie( temp_movie )
            break;

        case COPY_ITEM:
            temp_movie = MCCopy( The_Controller );
            error = PutMovieOnScrap( temp_movie,
                                        movieScrapOnlyPutMovie );
            DisposeMovie( temp_movie )
            break;

        case PASTE_ITEM:
            comp_result = MCPaste( The_Controller, nil );
            break;

        case CLEAR_ITEM:
            comp_result = MCClear( The_Controller );
            break;
    }
}
```

Saving a Movie

If your program allows movie editing, it should also allow the user to save the changes made to a movie. You'll typically have a **Save** item in the File menu to do that.

In this chapter's *Displaying the Standard Get File Dialog Box* section we mentioned that two variables used in opening and creating a movie were made global in this chapter's code. Here we'll see why.

You initially open a movie file with a call to *OpenMovieFile()*. One of the parameters to this routine—we called it *Movie_Res_File*—is a pointer to a variable of type *short*. *OpenMovieFile()* fills this parameter with a reference number to the resource file that contains the information used to create the movie. You'll be using this variable in a moment.

The Movie Toolbox routine you call after *OpenMovieFile()* is *NewMovieFromFile()*. This routine creates and loads a movie. It too returns a value to your program—*Movie_Res_ID*. You initially set the variable to the movie you want to use from within the movie file. *NewMovieFromFile()* will alter the value of this variable by changing it to the resource ID of the 'MooV' resource it uses to create the movie. You use both the reference number of the movie file and the movie resource ID to save a changed movie. Here's the call to the Movie Toolbox routine that saves a movie—*UpdateMovieResource()*:

```
OSErr error;

error = UpdateMovieResource( The_Movie, Movie_Res_File,
                    Movie_Res_ID, nil );
```

The first parameter to *UpdateMovieResource()* is the movie to be saved. The second and third parameters are those discussed above—the movie reference number and the movie resource ID. These were both obtained in a different routine, thus the necessity of making them global variables. The final parameter is a pointer to a new name for the resource. Note that this is the name of the 'MooV' resource itself, not the movie file as viewed in the Finder. If you don't want to change the name, set this parameter to *nil*.

Example Program: MovieViewer

This chapter's sample program is for the MovieViewer program included on the disk. You can study the source code and leave it as is, or you can add features to it to expand the capabilities of this QuickTime utility.

Figure 8.17 shows the menu items in the File, Edit, and Movie menus of MovieViewer.

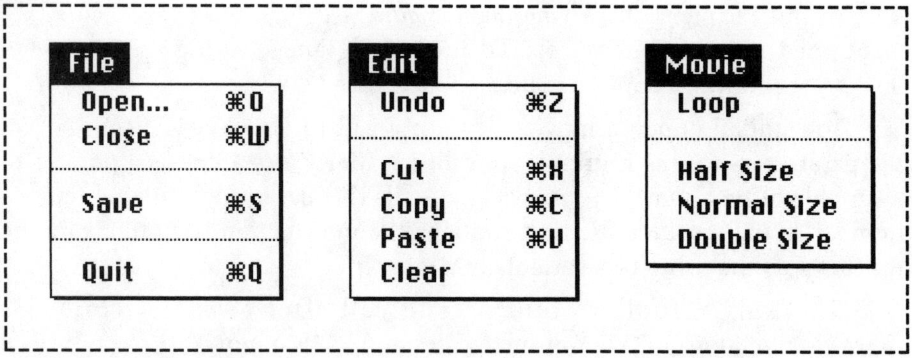

File		Edit		Movie
Open...	⌘O	Undo	⌘Z	Loop
Close	⌘W			
		Cut	⌘X	Half Size
Save	⌘S	Copy	⌘C	Normal Size
		Paste	⌘V	Double Size
Quit	⌘Q	Clear		

FIGURE 8.17
The Menus of MovieViewer

MovieViewer allows the user to open one movie. Editing for the movie is enabled, which means the user can change the movie by using the Edit menu commands. The user then has the option to save the changes. The Movie menu allows the user to run the movie in loop mode—when the movie controller Play button is clicked, the movie will loop repeatedly until the mouse is clicked. This menu also allows the user to resize the window to half or double its normal size.

Program Resources: MovieViewer.π.rsrc

MovieViewer has just four types of resources. There is one 'ALRT' and its accompanying 'DITL'. These two resources are used to display an alert when the user selects the About MovieViewer item from the Apple menu.

There are four 'MENU' resources, one per menu in the menu bar. They are for the Apple, File, Edit, and Movie menus. These four resources, with IDs of 128, 129, 130, and 131, respectively, are tied together by the one 'MBAR' resource.

Program Listing: MovieViewer.c

As in the last chapter, we'll first present the entire source code for the sample program, followed by details of what we're doing.

```
/*++++++++++++++++++++++++++++++++++++++++++++++++++++++++++++++++++*/

#include <GestaltEqu.h>
#include <Movies.h>

/*++++++++++++++++++++++++++++++++++++++++++++++++++++++++++++++++++*/

void   Initialize_Toolbox( void );
void   Initialize_Movies( void );
void   Set_Up_Menu_Bar( void );
void   Adjust_Menus_For_No_Window( void );
void   Adjust_Menus_For_Open_Window( void );
void   Handle_One_Event( void );
void   Handle_Keystroke( void );
void   Handle_Mouse_Down( void );
void   Handle_Menu_Choice( long );
void   Handle_Apple_Choice( short );
void   Handle_File_Choice( short );
void   Open_A_Movie( void );
Movie Get_A_Movie( void );
void   Open_And_Size_Window( void );
void   Close_A_Movie( void );
void   Handle_Edit_Choice( short );
void   Handle_Movie_Choice( short );
void   Handle_Loop_Item( void );

/*++++++++++++++++++++++++++++++++++++++++++++++++++++++++++++++++++*/

#define          ABOUT_ALRT_ID              128
#define          MENU_BAR_ID                128
#define          APPLE_MENU_ID              128
#define            ABOUT_ITEM                 1
#define          FILE_MENU_ID               129
#define            OPEN_ITEM                  1
#define            CLOSE_ITEM                 2
#define            SAVE_ITEM                  4
#define            QUIT_ITEM                  6
#define          EDIT_MENU_ID               130
#define            UNDO_ITEM                  1
#define            CUT_ITEM                   3
#define            COPY_ITEM                  4
#define            PASTE_ITEM                 5
#define            CLEAR_ITEM                 6
#define          MOVIE_MENU_ID              131
#define            LOOP_ITEM                  1
#define            HALF_SIZE_ITEM             3
#define            NORMAL_SIZE_ITEM           4
#define            DOUBLE_SIZE_ITEM           5

#define          IN_FRONT          (WindowPtr)-1L
```

```c
/*++++++++++++++++++++++++++++++++++++++++++++++++++++++++++++++++*/

EventRecord      The_Event;
Boolean          All_Done = false;
MenuHandle       Apple_Menu;
MenuHandle       File_Menu;
MenuHandle       Edit_Menu;
MenuHandle       Movie_Menu;
WindowPtr        The_Window = nil;
Movie            The_Movie = nil;
MovieController  The_Controller = nil;
Rect             Original_Rect;
short            Movie_Res_File;
short            Movie_Res_ID = 0;

/*++++++++++++++++++++++++++++++++++++++++++++++++++++++++++++++++*/

void  main( void )
{
   Initialize_Toolbox();

   Initialize_Movies();

   Set_Up_Menu_Bar();

   while ( All_Done == false )
      Handle_One_Event();
}

/*++++++++++++++++++++++++++++++++++++++++++++++++++++++++++++++++*/

void  Initialize_Toolbox( void )
{
   InitGraf( &thePort );
   InitFonts();
   InitWindows();
   InitMenus();
   TEInit();
   InitDialogs( nil );
   InitCursor();
}

/*++++++++++++++++++++++++++++++++++++++++++++++++++++++++++++++++*/

void  Initialize_Movies( void )
{
   OSErr  error;
   long   result;

   error = Gestalt( gestaltQuickTime, &result );
   if ( error != noErr )
```

```
            ExitToShell();

      error = EnterMovies();
      if ( error != noErr )
         ExitToShell();
}
/*+++++++++++++++++++++++++++++++++++++++++++++++++++++++++++++++++++++*/

void  Set_Up_Menu_Bar( void )
{
   Handle   menu_bar_handle;

   menu_bar_handle = GetNewMBar( MENU_BAR_ID );

   SetMenuBar( menu_bar_handle );
   DisposHandle( menu_bar_handle );

   Apple_Menu  = GetMHandle( APPLE_MENU_ID );
   File_Menu   = GetMHandle( FILE_MENU_ID  );
   Edit_Menu   = GetMHandle( EDIT_MENU_ID  );
   Movie_Menu  = GetMHandle( MOVIE_MENU_ID );

   Adjust_Menus_For_No_Window();

   AddResMenu( Apple_Menu, 'DRVR' );

   DrawMenuBar();
}

/*+++++++++++++++++++++++++++++++++++++++++++++++++++++++++++++++++++++*/

void  Adjust_Menus_For_No_Window( void )
{
   EnableItem( File_Menu, OPEN_ITEM );
   DisableItem( File_Menu, CLOSE_ITEM );
   DisableItem( File_Menu, SAVE_ITEM );
   DisableItem( Edit_Menu, 0 );
   DisableItem( Movie_Menu, 0 );
}

/*+++++++++++++++++++++++++++++++++++++++++++++++++++++++++++++++++++++*/

void  Adjust_Menus_For_Open_Window( void )
{
   DisableItem( File_Menu, OPEN_ITEM );
   EnableItem( File_Menu, CLOSE_ITEM );
   EnableItem( Edit_Menu, 0 );
   EnableItem( Movie_Menu, 0 );
}
```

```
/*++++++++++++++++++++++++++++++++++++++++++++++++++++++++++++++++++++*/

void  Handle_One_Event( void )
{
   WindowPtr   which_window;
   long        movie_related_event;

   WaitNextEvent(everyEvent, &The_Event, 0, nil);

   if ( The_Controller == nil )
      movie_related_event = 0;
   else
      movie_related_event = MCIsPlayerEvent(The_Controller,
                                            &The_Event);

   if ( movie_related_event == 0 )
   {
      switch (The_Event.what)
      {
         case keyDown:
            Handle_Keystroke();
            break;

         case updateEvt:
            which_window = (WindowPtr)The_Event.message;
            SetPort( which_window );
            BeginUpdate(which_window);
               EraseRgn( which_window->visRgn );
            EndUpdate(which_window);
            break;

         case mouseDown:
            Handle_Mouse_Down();
            break;
      }
   }
}

/*++++++++++++++++++++++++++++++++++++++++++++++++++++++++++++++++++++*/

void  Handle_Keystroke( void )
{
   short  chr;
   long   menu_choice;

   chr = The_Event.message & charCodeMask;

   if ( ( The_Event.modifiers & cmdKey ) != 0 )
   {
      if ( The_Event.what != autoKey )
      {
```

```
                menu_choice = MenuKey( chr );
                Handle_Menu_Choice( menu_choice );
            }
        }
    }

    /*+++++++++++++++++++++++++++++++++++++++++++++++++++++++++++++++++*/

    void  Handle_Mouse_Down( void )
    {
        WindowPtr  which_window;
        short      the_part;
        long       menu_choice;

        the_part = FindWindow( The_Event.where, &which_window );

        switch ( the_part )
        {
            case inMenuBar:
                menu_choice = MenuSelect( The_Event.where );
                Handle_Menu_Choice( menu_choice );
                break;

            case inSysWindow:
                SystemClick( &The_Event, which_window);
                break;

            case inDrag:
                DragWindow( which_window, The_Event.where,
                            &screenBits.bounds );
                break;

            case inGoAway:
                if ( TrackGoAway( which_window, The_Event.where ) )
                    Close_A_Movie();
                break;

            case inContent:
                SelectWindow( which_window );
                break;
        }
    }

    /*+++++++++++++++++++++++++++++++++++++++++++++++++++++++++++++++++*/

    void  Handle_Menu_Choice( long menu_choice )
    {
        int  the_menu;
        int  the_menu_item;

        if ( menu_choice != 0 )
```

```
    {
        the_menu = HiWord( menu_choice );
        the_menu_item = LoWord( menu_choice );

        switch ( the_menu )
        {
            case APPLE_MENU_ID:
                Handle_Apple_Choice( the_menu_item );
                break;

            case FILE_MENU_ID:
                Handle_File_Choice( the_menu_item );
                break;

            case EDIT_MENU_ID:
                Handle_Edit_Choice( the_menu_item );
                break;

            case MOVIE_MENU_ID:
                Handle_Movie_Choice( the_menu_item );
                break;
        }
        HiliteMenu( 0 );
    }
}

/*++++++++++++++++++++++++++++++++++++++++++++++++++++++++++++++++*/

void  Handle_Apple_Choice( short the_item )
{
    Str255  desk_acc_name;
    int     desk_acc_number;

    switch ( the_item )
    {
        case ABOUT_ITEM:
            Alert( ABOUT_ALRT_ID, nil );
            break;

        default:
            GetItem( Apple_Menu, the_item, desk_acc_name );
            desk_acc_number = OpenDeskAcc( desk_acc_name );
            break;
    }
}

/*++++++++++++++++++++++++++++++++++++++++++++++++++++++++++++++++*/

void  Handle_File_Choice( short the_item )
{
    OSErr  error;
```

```
   switch ( the_item )
   {
      case OPEN_ITEM:
         Open_A_Movie();
         break;

      case CLOSE_ITEM:
         Close_A_Movie();
         break;

      case SAVE_ITEM:
         error = UpdateMovieResource( The_Movie, Movie_Res_File,
                                      Movie_Res_ID, nil );
         DisableItem( File_Menu, SAVE_ITEM );
         break;

      case QUIT_ITEM:
         All_Done = TRUE;
         break;
   }
}

/*++++++++++++++++++++++++++++++++++++++++++++++++++++++++++++++++*/

void  Open_A_Movie( void )
{
   ComponentResult  comp_result;

   The_Movie = Get_A_Movie();

   if (The_Movie != nil)
   {
      Open_And_Size_Window();

      comp_result = MCDoAction(The_Controller,
                               mcActionSetKeysEnabled,
                               (Ptr)true);

      comp_result = MCEnableEditing( The_Controller, true );

      Adjust_Menus_For_Open_Window();
   }
}

/*++++++++++++++++++++++++++++++++++++++++++++++++++++++++++++++++*/

Movie Get_A_Movie( void )
{
   OSErr              error;
   Movie              get_movie = nil;
```

256 QuickTime: Macintosh Multimedia

\-

```
    SFTypeList          type_list = { MovieFileType, 0, 0, 0 };
    StandardFileReply   the_reply;
    Str255              movie_name;
    Boolean             was_changed;

    Movie_Res_ID = 0;

    StandardGetFilePreview( nil, 1, type_list, &the_reply );

    if ( the_reply.sfGood == true )
    {
        error = OpenMovieFile( &the_reply.sfFile, &Movie_Res_File,
                               fsRdWrPerm );
        if ( error == noErr )
            error = NewMovieFromFile( &get_movie, Movie_Res_File,
                                      &Movie_Res_ID,
                                      movie_name, newMovieActive,
                                      &was_changed );
    }
    return ( get_movie );
}

/*++++++++++++++++++++++++++++++++++++++++++++++++++++++++++++++++++++*/

void  Open_And_Size_Window( void )
{
    ComponentResult  comp_result;
    Rect             movie_box;
    Rect             the_rect;

    SetRect(&the_rect, 100, 100, 150, 150);
    The_Window = NewCWindow( nil, &the_rect, "\pMovie", false,
                             noGrowDocProc, IN_FRONT, true, 0 );

    SetMovieGWorld( The_Movie, ( CGrafPtr )The_Window, nil );

    GetMovieBox( The_Movie, &movie_box );

    The_Controller = NewMovieController(The_Movie, &movie_box,
                                        mcTopLeftMovie);
    if (The_Controller == nil)
        ExitToShell();

    comp_result = MCGetControllerBoundsRect(The_Controller,
                                            &the_rect);

    SizeWindow( The_Window, the_rect.right, the_rect.bottom,
                true );
    ShowWindow(The_Window);

    Original_Rect = the_rect;
```

```
}

/*++++++++++++++++++++++++++++++++++++++++++++++++++++++++++++++++++++*/

void  Close_A_Movie( void )
{
   CloseMovieFile( Movie_Res_File );
   The_Controller = nil;
   DisposeMovieController( The_Controller );
   DisposeMovie( The_Movie );
   DisposeWindow( The_Window );

   Adjust_Menus_For_No_Window();
}

/*++++++++++++++++++++++++++++++++++++++++++++++++++++++++++++++++++++*/

void  Handle_Edit_Choice( short the_item )
{
   Movie            temp_movie;
   OSErr            error;
   ComponentResult  comp_result;

   switch ( the_item )
   {
      case UNDO_ITEM:
         comp_result = MCUndo( The_Controller );
         break;

      case CUT_ITEM:
         temp_movie = MCCut( The_Controller );
         error = PutMovieOnScrap( temp_movie,
                                  movieScrapOnlyPutMovie );
         DisposeMovie( temp_movie );
         break;

      case COPY_ITEM:
         temp_movie = MCCopy( The_Controller );
         error = PutMovieOnScrap( temp_movie,
                                  movieScrapOnlyPutMovie );
         DisposeMovie( temp_movie );
         break;

      case PASTE_ITEM:
         comp_result = MCPaste( The_Controller, nil );
         break;

      case CLEAR_ITEM:
         comp_result = MCClear( The_Controller );
         break;
   }
```

```
    if ( HasMovieChanged( The_Movie ) == true )
        EnableItem( File_Menu, SAVE_ITEM );
}

/*++++++++++++++++++++++++++++++++++++++++++++++++++++++++++++++++++*/

void  Handle_Movie_Choice( short the_item )
{
    ComponentResult   comp_result;
    Rect              the_rect;
    short             width;
    short             height;

    switch ( the_item )
    {
        case LOOP_ITEM:
            Handle_Loop_Item();
            break;

        case HALF_SIZE_ITEM:
            the_rect.left = Original_Rect.left;
            the_rect.top  = Original_Rect.top;
            width = Original_Rect.right - Original_Rect.left;
            the_rect.right = the_rect.left + ( width/2 );
            height = Original_Rect.bottom - Original_Rect.top;
            the_rect.bottom = the_rect.top + ( height/2 );
            comp_result = MCSetControllerBoundsRect( The_Controller,
                                                    &the_rect );
            SizeWindow( The_Window, the_rect.right, the_rect.bottom,
                      true );
            break;

        case NORMAL_SIZE_ITEM:
            comp_result = MCSetControllerBoundsRect( The_Controller,
                                                    &Original_Rect);
            SizeWindow( The_Window, Original_Rect.right,
                      Original_Rect.bottom,
                      true );
            break;

        case DOUBLE_SIZE_ITEM:
            the_rect.left = Original_Rect.left;
            the_rect.top  = Original_Rect.top;
            width = Original_Rect.right - Original_Rect.left;
            the_rect.right = the_rect.left + ( 2 * width );
            height = Original_Rect.bottom - Original_Rect.top;
            the_rect.bottom = the_rect.top + ( 2 * height );
            comp_result = MCSetControllerBoundsRect( The_Controller,
                                                    &the_rect );
```

```
            SizeWindow( The_Window, the_rect.right, the_rect.bottom,
                        true );
            break;
    }
}

/*++++++++++++++++++++++++++++++++++++++++++++++++++++++++++++++*/

void  Handle_Loop_Item( void )
{
    ComponentResult   comp_result;
    Boolean           looping_on;

    comp_result = MCDoAction( The_Controller, mcActionGetLooping,
                              &looping_on );

    if ( looping_on == true )
    {
        CheckItem( Movie_Menu, LOOP_ITEM, false );
        comp_result = MCDoAction( The_Controller,
                                  mcActionSetLooping,
                                  (Ptr)false );
    }
    else
    {
        CheckItem( Movie_Menu, LOOP_ITEM, true );
        comp_result = MCDoAction( The_Controller,
                                  mcActionSetLooping,
                                  (Ptr)true );
    }
}
```

Stepping Through the Code

Some of the MovieViewer source code is code common to all Mac programs,
such as event and menu handling. Other code was covered thoroughly in
this chapter. Our emphasis here will be on the code you're seeing for the first
time.

The Preliminary Stuff

MovieViewer uses the same two header files as last chapter's program:
GestaltEqu.h and Movies.h.

Each function has a prototype up front to help catch bugs when we
compile the source code.

All but one of the #*define* directives pertains to resources. Each 'MENU' resource ID is given a #*define*, along with the item number of each item in the menu.

All of the global variables, with the exception of the *Rect* variable *Original_Rect*, have been discussed in this chapter. *Original_Rect* holds the normal size of the open movie window. It will be used as a reference when resizing the window.

The main() Function

After initializing the Toolbox and the Movie Toolbox, the *main()* function calls *Set_Up_Menu_Bar()* to load all the menus and place them in the menu bar. Then, it's on to the *while* loop that will call *Handle_One_Event()* repeatedly until the program ends.

```
void  main( void )
{
    Initialize_Toolbox();

    Initialize_Movies();

    Set_Up_Menu_Bar();

    while ( All_Done == false )
        Handle_One_Event();
}
```

Setting Up the Menus

The *Set_Up_Menu_Bar()* function loads the menus and displays them. It also gets a handle to each menu and saves them in global variables. Any time the program wants to make a change to a menu item, we'll use the appropriate *MenuHandle* variable.

```
void  Set_Up_Menu_Bar( void )
{
    Handle  menu_bar_handle;

    menu_bar_handle = GetNewMBar( MENU_BAR_ID );

    SetMenuBar( menu_bar_handle );
    DisposHandle( menu_bar_handle );

    Apple_Menu  = GetMHandle( APPLE_MENU_ID );
```

```
   File_Menu   = GetMHandle( FILE_MENU_ID  );
   Edit_Menu   = GetMHandle( EDIT_MENU_ID  );
   Movie_Menu  = GetMHandle( MOVIE_MENU_ID );

   Adjust_Menus_For_No_Window();

   AddResMenu( Apple_Menu, 'DRVR' );

   DrawMenuBar();
}
```

Adjusting the Menus

When MovieViewer has no open movie, we'll want to dim, or disable, most of the menu options. If there is no movie, there is no movie to close or save, so we disable these two menu items from the File menu. There is nothing to edit, and no movie to loop through or resize, so we disable the entire Edit and Movie menus. Setting the second parameter to *DisableItem()* to 0 tells the Toolbox to disable the entire menu named in the first parameter to *DisableItem()*.

```
void  Adjust_Menus_For_No_Window( void )
{
   EnableItem( File_Menu, OPEN_ITEM );
   DisableItem( File_Menu, CLOSE_ITEM );
   DisableItem( File_Menu, SAVE_ITEM );
   DisableItem( Edit_Menu, 0 );
   DisableItem( Movie_Menu, 0 );
}
```

Once a movie is opened, we'll want to enable most of the menu items. A few calls to *EnableItem()* does this. Since MovieViewer allows just one movie to be open, we'll disable the Open menu item.

```
void  Adjust_Menus_For_Open_Window( void )
{
   DisableItem( File_Menu, OPEN_ITEM );
   EnableItem( File_Menu, CLOSE_ITEM );
   EnableItem( Edit_Menu, 0 );
   EnableItem( Movie_Menu, 0 );
}
```

The Main Event Loop

This chapter's *Movies and the Event Loop* section discussed how to use a call to *MCIsPlayerEvent()* to allow the Movie Toolbox to handle a movie-related event. MovieViewer does just that. If the event isn't movie-related, the event is further examined and handled in a switch section—just as it would be in a Macintosh program that didn't use QuickTime.

```
void  Handle_One_Event( void )
{
   WindowPtr  which_window;
   long       movie_related_event;

   WaitNextEvent(everyEvent, &The_Event, 0, nil);

   if ( The_Controller == nil )
      movie_related_event = 0;
   else
      movie_related_event = MCIsPlayerEvent(The_Controller,
                               &The_Event);

   if ( movie_related_event == 0 )
   {
      switch (The_Event.what)
      {
         case keyDown:
            Handle_Keystroke();
            break;

         case updateEvt:
            which_window = (WindowPtr)The_Event.message;
            SetPort( which_window );
            BeginUpdate(which_window);
               EraseRgn( which_window->visRgn );
            EndUpdate(which_window);
            break;

         case mouseDown:
            Handle_Mouse_Down();
            break;
      }
   }
}
```

Handling a Keystroke

MovieViewer has several menu options that have Command key equivalents. So every keystroke is checked to see if the Command key is pressed.

The *message* field of the event record holds the pressed key, along with other information. We mask out the extraneous information using the constant *charCodeMask*—leaving the typed character.

We're only interested in a keystroke that is paired with a press of the Command key. The *modifiers* field of the event record holds this information. Using the *&* operator on the *modifiers* field and the constant *cmdKey* will result in a nonzero value—if the Command key was pressed.

The final check is to verify that the key was not pressed and held down. An autoKey does not qualify as a Command key equivalent and is ignored.

If all three tests pass, the event is treated like a menu selection.

```
void  Handle_Keystroke( void )
{
   short   chr;
   long    menu_choice;

   chr = The_Event.message & charCodeMask;

   if ( ( The_Event.modifiers & cmdKey ) != 0 )
   {
      if ( The_Event.what != autoKey )
      {
         menu_choice = MenuKey( chr );
         Handle_Menu_Choice( menu_choice );
      }
   }
}
```

Handling a Mouse Down Event

If *Handle_Mouse_Down()* is called, the event was not handled by the Movie Toolbox routine *MCIsPlayerEvent()* in the main event loop. *Handle_Mouse_Down()* contains no code specific to QuickTime—it's a run-of-the-mill mouse-handling routine.

A click in the menu bar results in a call to *Handle_Menu_Choice()*. A click in a desk accessory, or system window, is handled by a call to the Toolbox routine *SystemClick()*. If the window is being dragged, the Toolbox routine *DragWindow()* handles everything. A click in the go-away box of the window that is displaying the movie results in a call to our own *Close_A_Window()* routine (we'll discuss that a little later). If the user clicks in the content area of the movie window, we simply call *SelectWindow()* to bring that window to the front (if it's not there already).

```
void  Handle_Mouse_Down( void )
```

```
{
    WindowPtr   which_window;
    short       the_part;
    long        menu_choice;

    the_part = FindWindow( The_Event.where, &which_window );

    switch ( the_part )
    {
        case inMenuBar:
            menu_choice = MenuSelect( The_Event.where );
            Handle_Menu_Choice( menu_choice );
            break;

        case inSysWindow:
            SystemClick( &The_Event, which_window);
            break;

        case inDrag:
            DragWindow( which_window, The_Event.where,
            &screenBits.bounds );
            break;

        case inGoAway:
            if ( TrackGoAway( which_window, The_Event.where ) )
                Close_A_Movie();
            break;

        case inContent:
            SelectWindow( which_window );
            break;
    }
}
```

Handling a Menu Choice

A menu selection brings us to *Handle_Menu_Choice()*. The passed-in value *menu_choice* has two values embedded in it: the menu and the menu item. Calls to the Toolbox routines *HiWord()* and *LoWord()* extract these values. Then *Handle_Menu_Choice()* branches off to the routine written to expressly handle selections in each menu.

```
void  Handle_Menu_Choice( long menu_choice )
{
    int   the_menu;
    int   the_menu_item;

    if ( menu_choice != 0 )
```

```
{
    the_menu = HiWord( menu_choice );
    the_menu_item = LoWord( menu_choice );

    switch ( the_menu )
    {
        case APPLE_MENU_ID:
            Handle_Apple_Choice( the_menu_item );
            break;

        case FILE_MENU_ID:
            Handle_File_Choice( the_menu_item );
            break;

        case EDIT_MENU_ID:
            Handle_Edit_Choice( the_menu_item );
            break;

        case MOVIE_MENU_ID:
            Handle_Movie_Choice( the_menu_item );
            break;
    }
    HiliteMenu( 0 );
    }
}
```

Handling the Apple Menu

Almost all Mac programs handle a selection in the Apple menu the same
way. The first item, About, simply displays an alert with some information
about the program. Any other item is a desk accessory, or, under System 7,
anything placed in the Apple Menu Items folder in the System folder. Call
GetItem() to get the name of the menu item, then call *OpenDeskAcc()* to
open that item.

```
void  Handle_Apple_Choice( short the_item )
{
    Str255  desk_acc_name;
    int     desk_acc_number;

    switch ( the_item )
    {
        case ABOUT_ITEM:
            Alert( ABOUT_ALRT_ID, nil );
            break;

        default:
            GetItem( Apple_Menu, the_item, desk_acc_name );
```

```
        desk_acc_number = OpenDeskAcc( desk_acc_name );
        break;
    }
}
```

Handling the File Menu

The File menu has three menu commands that concern movies: Open, Close, and Save. The last command, Quit, sets the global variable *All_Done* to *true*, ending the program at the next pass through the main event loop.

```
void  Handle_File_Choice( short the_item )
{
    OSErr  error;

    switch ( the_item )
    {
        case OPEN_ITEM:
            Open_A_Movie();
            break;

        case CLOSE_ITEM:
            Close_A_Movie();
            break;

        case SAVE_ITEM:
            error = UpdateMovieResource( The_Movie, Movie_Res_File,
                                         Movie_Res_ID, nil );
            DisableItem( File_Menu, SAVE_ITEM );
            break;

        case QUIT_ITEM:
            All_Done = TRUE;
            break;
    }
}
```

Opening a Movie

A movie is opened with a call to *Open_A_Movie()*. The movie itself is created by a call to *Get_A_Movie()*. If the user doesn't click the Cancel button in the standard Get File dialog box that opens, *Open_And_Size_Window()* will be called to open a window and attach a controller to it. With the display window open, the controller is set to recognize keystrokes and to accept editing commands. Finally, the menus are adjusted to reflect the fact that a movie window is open.

```
void  Open_A_Movie( void )
{
   ComponentResult  comp_result;

   The_Movie = Get_A_Movie();

   if (The_Movie != nil)
   {
      Open_And_Size_Window();

      comp_result = MCDoAction(The_Controller,
                               mcActionSetKeysEnabled,
                               (Ptr)true);

      comp_result = MCEnableEditing( The_Controller, true );

      Adjust_Menus_For_Open_Window();
   }
}
```

The *Get_A_Movie()* routine was covered in depth in this chapter's *Displaying the Standard Get File Dialog* Box section. It appears in MovieViewer exactly as it does in that section.

```
Movie Get_A_Movie( void )
{
   OSErr               error;
   Movie               get_movie = nil;
   SFTypeList          type_list = { MovieFileType, 0, 0, 0 };
   StandardFileReply   the_reply;
   Str255              movie_name;
   Boolean             was_changed;

   Movie_Res_ID = 0;

   StandardGetFilePreview( nil, 1, type_list, &the_reply );

   if ( the_reply.sfGood == true )
   {
      error = OpenMovieFile( &the_reply.sfFile, &Movie_Res_File,
                             fsRdWrPerm );
      if ( error == noErr )
         error = NewMovieFromFile( &get_movie, Movie_Res_File,
                                   &Movie_Res_ID,
                                   movie_name, newMovieActive,
                                   &was_changed );
   }
   return ( get_movie );
}
```

Except for one line, the *Open_And_Size_Window()* routine is identical to the one developed in this chapter's *Attaching a Controller to a Movie* section. While we have the size of the newly opened window, we save its rectangle to the global *Rect* variable *Original_Rect*. We'll use it later when we resize the window.

```
void  Open_And_Size_Window( void )
{
    ComponentResult   comp_result;
    Rect              movie_box;
    Rect              the_rect;

    SetRect(&the_rect, 100, 100, 150, 150);
    The_Window = NewCWindow( nil, &the_rect, "\pMovie", false,
                             noGrowDocProc, IN_FRONT, true, 0 );

    SetMovieGWorld( The_Movie, ( CGrafPtr )The_Window, nil );

    GetMovieBox( The_Movie, &movie_box );

    The_Controller = NewMovieController(The_Movie, &movie_box,
                                        mcTopLeftMovie);
    if (The_Controller == nil)
        ExitToShell();

    comp_result = MCGetControllerBoundsRect(The_Controller,
                                            &the_rect);

    SizeWindow( The_Window, the_rect.right, the_rect.bottom,
                true );
    ShowWindow(The_Window);

    Original_Rect = the_rect;
}
```

Closing a Movie

The Close item in the File menu results in a call to *Close_A_Movie()*. First, the movie file is closed. We kept it open in case the user wanted to save the movie back to its file after editing. Next, we set the movie controller to *nil*. The main event loop will be testing *The_Controller* for a value of *nil* to determine how it should handle an event. To free memory, we dispose of the movie, and the window and controller associated with it. Finally, we adjust the menus to disable menu commands that aren't appropriate for the empty screen.

```
void  Close_A_Movie( void )
{
```

```
CloseMovieFile( Movie_Res_File );
The_Controller = nil;
DisposeMovieController( The_Controller );
DisposeMovie( The_Movie );
DisposeWindow( The_Window );

Adjust_Menus_For_No_Window();
}
```

Handling the Edit Menu

In the *Application Editing Function* section of this chapter we developed a routine to handle each of the standard editing commands. That same function, with two additional lines, is used by MovieViewer.

Handle_Edit_Choice() closes with a call to the Movie Toolbox routine *HasMovieChanges()*. Given a movie, this routine will return a *Boolean* value that tells your program whether the movie has been changed since it was last examined. If it returns *true*, we enable the **Save** command in the File menu—it is now appropriate to allow the user to save the movie. All editing actions performed on a movie, except for copy, will result in this function returning *true*.

```
void  Handle_Edit_Choice( short the_item )
{
   Movie             temp_movie;
   OSErr             error;
   ComponentResult   comp_result;

   switch ( the_item )
   {
      case UNDO_ITEM:
         comp_result = MCUndo( The_Controller );
         break;

      case CUT_ITEM:
         temp_movie = MCCut( The_Controller );
         error = PutMovieOnScrap( temp_movie,
                                  movieScrapOnlyPutMovie );
         DisposeMovie( temp_movie );
         break;

      case COPY_ITEM:
         temp_movie = MCCopy( The_Controller );
         error = PutMovieOnScrap( temp_movie,
                                  movieScrapOnlyPutMovie );
         DisposeMovie( temp_movie );
```

```
        break;

    case PASTE_ITEM:
        comp_result = MCPaste( The_Controller, nil );
        break;

    case CLEAR_ITEM:
        comp_result = MCClear( The_Controller );
        break;
    }

    if ( HasMovieChanged( The_Movie ) == true )
        EnableItem( File_Menu, SAVE_ITEM );
}
```

Handling the Movie Menu

A menu selection from the Movie menu brings the program to *Handle_Movie_Choice()*. If the first item, **Loop**, was selected, we branch off to *Handle_Loop_Item()* (discussed next). Any other menu choice is carried out in *Handle_Movie_Choice()*.

Resizing the movie window boils down to resetting the right and bottom coordinates of the movie window's boundary rectangle. A call to *MCSetControllerBoundsRect()* resizes the controller to this new rectangle. Then the window is resized using a call to *SizeWindow()*.

We use *Original_Rect* as the reference for what is the "normal" size of the window—the size it opened up to. When resizing the window, we don't ever change the coordinates of *Original_Rect*.

```
void  Handle_Movie_Choice( short the_item )
{
    ComponentResult   comp_result;
    Rect              the_rect;
    short             width;
    short             height;

    switch ( the_item )
    {
        case LOOP_ITEM:
            Handle_Loop_Item();
            break;

        case HALF_SIZE_ITEM:
            the_rect.left = Original_Rect.left;
            the_rect.top  = Original_Rect.top;
            width = Original_Rect.right - Original_Rect.left;
```

```
        the_rect.right = the_rect.left + ( width/2 );
        height = Original_Rect.bottom - Original_Rect.top;
        the_rect.bottom = the_rect.top + ( height/2 );
        comp_result = MCSetControllerBoundsRect( The_Controller,
                                                 &the_rect );
        SizeWindow( The_Window, the_rect.right, the_rect.bottom,
                    true );
        break;

    case NORMAL_SIZE_ITEM:
        comp_result = MCSetControllerBoundsRect( The_Controller,
                                                 &Original_Rect
        );
        SizeWindow( The_Window, Original_Rect.right,
                    Original_Rect.bottom,
                    true );
        break;

    case DOUBLE_SIZE_ITEM:
        the_rect.left = Original_Rect.left;
        the_rect.top  = Original_Rect.top;
        width = Original_Rect.right - Original_Rect.left;
        the_rect.right = the_rect.left + ( 2 * width );
        height = Original_Rect.bottom - Original_Rect.top;
        the_rect.bottom = the_rect.top + ( 2 * height );
        comp_result = MCSetControllerBoundsRect( The_Controller,
                                                 &the_rect );
        SizeWindow( The_Window, the_rect.right, the_rect.bottom,
                    true );
        break;
    }
}
```

If the Loop menu item is selected, *Handle_Loop_Item()* is called. This menu item toggles looping on and off for the open movie. A call to *MCDoAction()* is made to see if looping is currently on or off. Notice that the action constant *mcActionGetLooping* is passed. *MCDoAction()* fills in the third parameter with *true* if looping is on, *false* if looping is not currently set. Our decision to turn looping on or off is based on this returned value. Additionally, we either check or uncheck the menu item with a call to *CheckItem()*.

```
void  Handle_Loop_Item( void )
{
    ComponentResult  comp_result;
    Boolean          looping_on;

    comp_result = MCDoAction( The_Controller, mcActionGetLooping,
                              &looping_on );
```

```
    if ( looping_on == true )
    {
       CheckItem( Movie_Menu, LOOP_ITEM, false );
       comp_result = MCDoAction( The_Controller,
                                 mcActionSetLooping,
                                 (Ptr)false );
    }
    else
    {
       CheckItem( Movie_Menu, LOOP_ITEM, true );
       comp_result = MCDoAction( The_Controller,
                                 mcActionSetLooping,
                                 (Ptr)true );
    }
}
```

Chapter Summary

A movie controller is attached to the bottom of a movie, and is used to control the playing of that movie. Attaching movie controllers to the movies in your program will give your application a standardized look and feel. Routines in the Movie Toolbox make creating and working with movie controllers easy.

To allow the user to select a movie to open—with or without a controller—you can use the *StandardGetFilePreview()* routine. This function displays a standard Get File dialog box with a scrollable list of movie files in it. The *StandardGetFilePreview()* will return the name of the selected file, and you can then open it as you did in Chapter 7.

When you open a movie, you can attach a controller to the bottom of it by using the Movie Toolbox routine *NewMovieController()*. Once a movie with a controller is present, call *MCIsPlayerEvent()* from within your program's main event loop. This powerful routine will do most of the work of playing and stepping through a movie. Any time the user clicks on a movie controller button, *MCIsPlayerEvent()* will take over and handle the event.

You can use the *MCDoAction()* routine to change many of the settings of a movie controller. By passing this routine different parameter values, you tell it what changes to make. One such change is in the way the controller plays a movie. By passing *MCDoAction()* a value of *mcActionSetLooping*, you tell the controller to loop through the movie when the user clicks the controller's Play button.

Allowing users to edit QuickTime movies adds a great deal to the usefulness of your programs. First, call *MCEnableEditing()* to allow editing to take place. Then, in response to a user's selection from the standard Edit menu, call the appropriate Movie Toolbox routine to perform the editing. To cut part of a movie, call *MCCut()*. Follow this call with one to *PutMovieOnScrap()* to store the cut frames to the Clipboard. Use *MCCopy()*, *MCPaste()*, *MCClear()*, and *MCUndo()* in a similar fashion.

Once a change to a movie has been made, allow the user to save the revised movie. Call *UpdateMovieResource()* to write the new movie to the file the movie originally came from.

More Movie Toolbox

n the previous chapter you learned how to attach a movie controller to a movie. You also saw that it is possible to change how a movie looks by changing its size. In this chapter you'll learn much more about changing movie characteristics.

Parts of a movie controller, and the entire controller itself, can be hidden. If there are reasons to prevent the user of your application from using either the Speaker button or Step buttons, you can easily hide them (and, just as easily, redisplay them). The same holds true for the entire movie controller. This chapter shows you how to do this.

In this chapter you'll learn about QuickTime's dependence on time. You can use this information to determine the length of a movie, and to copy a single frame—any frame—and convert it to a picture in the Clipboard.

Here you'll see how to change the rate at which a movie is played. You'll be able to speed it up or slow it down—or even play it backwards. You will also learn how to constrain playback to just a portion of a movie. In the previous chapter we covered looping. Here you'll learn to use a different type of looping to loop in both directions.

Changing the Look of a Controller

When your program opens a movie, you may want to give the program user full access to movie-playing options, such as playing the movie, stepping through it, and listening to the sound track (if there is one). Then again, you might not. If for some reason you want your program to suppress certain play features, you can do so. The Movie Toolbox provides routines that allow you to hide some of the movie controller buttons, or even the entire controller. Of course, the Movie Toolbox also provides a way for you to redisplay these things.

Hiding Controller Buttons

You can use *MCDoAction()* to set a movie controller's *control flags*. Use the action *mcActionSetFlags* to do this. As the third parameter to *MCDoAction()*, pass a pointer to one of the following predefined constants:

- *mcFlagSuppressStepButtons*—don't display the step buttons.
- *mcFlagSuppressSpeakerButton*—don't display the speaker button.

Figure 9.1 shows the effects you can achieve by using *MCDoAction()* with the *mcActionSetFlags* action.

Here's how you would suppress the drawing of the Step buttons:

```
comp_error = MCDoAction( The_Controller, mcActionSetFlags,
                         (Ptr)mcFlagSuppressStepButtons );
```

If you want to use more than one of the constants, you may be tempted to call *MCDoAction()* more than once, passing a different constant each time. Don't. Each call to *MCDoAction()* that uses the *mcActionSetFlags* action overrides any previous calls. So to set a controller to suppress both the Speaker and Step buttons, the following will *not* work:

```
/* The following is incorrect! */

comp_error = MCDoAction( The_Controller, mcActionSetFlags,
                         (Ptr)mcFlagSuppressSpeakerButton );
```

```
comp_error = MCDoAction( The_Controller, mcActionSetFlags,
                         (Ptr)mcFlagSuppressStepButtons );
```

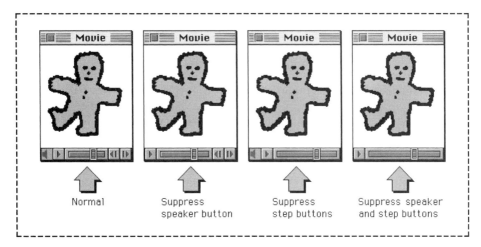

FIGURE 9.1
Changing the Look of the Controller Using MCDoAction()

Instead, declare a variable of type *long* and then use the Toolbox routine *BitOr()* to combine two flags into one value. Here's the correct way to suppress the Speaker and Step buttons:

```
/* The following is the correct method to use two flags */

long  controller_flags;

controller_flags = BitOr( mcFlagSuppressStepButtons,
                          mcFlagSuppressSpeakerButton );

comp_error = MCDoAction( The_Controller, mcActionSetFlags,
                         (Ptr)controller_flags );
```

Hiding the Controller

You just saw how to hide and show controller buttons. You can also hide and show the entire controller itself. Use the Movie Toolbox routine *MCSetVisible()* to do this. Pass the controller as the first parameter, and a Boolean value as the second parameter. A value of *true* sets the controller to visible; a value of *false* hides it. Here's the code to hide the controller:

```
MCSetVisible( The_Controller, false );
```

Once you hide the controller, you'll want to resize the movie window. Remember, both the movie and the movie controller are seated within the window. If you remove one, you'll want to eliminate the area it occupied. Call *GetMovieBox()* to receive a rectangle that gives the movie's size—without the controller. Then call *SizeWindow()* to resize the window to this rectangle. Here's the code to do that:

```
Rect   the_rect;

MCSetVisible( The_Controller, false );

GetMovieBox( The_Movie, &the_rect );

SizeWindow( The_Window, the_rect.right, the_rect.bottom, true );
```

To display the controller, again call *MCSetVisible()*. This time set the second parameter to *false*. To get the window size, call *MCGetControllerBounds-Rect()*—not *GetMovieBox()*. The *GetMovieBox()* routine returns the boundary rectangle of only the movie—not both the movie and the movie controller. Figure 9.2 illustrates the difference.

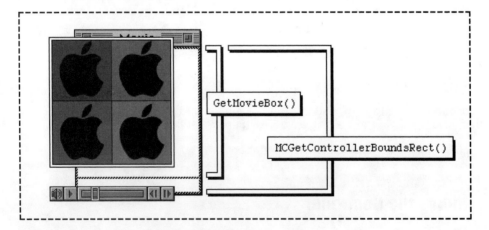

FIGURE 9.2
Getting the Size of the Movie and the Movie and Controller

```
ComponentResult   comp_result;
Rect              the_rect;
```

```
MCSetVisible( The_Controller, false );

comp_result=MCGetControllerBoundsRect(The_Controller, &the_rect);

SizeWindow( The_Window, the_rect.right, the_rect.bottom, true );
```

This chapter's sample program provides a menu item that allows the user to toggle back and forth between hiding and displaying the movie controller.

Movie Frames

The video sequences that make up a QuickTime movie consist of *time-based* data. A particular point in a movie is also a point in time, and is represented using a *time value*. The time can be expressed in different *time scales*. Seconds, sixtieths of a second, and milliseconds are all time scales.

In this section we'll use QuickTime's dependence on time to determine the length of a movie and to select a particular frame to convert to a 'PICT' and store in the scrap—the Clipboard.

Determining the Length of a Movie

You can use the Movie Toolbox routine *GetMovieDuration()* to determine the duration, or length, of a movie. This routine returns the time as a *TimeValue* variable.

```
TimeValue  duration_time;

duration_time = GetMovieDuration( The_Movie );
```

The duration is only meaningful if you know the time scale. That is, a duration of 600 means the movie is 1 second in length if the time scale is 600, but is 10 seconds in length if the time scale is 60. After getting the duration, get the time scale by using the Movie Toolbox routine *GetMovieTimeScale()*:

```
TimeScale  the_scale;

the_scale = GetMovieTimeScale( The_Movie );
```

Once you know both the duration and the time scale, you can determine the movie length in seconds by dividing the duration by the scale.

A *TimeValue* is simply a *long* with a fancy name. And, as it turns out, so is a *TimeScale*. Before calculating the movie duration from these values, keep in mind that if you divide one *long* by another, your C compiler will return a *long*—even if you assign the result to a variable of type *float*. If you want a more accurate movie duration, convert the *TimeValue* and *TimeScale* to floating-point values by multiplying each by 1.0. Here's the code that will give you a movie's length in seconds:

```
TimeScale    the_scale;
TimeValue    duration_time;
float        movie_length;

duration_time = GetMovieDuration( The_Movie );
the_scale = GetMovieTimeScale( The_Movie );

movie_length = (duration_time * 1.0)/(the_scale * 1.0);
```

Copying a Single Frame as a 'PICT'

You can use the standard edit command **Copy** to copy a single frame of a movie to the Clipboard. However, it will be stored in the Clipboard as a single frame movie—not always the desired way to save it. Many programs don't support QuickTime movies, and won't paste them into their documents. Additionally, you might just want the single frame as a picture rather than a movie. We'll address that issue now.

You can use the Movie Toolbox routine *GetMoviePict()* to get a 'PICT' of a single movie frame. Pass *GetMoviePict()* a movie and a time value, and the routine will return a handle to the picture that is located at the specified time value.

Each frame in a movie has a time value that corresponds to it. QuickTime movies, regardless of the time scale used, always start at time 0. Thus the first frame of a movie is at time value 0.

To obtain the second parameter to *GetMoviePict()*, the *TimeValue*, you'll need to get the time associated with the current frame. *GetMovieTime()* does that for you. Pass this routine the movie, and it will return the time of the current frame. The second parameter to *GetMovieTime()* is the time expressed in a different format—a *TimeRecord*.

We'll pass a value of *nil* here to ignore this format and just use the return value, the time in *TimeValue* format.

```
TimeValue   frame_time;

frame_time = GetMovieTime( The_Movie, nil );
```

Now that we have the time value of the current frame, we're all set to get a handle to the picture that makes up the frame.

```
TimeValue   frame_time;
PicHandle   pic_handle;

frame_time = GetMovieTime( The_Movie, nil );
pic_handle = GetMoviePict( The_Movie, frame_time );
```

You can use this *PicHandle* as you would any handle to a picture. You could use the Toolbox routine *DrawPicture()* to draw it into a different window or dialog. Or, you could save the picture that the handle points to in the scrap (as we'll do next). Once the picture is stored in the Clipboard, a user of your program can paste the picture into the Scrapbook, or any other program or document that supports pictures.

To get the picture into the scrap we'll rely on the Toolbox routine *PutScrap()*. Because *PutScrap()* adds to whatever is already in the Clipboard, we'll first call the Toolbox routine *ZeroScrap()* to empty out the Clipboard. And, since we're working with a handle, we'll nest our actions between calls to *HLock()* and *HUnlock()* to ensure that the picture we're pointing to doesn't get shifted about in memory.

```
PicHandle   pic_handle;
long        pic_size;

ZeroScrap();
HLock( pic_handle );
   pic_size = GetHandleSize( pic_handle );
   PutScrap( pic_size, 'PICT', *pic_handle );
HUnlock( pic_handle );
```

After locking the handle, the first thing we do is determine the size, in bytes, that the picture occupies. *GetHandleSize()* tells us that. Then, we call *PutScrap()* to place the picture in the scrap.

The first parameter to *PutScrap()* is the size of the object that's going into the scrap. The second parameter is the type of the object—*PutScrap()* can also put 'TEXT' into the Clipboard. The last parameter is a pointer to the object going in. We have a handle, so we dereference it once to get a pointer.

Let's look at the entire code that gets the time of the current frame, gets a handle to the picture that makes up that frame, and then places that picture onto the scrap:

```
TimeValue   frame_time;
PicHandle   pic_handle;
long        pic_size;

frame_time = GetMovieTime( The_Movie, nil );
pic_handle = GetMoviePict( The_Movie, frame_time );

ZeroScrap();
HLock( pic_handle );
    pic_size = GetHandleSize( pic_handle );
    PutScrap( pic_size, 'PICT', *pic_handle );
HUnlock( pic_handle );
```

In this chapter's sample program we bundle the above code into a function used in our implementation of a Copy Current Frame As PICT menu item. The user can select this item to copy a frame to the Clipboard.

Changing the Movie Playing Rate

In the last section we mentioned that movies are time-based. Time is a crucial element of QuickTime movies—the effect of motion in a movie is achieved by quickly displaying a series of pictures. Just how quickly the pictures are displayed greatly influences the look of the movie.

Allowing the user to select the rate at which a movie plays is something that many QuickTime programs don't do. But it's an easy feat to accomplish, and it gives the user one more way of controlling a movie. You might want to consider adding functionality to your program by including a menu like one of the two examples we show in Figure 9.3.

As you've done in the past, you'll use the Movie Toolbox routine *MCDoAction()* to change a feature of a controller. Here, you'll use the routine to change the rate in which a movie is played. To specify the rate of play, you'll need to be familiar with the *Fixed* data type.

```
┌─────────────────┐        ┌──────────────────────┐
│ Play            │        │ Play                 │
├─────────────────┤        ├──────────────────────┤
│ Half Speed      │        │ Super Slow Motion    │
│ Double Speed    │        │ Slow Motion          │
│ Triple Speed    │        │ Fast Motion          │
│ Backwards Normal Speed │ │ Super Fast Motion    │
└─────────────────┘        └──────────────────────┘
```

FIGURE 9.3
Typical Menus Allowing Users to Change the Movie Rate

The Fixed Data Type

Movie rates are given in a format that use the *Fixed* data type. A *Fixed* number is 32 bits in size, with the upper 16 bits devoted to the integer portion of a number, and the lower 16 bits devoted to the fractional part of the same number.

In the C language, you can express a constant *Fixed* number by a leading 0x, followed by eight hexadecimal digits. Here's an example that defines the *Fixed* representation of the number 2:

```
#define    FIXED_2    0x00020000
```

To play a movie at other than its normal rate, you'll use a *Fixed* number in a call to *MCDoAction()*. To play the movie at double its normal rate, you'd use 0x00020000—the *FIXED_2* defined above. Converting numbers to *Fixed* notation involves binary representation, and two's complement—topics that are beyond the scope of this book. Instead, we've done the conversions of some of the most common values for you. They're listed in the next section.

Changing the Rate of Play

To change the rate of play of a movie, call *MCDoAction()* with the action *mcActionPlay* as the second parameter. The last parameter specifies the rate to play the movie. It must be in *Fixed* notation, as discussed in the previous section. Here's an example that plays a movie at double its normal rate:

```
#define              F_TIMES_2_SPEED              0x00020000

ComponentResult   comp_result;

comp_result = MCDoAction( The_Controller, mcActionPlay,
                          (Ptr)F_TIMES_2_SPEED );
```

Once you make the call to *MCDoAction()*, the movie associated with *The_Controller* will immediately play.

As promised, here are the *#define* directives for many of the rates you might want to play a movie at. Constants that begin with "F_" play the movie in the forward direction at the specified rate. Constants beginning with "B_" play the movie in the backwards direction at the given rate.

```
#define              F_TIMES_EIGHTH_SPEED         0x00002000
#define              F_TIMES_QUARTER_SPEED        0x00004000
#define              F_TIMES_HALF_SPEED           0x00008000
#define              F_TIMES_1_SPEED              0x00010000
#define              F_TIMES_2_SPEED              0x00020000
#define              F_TIMES_3_SPEED              0x00030000
#define              F_TIMES_4_SPEED              0x00040000
#define              F_TIMES_5_SPEED              0x00050000
#define              F_TIMES_10_SPEED             0x000A0000
#define              B_TIMES_HALF_SPEED           0xFFFF8000
#define              B_TIMES_1_SPEED              0xFFFF0000
#define              B_TIMES_2_SPEED              0xFFFE0000
```

To make use of any or all of the above *Fixed* values, add them to your source code. Then use them in calls to *MCDoAction()*. Here's a few more examples:

```
/* play movie forward, half speed:  */
comp_result = MCDoAction( The_Controller, mcActionPlay,
                          (Ptr)F_TIMES_HALF_SPEED );

/* play movie backwards, normal speed:  */
comp_result = MCDoAction( The_Controller, mcActionPlay,
                          (Ptr)B_TIMES_1_SPEED );
```

The sample program at the end of this chapter implements the menu shown on the left side of Figure 9.3 using *MCDoAction()* and the above *#define* directives.

Playing Movie Selections

Normally, when you click on the **Play** button of a movie controller, the movie will play from the current frame to the end of the movie. You can set a controller so that it will play only a selected portion of a movie. The portion played will be that part of the movie the user selects by holding the **Shift** key and moving the slider along the slide bar. See Figure 9.4.

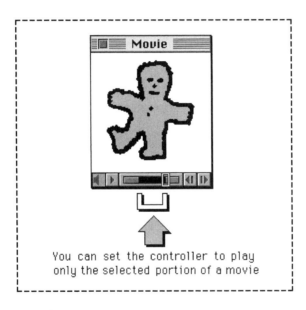

You can set the controller to play
only the selected portion of a movie

FIGURE 9.4

Playing Only the Selected Portion of a Movie

You can set a controller to play the selected part of its movie by calling the *MCDoAction()* routine with an action of *mcActionSetPlaySelection*. Here's an example:

```
ComponentResult  comp_result;

comp_result=MCDoAction(The_Controller, mcActionSetPlaySelection,
                  (Ptr)true );
```

For this action, *MCDoAction()* does not play the movie. Instead, it changes the way the Play button behaves. Each time the user clicks the **Play** button, it will play only the selected part of the movie. If no part is selected, the movie will play as normal—from the point of the slider to the end of the movie. The Play button will behave this way, for the movie associated with *The_Controller*, until another call to *MCDoAction()* is made—this time with the last parameter set to *false*:

```
comp_result=MCDoAction(The_Controller, mcActionSetPlaySelection,
                (Ptr)false );
```

Because the *mcActionSetPlaySelection* action changes the controller for more than one playing of a movie, you'll want to indicate to the user that the controller has been changed. If the user made the change through a menu item, set a check mark next to that item.

You can use the *mcActionGetPlaySelection* action to determine if play selection is on. *MCDoAction()* will return a value of *true* if it is, *false* if it isn't.

```
Boolean  play_selection_on;

comp_error=MCDoAction( The_Controller, mcActionGetPlaySelection,
                &play_selection_on );
```

Looping, Revisited

In the previous chapter you saw how to use *MCDoAction()* to turn looping on and off:

```
ComponentResult  comp_error;

comp_error = MCDoAction( The_Controller, mcActionSetLooping,
                (Ptr)true );
```

The above call sets *The_Controller* to loop through its movie whenever the **Play** button is clicked. When the movie reaches the end, it will jump back to the start and play again.

You can also use *MCDoAction()* to set a controller for a different kind of looping—*palindrome looping*. This type of looping causes a movie to alternately play forward and backward. When the movie reaches the end, it won't jump back to the beginning to play again. Instead, it plays backwards to the beginning.

To set a controller to palindrome looping, the controller must also be set to normal looping. Here's how that's done:

```
comp_error = MCDoAction( The_Controller, mcActionSetLooping,
                         (Ptr)true );
comp_error = MCDoAction( The_Controller,
                         mcActionSetLoopIsPalindrome,
                         (Ptr)true );
```

Like normal looping, you should set a check mark next to the menu item that initiates palindrome looping, as we do in the sample program we discuss next.

Sample Program: MovieFeatures

This chapter's sample program is for the MovieFeatures included on the disk that accompanies this book. Like the other examples, we've included the C language source code. The MovieFeatures program is another movie viewer. It has an array of new features not found in last chapter's viewer, MovieViewer.

Rather than repeat much of the source code from last chapter's program, we've eliminated several menu options that appeared in MovieViewer. The File menu has Open, Close, and Quit items, but no Save item. The Edit menu has been disabled—MovieFeatures doesn't support editing. Refer to Chapter 8 if you'd like to include these functions in your own QuickTime program. Figure 9.5 shows the menu items in the Movie and Play menus of MovieFeatures.

MovieFeatures uses menu items to implement all of the features discussed in this chapter. That gives you a chance to experiment by trying things out again and again. Your program may bury some of these features out of reach of the user, such as hiding the **Speaker** button of the controller. If you don't want the user to be able to play the sound track of a movie, you can suppress the **Speaker** button right after you open the window.

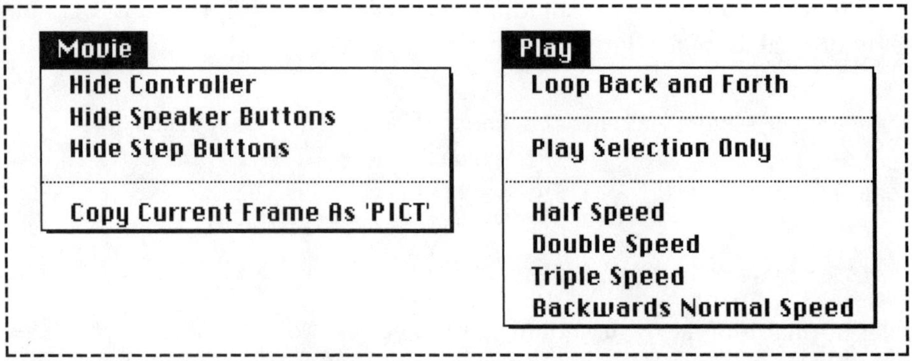

Movie
Hide Controller
Hide Speaker Buttons
Hide Step Buttons
Copy Current Frame As 'PICT'

Play
Loop Back and Forth
Play Selection Only
Half Speed
Double Speed
Triple Speed
Backwards Normal Speed

FIGURE 9.5
The Movie and Play Menus of MovieFeatures

Program Resources: MovieFeatures.π.rsrc

MovieFeatures has the same four resource types as MovieViewer. There is the one 'ALRT' and its accompanying 'DITL' used to display the About alert.

There are five 'MENU' resources. They are for the Apple, File, Edit, Movie, and Play menus. MovieFeatures uses the Movie menu for items that don't affect the playing of a movie, and the Play menu for items that do affect movie playing. The 'MENU's are grouped together by the one 'MBAR' resource.

Program Listing: MovieFeatures.c

After this listing of the entire MovieFeatures source code, we'll discuss the code that pertains to this chapter.

```
/*++++++++++++++++++++++++++++++++++++++++++++++++++++++++++++++++++++++*/

#include <GestaltEqu.h>
#include <Movies.h>

/*++++++++++++++++++++++++++++++++++++++++++++++++++++++++++++++++++++++*/

void    Initialize_Toolbox( void );
void    Initialize_Movies( void );
void    Set_Up_Menu_Bar( void );
void    Adjust_Menus_For_No_Window( void );
```

```
void   Adjust_Menus_For_Open_Window( void );
void   Handle_One_Event( void );
void   Handle_Mouse_Down( void );
void   Handle_Menu_Choice( long );
void   Handle_Apple_Choice( short );
void   Handle_File_Choice( short );
void   Open_A_Movie( void );
Movie Get_A_Movie( void );
void   Open_And_Size_Window( void );
void   Close_A_Movie( void );
void   Handle_Movie_Choice( short );
void   Show_Hide_Controller( void );
void   Show_Speaker( void );
void   Hide_Speaker( void );
void   Show_Steps( void );
void   Hide_Steps( void );
void   Copy_Current_Frame_To_Scrap( void );
void   Handle_Play_Choice( short );
void   Handle_Palindrome_Loop_Item( void );
void   Handle_Play_Selection_Item( void );


/*++++++++++++++++++++++++++++++++++++++++++++++++++++++++++++++++*/

#define           ABOUT_ALRT_ID                  128
#define           MENU_BAR_ID                    128
#define           APPLE_MENU_ID                  128
#define             ABOUT_ITEM                     1
#define           FILE_MENU_ID                   129
#define             OPEN_ITEM                      1
#define             CLOSE_ITEM                     2
#define             QUIT_ITEM                      4
#define           EDIT_MENU_ID                   130
#define           MOVIE_MENU_ID                  131
#define             HIDE_CONTROLLER_ITEM           1
#define             HIDE_SPEAKER_ITEM              2
#define             HIDE_STEPS_ITEM                3
#define             COPY_FRAME_ITEM                5
#define           PLAY_MENU_ID                   132
#define             PAL_LOOP_ITEM                  1
#define             PLAY_SELECTION_ITEM            3
#define             HALF_SPEED_ITEM                5
#define             DOUBLE_SPEED_ITEM              6
#define             TRIPLE_SPEED_ITEM              7
#define             BACK_SPEED_ITEM                8

#define           F_TIMES_EIGHTH_SPEED    0x00002000
#define           F_TIMES_QUARTER_SPEED   0x00004000
#define           F_TIMES_HALF_SPEED      0x00008000
#define           F_TIMES_1_SPEED         0x00010000
#define           F_TIMES_2_SPEED         0x00020000
#define           F_TIMES_3_SPEED         0x00030000
```

```
#define          F_TIMES_4_SPEED          0x00040000
#define          F_TIMES_5_SPEED          0x00050000
#define          F_TIMES_10_SPEED         0x000A0000
#define          B_TIMES_HALF_SPEED       0xFFFF8000
#define          B_TIMES_1_SPEED          0xFFFF0000
#define          B_TIMES_2_SPEED          0xFFFE0000

#define          IN_FRONT                 (WindowPtr)-1L

/*++++++++++++++++++++++++++++++++++++++++++++++++++++++++++++++++*/

EventRecord      The_Event;
Boolean          All_Done = false;
MenuHandle       Apple_Menu;
MenuHandle       File_Menu;
MenuHandle       Edit_Menu;
MenuHandle       Movie_Menu;
MenuHandle       Play_Menu;
WindowPtr        The_Window = nil;
Movie            The_Movie = nil;
MovieController  The_Controller = nil;
short            Movie_Res_File;
short            Movie_Res_ID = 0;
Boolean          Speaker_Hidden = false;
Boolean          Steps_Hidden = false;

/*++++++++++++++++++++++++++++++++++++++++++++++++++++++++++++++++*/

void   main( void )
{
   Initialize_Toolbox();

   Initialize_Movies();

   Set_Up_Menu_Bar();

   while ( All_Done == false )
      Handle_One_Event();
}

/*++++++++++++++++++++++++++++++++++++++++++++++++++++++++++++++++*/

void   Initialize_Toolbox( void )
{
   InitGraf( &thePort );
   InitFonts();
   InitWindows();
   InitMenus();
   TEInit();
   InitDialogs( nil );
   InitCursor();
}
```

```
/*+++++++++++++++++++++++++++++++++++++++++++++++++++++++++++++++++++*/

void   Initialize_Movies( void )
{
   OSErr   error;
   long    result;

   error = Gestalt( gestaltQuickTime, &result );
   if ( error != noErr )
      ExitToShell();

   error = EnterMovies();
   if ( error != noErr )
      ExitToShell();
}

/*+++++++++++++++++++++++++++++++++++++++++++++++++++++++++++++++++++*/

void   Set_Up_Menu_Bar( void )
{
   Handle   menu_bar_handle;

   menu_bar_handle = GetNewMBar( MENU_BAR_ID );

   SetMenuBar( menu_bar_handle );
   DisposHandle( menu_bar_handle );

   Apple_Menu = GetMHandle( APPLE_MENU_ID );
   File_Menu  = GetMHandle( FILE_MENU_ID  );
   Edit_Menu  = GetMHandle( EDIT_MENU_ID  );
   Movie_Menu = GetMHandle( MOVIE_MENU_ID );
   Play_Menu  = GetMHandle( PLAY_MENU_ID );

   DisableItem( Edit_Menu, 0 );

   Adjust_Menus_For_No_Window();

   AddResMenu( Apple_Menu, 'DRVR' );

   DrawMenuBar();
}

/*+++++++++++++++++++++++++++++++++++++++++++++++++++++++++++++++++++*/

void   Adjust_Menus_For_No_Window( void )
{
   EnableItem( File_Menu, OPEN_ITEM );
   DisableItem( File_Menu, CLOSE_ITEM );
   DisableItem( Movie_Menu, 0 );
   DisableItem( Play_Menu, 0 );
}
```

```
/*+++++++++++++++++++++++++++++++++++++++++++++++++++++++++++++++++++++*/

void   Adjust_Menus_For_Open_Window( void )
{
    DisableItem( File_Menu, OPEN_ITEM );
    EnableItem( File_Menu, CLOSE_ITEM );
    EnableItem( Movie_Menu, 0 );
    EnableItem( Play_Menu, 0 );
}

/*+++++++++++++++++++++++++++++++++++++++++++++++++++++++++++++++++++++*/

void   Handle_One_Event( void )
{
    WindowPtr    which_window;
    long         movie_related_event;

    WaitNextEvent(everyEvent, &The_Event, 0, nil);

    if ( The_Controller == nil )
        movie_related_event = 0;
    else
        movie_related_event = MCIsPlayerEvent(The_Controller,
                                              &The_Event);

    if ( movie_related_event == 0 )
    {
        switch (The_Event.what)
        {
            case updateEvt:
                which_window = (WindowPtr)The_Event.message;
                SetPort( which_window );
                BeginUpdate(which_window);
                    EraseRgn( which_window->visRgn );
                EndUpdate(which_window);
                break;

            case mouseDown:
                Handle_Mouse_Down();
                break;
        }
    }
}

/*+++++++++++++++++++++++++++++++++++++++++++++++++++++++++++++++++++++*/

void   Handle_Mouse_Down( void )
{
    WindowPtr    which_window;
    short        the_part;
```

```
    long       menu_choice;

    the_part = FindWindow( The_Event.where, &which_window );

    switch ( the_part )
    {
        case inMenuBar:
            menu_choice = MenuSelect( The_Event.where );
            Handle_Menu_Choice( menu_choice );
            break;

        case inSysWindow:
            SystemClick( &The_Event, which_window);
            break;

        case inDrag:
            DragWindow( which_window, The_Event.where,
                        &screenBits.bounds );
            break;

        case inGoAway:
            if ( TrackGoAway( which_window, The_Event.where ) )
                Close_A_Movie();
            break;

        case inContent:
            SelectWindow( which_window );
            break;
    }
}

/*+++++++++++++++++++++++++++++++++++++++++++++++++++++++++++++++++++++*/

void  Handle_Menu_Choice( long menu_choice )
{
    int  the_menu;
    int  the_menu_item;

    if ( menu_choice != 0 )
    {
        the_menu = HiWord( menu_choice );
        the_menu_item = LoWord( menu_choice );

        switch ( the_menu )
        {
            case APPLE_MENU_ID:
                Handle_Apple_Choice( the_menu_item );
                break;

            case FILE_MENU_ID:
                Handle_File_Choice( the_menu_item );
```

```
                        break;

                case EDIT_MENU_ID:
                    /* disabled menu */
                    break;

                case MOVIE_MENU_ID:
                    Handle_Movie_Choice( the_menu_item );
                    break;

                case PLAY_MENU_ID:
                    Handle_Play_Choice( the_menu_item );
                    break;
            }
            HiliteMenu( 0 );
        }
}

/*+++++++++++++++++++++++++++++++++++++++++++++++++++++++++++++++++*/

void   Handle_Apple_Choice( short the_item )
{
    Str255   desk_acc_name;
    int      desk_acc_number;

    switch ( the_item )
    {
        case ABOUT_ITEM:
            Alert( ABOUT_ALRT_ID, nil );
            break;

        default:
            GetItem( Apple_Menu, the_item, desk_acc_name );
            desk_acc_number = OpenDeskAcc( desk_acc_name );
            break;
    }
}

/*+++++++++++++++++++++++++++++++++++++++++++++++++++++++++++++++++*/

void   Handle_File_Choice( short the_item )
{
    OSErr   error;

    switch ( the_item )
    {
        case OPEN_ITEM:
            Open_A_Movie();
            break;

        case CLOSE_ITEM:
```

```
            Close_A_Movie();
            break;

        case QUIT_ITEM:
            All_Done = TRUE;
            break;
    }
}

/*+++++++++++++++++++++++++++++++++++++++++++++++++++++++++++++++++++++*/

void  Open_A_Movie( void )
{
    ComponentResult  comp_result;

    The_Movie = Get_A_Movie();

    if (The_Movie != nil)
    {
        Open_And_Size_Window();

        comp_result = MCDoAction( The_Controller,
                                  mcActionSetKeysEnabled,
                                  (Ptr)true);

        comp_result = MCEnableEditing( The_Controller, true );

        Adjust_Menus_For_Open_Window();
    }
}

/*+++++++++++++++++++++++++++++++++++++++++++++++++++++++++++++++++++++*/

Movie Get_A_Movie( void )
{
    OSErr              error;
    Movie              get_movie = nil;
    SFTypeList         type_list = { MovieFileType, 0, 0, 0 };
    StandardFileReply  the_reply;
    Str255             movie_name;
    Boolean            was_changed;

    Movie_Res_ID = 0;

    StandardGetFilePreview( nil, 1, type_list, &the_reply );

    if ( the_reply.sfGood == true )
    {
        error = OpenMovieFile( &the_reply.sfFile, &Movie_Res_File,
                               fsRdPerm );
        if ( error == noErr )
```

```
           error = NewMovieFromFile( &get_movie, Movie_Res_File,
                                      &Movie_Res_ID,
                                      movie_name, newMovieActive,
                                      &was_changed );

      CloseMovieFile( Movie_Res_File );
   }
   return ( get_movie );
}

/*++++++++++++++++++++++++++++++++++++++++++++++++++++++++++++++++++++*/

void   Open_And_Size_Window( void )
{
   ComponentResult  comp_result;
   Rect             movie_box;
   Rect             the_rect;

long   controller_flags;

   SetRect(&the_rect, 100, 100, 150, 150);
   The_Window = NewCWindow( nil, &the_rect, "\pMovie", false,
                            noGrowDocProc, IN_FRONT, true, 0 );

   SetMovieGWorld( The_Movie, ( CGrafPtr )The_Window, nil );

   GetMovieBox( The_Movie, &movie_box );

   The_Controller = NewMovieController( The_Movie, &movie_box,
                                        mcTopLeftMovie );
   if (The_Controller == nil)
      ExitToShell();

   comp_result = MCGetControllerBoundsRect( The_Controller,
                                            &the_rect );

   SizeWindow( The_Window, the_rect.right, the_rect.bottom,
               true );
   ShowWindow( The_Window );
}

/*++++++++++++++++++++++++++++++++++++++++++++++++++++++++++++++++++++*/

void   Close_A_Movie( void )
{
   The_Controller = nil;
   DisposeMovieController( The_Controller );
   DisposeMovie( The_Movie );
   DisposeWindow( The_Window );

   Adjust_Menus_For_No_Window();
```

```
}
/*++++++++++++++++++++++++++++++++++++++++++++++++++++++++++++++++++++++*/

void   Handle_Movie_Choice( short the_item )
{
   switch ( the_item )
   {
      case HIDE_CONTROLLER_ITEM:
         Show_Hide_Controller();
         break;

      case HIDE_SPEAKER_ITEM:
         if ( Speaker_Hidden == true )
            Show_Speaker();
         else
            Hide_Speaker();
         break;

      case HIDE_STEPS_ITEM:
         if ( Steps_Hidden == true )
            Show_Steps();
         else
            Hide_Steps();
         break;

      case COPY_FRAME_ITEM:
         Copy_Current_Frame_To_Scrap();
         break;
   }
}

/*++++++++++++++++++++++++++++++++++++++++++++++++++++++++++++++++++++++*/

void   Show_Hide_Controller( void )
{
Rect   the_rect;

   ComponentResult   comp_result;

   comp_result = MCGetVisible( The_Controller );
   if ( comp_result == 1 )
   {
       comp_result = MCSetVisible( The_Controller, false );
       SetItem( Movie_Menu, HIDE_CONTROLLER_ITEM,
               "\pShow Controller" );

       GetMovieBox( The_Movie, &the_rect );
   }
   else
   {
```

```
        comp_result = MCSetVisible( The_Controller, true );
        SetItem( Movie_Menu, HIDE_CONTROLLER_ITEM,
                "\pHide Controller" );

        comp_result = MCGetControllerBoundsRect( The_Controller,
                                                 &the_rect );
    }

    SizeWindow( The_Window, the_rect.right, the_rect.bottom,
            true );
}

/*++++++++++++++++++++++++++++++++++++++++++++++++++++++++++++++++++++*/

void  Show_Speaker( void )
{
    ComponentResult  comp_result;

    if ( Steps_Hidden == true )
        comp_result = MCDoAction( The_Controller, mcActionSetFlags,
                                  (Ptr)mcFlagSuppressStepButtons );
    else
        comp_result = MCDoAction( The_Controller, mcActionSetFlags,
                                  (Ptr)0 );
    Speaker_Hidden = false;

    SetItem( Movie_Menu, HIDE_SPEAKER_ITEM,
            "\pHide Speaker Button" );
}

/*++++++++++++++++++++++++++++++++++++++++++++++++++++++++++++++++++++*/

void  Hide_Speaker( void )
{
    ComponentResult  comp_result;
    long             controller_flags;

    if ( Steps_Hidden == true )
    {
        controller_flags = BitOr( mcFlagSuppressStepButtons,
                                  mcFlagSuppressSpeakerButton );

        comp_result = MCDoAction( The_Controller, mcActionSetFlags,
                                  (Ptr)controller_flags );
    }
    else
    {
        comp_result = MCDoAction( The_Controller, mcActionSetFlags,
                                  (Ptr)mcFlagSuppressSpeakerButton);
    }
```

```
      Speaker_Hidden = true;

      SetItem( Movie_Menu, HIDE_SPEAKER_ITEM,
               "\pShow Speaker Button" );
}

/*+++++++++++++++++++++++++++++++++++++++++++++++++++++++++++++++++*/

void  Show_Steps( void )
{
   ComponentResult  comp_result;

   if ( Speaker_Hidden == true )
      comp_result = MCDoAction( The_Controller, mcActionSetFlags,
                                (Ptr)mcFlagSuppressSpeakerButton);
   else
      comp_result = MCDoAction( The_Controller, mcActionSetFlags,
                                (Ptr)0 );
   Steps_Hidden = false;

   SetItem( Movie_Menu, HIDE_STEPS_ITEM, "\pHide Step Buttons" );
}

/*+++++++++++++++++++++++++++++++++++++++++++++++++++++++++++++++++*/

void  Hide_Steps( void )
{
   ComponentResult  comp_result;
   long             controller_flags;

   if ( Speaker_Hidden == true )
   {
      controller_flags = BitOr( mcFlagSuppressStepButtons,
                                mcFlagSuppressSpeakerButton );

      comp_result = MCDoAction( The_Controller, mcActionSetFlags,
                                (Ptr)controller_flags );
   }
   else
   {
      comp_result = MCDoAction( The_Controller, mcActionSetFlags,
                                (Ptr)mcFlagSuppressStepButtons );
   }

   Steps_Hidden = true;

   SetItem( Movie_Menu, HIDE_STEPS_ITEM, "\pShow Step Buttons" );
}

/*+++++++++++++++++++++++++++++++++++++++++++++++++++++++++++++++++*/
```

```
void   Copy_Current_Frame_To_Scrap( void )
{
   TimeValue   frame_time;
   PicHandle   pic_handle;
   long        pic_size;

   frame_time = GetMovieTime( The_Movie, nil );
   pic_handle = GetMoviePict( The_Movie, frame_time );

   ZeroScrap();
   HLock( pic_handle );
      pic_size = GetHandleSize( pic_handle );
      PutScrap( pic_size, 'PICT', *pic_handle );
   HUnlock( pic_handle );
}

/*++++++++++++++++++++++++++++++++++++++++++++++++++++++++++++++++++++++*/

void   Handle_Play_Choice( short the_item )
{
   ComponentResult   comp_result;
   Rect              the_rect;
   short             width;
   short             height;

   switch ( the_item )
   {
      case PAL_LOOP_ITEM:
         Handle_Palindrome_Loop_Item();
         break;

      case PLAY_SELECTION_ITEM:
         Handle_Play_Selection_Item();
         break;

      case HALF_SPEED_ITEM:
         comp_result = MCDoAction( The_Controller, mcActionPlay,
                                   (Ptr)F_TIMES_HALF_SPEED );
         break;

      case DOUBLE_SPEED_ITEM:
         comp_result = MCDoAction( The_Controller, mcActionPlay,
                                   (Ptr)F_TIMES_2_SPEED );
         break;

      case TRIPLE_SPEED_ITEM:
         comp_result = MCDoAction( The_Controller, mcActionPlay,
                                   (Ptr)F_TIMES_3_SPEED );
         break;

      case BACK_SPEED_ITEM :
```

```
           comp_result = MCDoAction( The_Controller, mcActionPlay,
                                       (Ptr)B_TIMES_1_SPEED );
           break;
   }
}

/*++++++++++++++++++++++++++++++++++++++++++++++++++++++++++++++++*/

void  Handle_Palindrome_Loop_Item( void )
{
   ComponentResult  comp_result;
   Boolean          pal_looping_on;

   comp_result = MCDoAction( The_Controller,
                             mcActionGetLoopIsPalindrome,
                             &pal_looping_on );

   if ( pal_looping_on == true )
   {
      CheckItem( Play_Menu, PAL_LOOP_ITEM, false );
      comp_result = MCDoAction( The_Controller,
                                mcActionSetLooping,
                                (Ptr)false );
      comp_result = MCDoAction( The_Controller,
                                mcActionSetLoopIsPalindrome,
                                (Ptr)false );
   }
   else
   {
      CheckItem( Play_Menu, PAL_LOOP_ITEM, true );
      comp_result = MCDoAction( The_Controller,
                                mcActionSetLooping,
                                (Ptr)true );
      comp_result = MCDoAction( The_Controller,
                                mcActionSetLoopIsPalindrome,
                                (Ptr)true );
   }
}

/*++++++++++++++++++++++++++++++++++++++++++++++++++++++++++++++++*/

void  Handle_Play_Selection_Item( void )
{
   ComponentResult  comp_result;
   Boolean          play_selection_on;

   comp_result = MCDoAction( The_Controller,
                             mcActionGetPlaySelection,
                             &play_selection_on );

   if ( play_selection_on == true )
```

```
{
    CheckItem( Play_Menu, PLAY_SELECTION_ITEM, false );
    comp_result = MCDoAction( The_Controller,
                              mcActionSetPlaySelection,
                              (Ptr)false );
}
else
{
    CheckItem( Play_Menu, PLAY_SELECTION_ITEM, true );
    comp_result = MCDoAction( The_Controller,
                              mcActionSetPlaySelection,
                              (Ptr)true );
}
}
```

Stepping Through the Code

Much of the MovieFeatures source code is identical to that found in last chapter's MovieViewer program. We'll tell you when it is.

The Preliminary Stuff

MovieFeatures uses the same two header files as last chapter's program: GestaltEqu.h and Movies.h.

We've added the constants that were described in this chapter's Changing the Rate of Play section to the list of *#define* directives. They'll allow us to change the movie playback rate.

You should be familiar with most of the global variables; many of them appeared in MovieViewer. We've added two *Boolean* variables, *Speaker_Hidden* and *Steps_Hidden*, to keep track of which buttons to display in the movie controller.

Program Setup

The *main()* function of MovieFeatures is identical to that of MovieViewer. There's Toolbox initialization, menu setup, and then it's off and running. We've covered initializations in Chapter 7, and menus in Chapter 8. To keep the menus properly enabled and disabled, MovieFeatures has an *Adjust_Menus_For_No_Window()* and *Adjust_Menus_For_Open_Window()* routine—just as MovieViewer does.

```
void  main( void )
{
   Initialize_Toolbox();

   Initialize_Movies();

   Set_Up_Menu_Bar();

   while ( All_Done == false )
      Handle_One_Event();
}
```

The Main Event Loop

This main event loop, and the chain of routines it calls, is very similar to MovieViewer's. *Handle_One_Event()* is called repeatedly to grab the next event and process it. *Handle_Mouse_Down()*, *Handle_Menu_Choice()*, *Handle_Apple_Choice()*, and *Handle_File_Choice()* all closely match their counterparts in MovieViewer.

Opening and Closing a Movie

MovieFeatures opens and closes a movie as MovieViewer does. It allows the user to select the movie to open by using the standard Get File dialog box.

Handling the Movie Menu

Now comes the new stuff. Three of the four menu items in the Movie menu are used to hide or display parts of the movie controller. The first item hides the entire controller if it's visible. If it's already hidden, this menu item will instead be used to display the controller. We toggle the name of the menu item to let the user know which action will be taken. Figure 9.6 shows how the menu item can change.

A mouse click on the first item in the Movie menu takes the program to the *Show_Hide_Controller()* function, described below.

```
void  Handle_Movie_Choice( short the_item )
{
   switch ( the_item )
   {
      case HIDE_CONTROLLER_ITEM:
         Show_Hide_Controller();
```

```
            break;

        [ other case statements here ]
    }
}

void  Show_Hide_Controller( void )
{
    Rect              the_rect;
    ComponentResult   comp_result;

    comp_result = MCGetVisible( The_Controller );
    if ( comp_result == 1 )
    {
        comp_result = MCSetVisible( The_Controller, false );
        SetItem( Movie_Menu, HIDE_CONTROLLER_ITEM,
                "\pShow Controller" );

        GetMovieBox( The_Movie, &the_rect );
    }
    else
    {
        comp_result = MCSetVisible( The_Controller, true );
        SetItem( Movie_Menu, HIDE_CONTROLLER_ITEM,
                "\pHide Controller" );

        comp_result = MCGetControllerBoundsRect( The_Controller,
                                                 &the_rect );
    }

    SizeWindow( The_Window, the_rect.right, the_rect.bottom,
                true );
}
```

In this chapter's *Hiding the Controller* section, we discussed using *MCSetVisible()* to hide or display the movie controller. That's the routine we use here. But before doing so, we use the companion routine *MCGetVisible()* to determine the current state of the controller. This routine returns a 1 if the controller is visible, a 0 if it's not. Based on the return value of *MCGetVisible()*, we either display or hide the controller.

To let the user know which action will next be performed by the menu item, we set the menu item text with a call to the Toolbox routine *SetItem()*. We haven't used this routine yet, so we'll discuss it now.

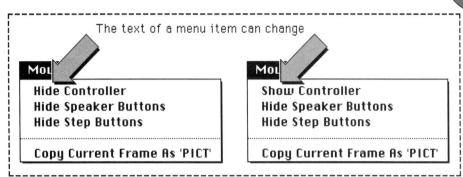

FIGURE 9.6
The Name of a Menu Item Can Change as a Program Runs

Pass *SetItem()* a *MenuHandle* and an item number to let it know which menu item is to be changed. The last parameter is the new text. If we've just hidden the controller, we'll change the text so the user knows that the next selection of this menu item will redisplay the controller. If we've just displayed the controller, we'll toggle the text the other way:

```
[ determine if controller is visible ]

if [ controller is visible ]
{
   [ set controller to invisible — hide it ]

   SetItem( Movie_Menu, HIDE_CONTROLLER_ITEM, "\pShow Controller" );

   [ get the size of the movie box ]
}
else
{
   [ set controller to visible - show it ]

   SetItem( Movie_Menu, HIDE_CONTROLLER_ITEM, "\pHide Controller" );

   [ get the size of both the movie box and the controller ]
}

[ size the window ]
```

The second and third menu items in the Movie menu work in a way similar to hiding the controller. The second item hides or displays the speaker; the third item hides or displays the step buttons. The text of both of these menu items changes, as it does for the Hide Controller item. Because there's a little more code involved than for hiding the entire controller, we've divided it into two functions: *Show_Speaker()* and *Hide_Speaker()*.

```
void  Handle_Movie_Choice( short the_item )
{
   switch ( the_item )
   {
      [ other case statements here ]

      case HIDE_SPEAKER_ITEM:
         if ( Speaker_Hidden == true )
            Show_Speaker();
         else
            Hide_Speaker();
         break;

      [ other case statements here ]
   }
}
```

Because one call to *MCDoAction()* with the *mcActionSetFlags* action overwrites any previous calls, we have to keep track of the current state of both the Speaker and the Step buttons. For that we use two global *Boolean* variables: *Speaker_Hidden* and *Steps_Hidden*. If the Speaker button is hidden and the user selects **Show Speaker button**, we'll arrive at *Show_Speaker()*. Before showing the speaker, we set the flags that will be passed to *MCDoAction()*. If the Step buttons are hidden, we'll pass just this flag. If they aren't, we set the flags to zero. That tells *MCDoAction()* to display everything. We then update the *Speaker_Hidden* variable and change the text of the menu item using *SetItem()*.

```
void  Show_Speaker( void )
{
   ComponentResult  comp_result;

   if ( Steps_Hidden == true )
      comp_result = MCDoAction( The_Controller, mcActionSetFlags,
                                (Ptr)mcFlagSuppressStepButtons );
   else
      comp_result = MCDoAction( The_Controller, mcActionSetFlags,
                                (Ptr)0 );
   Speaker_Hidden = false;

   SetItem( Movie_Menu, HIDE_SPEAKER_ITEM,
            "\pHide Speaker Button" );
}
```

Hide_Speaker() works much as *Show_Speaker()*. If the Step buttons are hidden and the Speaker button is to be hidden, we have to use the *BitOr()* routine to set both flags within the one long variable *controller_flags*.

```
void  Hide_Speaker( void )
{
    ComponentResult   comp_result;
    long              controller_flags;

    if ( Steps_Hidden == true )
    {
        controller_flags = BitOr( mcFlagSuppressStepButtons,
                                   mcFlagSuppressSpeakerButton );

        comp_result = MCDoAction( The_Controller, mcActionSetFlags,
                                   (Ptr)controller_flags );
    }
    else
    {
        comp_result = MCDoAction( The_Controller, mcActionSetFlags,
                                   (Ptr)mcFlagSuppressSpeakerButton);
    }

    Speaker_Hidden = true;

    SetItem( Movie_Menu, HIDE_SPEAKER_ITEM,
             "\pShow Speaker Button" );
}
```

If you understand how the Hide Speaker Button menu item works, you'll also be able to follow the Hide Step Buttons menu item code—it works in the exact same manner.

```
void  Show_Steps( void )
{
    ComponentResult   comp_result;

    if ( Speaker_Hidden == true )
        comp_result = MCDoAction( The_Controller, mcActionSetFlags,
                                   (Ptr)mcFlagSuppressSpeakerButton);
    else
        comp_result = MCDoAction( The_Controller, mcActionSetFlags,
                                   (Ptr)0 );
    Steps_Hidden = false;

    SetItem( Movie_Menu, HIDE_STEPS_ITEM, "\pHide Step Buttons" );
}
```

```
void  Hide_Steps( void )
{
   ComponentResult  comp_result;
   long             controller_flags;

   if ( Speaker_Hidden == true )
   {
      controller_flags = BitOr( mcFlagSuppressStepButtons,
                                mcFlagSuppressSpeakerButton );

      comp_result = MCDoAction( The_Controller, mcActionSetFlags,
                                (Ptr)controller_flags );
   }
   else
   {
      comp_result = MCDoAction( The_Controller, mcActionSetFlags,
                                (Ptr)mcFlagSuppressStepButtons );
   }

   Steps_Hidden = true;

   SetItem( Movie_Menu, HIDE_STEPS_ITEM, "\pShow Step Buttons" );
}
```

The last menu item in the Movies menu copies the current movie frame, saves it as a 'PICT', and transfers it to the scrap. This feature allows a user to save any frame in a format that can be pasted into a word processor or graphics program. The code for *Copy_Current_Frame_To_Scrap()* was developed in this chapter's *Copying a Single Frame as a 'PICT'* section, and appears here exactly as shown in that section.

```
void  Handle_Movie_Choice( short the_item )
{
   switch ( the_item )
   {
      [ other case statements here ]

      case COPY_FRAME_ITEM:
         Copy_Current_Frame_To_Scrap();
         break;

   }
}

void  Copy_Current_Frame_To_Scrap( void )
{
   TimeValue  frame_time;
```

```
   PicHandle   pic_handle;
   long        pic_size;

   frame_time = GetMovieTime( The_Movie, nil );
   pic_handle = GetMoviePict( The_Movie, frame_time );

   ZeroScrap();
   HLock( pic_handle );
      pic_size = GetHandleSize( pic_handle );
      PutScrap( pic_size, 'PICT', *pic_handle );
   HUnlock( pic_handle );
}
```

Handling the Play Menu

The Play menu of MovieFeatures allows the user to use palindrome looping,
play only the selected portion of a movie, or run the movie at different rates
of speed.

MovieFeatures handles looping just as MovieViewer does. First, use
MCDoAction() to see if looping is on or off, then use it again to toggle looping to the opposite state. Remember: to turn palindrome looping on, normal
looping must also be turned on.

```
void  Handle_Play_Choice( short the_item )
{
   [ variable declarations ]

   switch ( the_item )
   {
      case PAL_LOOP_ITEM:
         Handle_Palindrome_Loop_Item();
         break;

      [ other case statements here ]
   }
}


void  Handle_Palindrome_Loop_Item( void )
{
   ComponentResult  comp_result;
   Boolean          pal_looping_on;

   comp_result = MCDoAction( The_Controller,
        mcActionGetLoopIsPalindrome,
                            &pal_looping_on );
```

```
if ( pal_looping_on == true )
{
   CheckItem( Play_Menu, PAL_LOOP_ITEM, false );
   comp_result = MCDoAction( The_Controller,
                             mcActionSetLooping,
                             (Ptr)false );
   comp_result = MCDoAction( The_Controller,
                             mcActionSetLoopIsPalindrome,
                             (Ptr)false );
}
else
{
   CheckItem( Play_Menu, PAL_LOOP_ITEM, true );
   comp_result = MCDoAction( The_Controller,
                             mcActionSetLooping,
                             (Ptr)true );
   comp_result = MCDoAction( The_Controller,
                             mcActionSetLoopIsPalindrome,
                             (Ptr)true );
}
}
```

Playing only a selection of a movie involves a call to *MCDoAction()* with the
mcActionSetPlaySelection action. The Play Selection Only menu item is
another menu option that uses a check mark, as the Loop Back and Forth
item is. Instead of using a check mark, you could make this item change
text, from Play Selection Only to Play Entire Movie. The choice is yours.

```
void  Handle_Play_Choice( short the_item )
{
   [ variable declarations ]

   switch ( the_item )
   {
      [ other case statements here ]

      case PLAY_SELECTION_ITEM:
         Handle_Play_Selection_Item();
         break;

      [ other case statements here ]
   }
}


void  Handle_Play_Selection_Item( void )
{
```

```
ComponentResult   comp_result;
Boolean           play_selection_on;

comp_result = MCDoAction( The_Controller,
                          mcActionGetPlaySelection,
                          &play_selection_on );

if ( play_selection_on == true )
{
   CheckItem( Play_Menu, PLAY_SELECTION_ITEM, false );
   comp_result = MCDoAction( The_Controller,
                             mcActionSetPlaySelection,
                             (Ptr)false );
}
else
{
   CheckItem( Play_Menu, PLAY_SELECTION_ITEM, true );
   comp_result = MCDoAction( The_Controller,
                             mcActionSetPlaySelection,
                             (Ptr)true );
}
}
```

The last four menu items all work in exactly the same way. A call to
MCDoAction() immediately plays the movie specified by *The_Controller*. The
movie is played at the rate given in the last parameter.

```
void  Handle_Play_Choice( short the_item )
{
   [ variable declarations ]

   switch ( the_item )
   {
      [ other case statements here ]

      case HALF_SPEED_ITEM:
         comp_result = MCDoAction( The_Controller, mcActionPlay,
                                   (Ptr)F_TIMES_HALF_SPEED );
         break;

      [ other case statements here ]
   }
}
```

We've given the user four different speeds to run a movie (including backwards). You can provide as many different speeds as you want using any of
the *#defines* listed in the *Changing the Rate of Play* section of this chapter.

Chapter Summary

In the previous chapter you saw how to create a movie controller and attach it to a movie. Here, you've seen that you have a great deal of control over the way the controller is displayed, and how it plays a movie.

You can use *MCDoAction()* with the *mcActionSetFlags* action to either hide or display the Speaker button or the Step buttons of a controller. You can use the *MCSetVisible()* routine to hide or display the entire controller. If your QuickTime application has a need to prevent the user from using certain controller functions, these routines can suppress features of the controller.

QuickTime relies on time to properly display a movie. Because QuickTime keeps careful track of timing, you can determine how long a movie will run using the *GetMovieDuration()* routine. You can also use timing information to get the time associated with any single frame of a movie. You then pass this information on to the Movie Toolbox routine *GetMoviePict()* to obtain a picture of a frame. From there, copy the picture to the Clipboard using the Toolbox routine *PutScrap()*. That allows users of your program to save any frame as a picture, and transfer it to the Scrapbook, a word processor, or any other program that accepts the 'PICT' format.

You can use the Movie Toolbox to easily change the rate of play of a movie. You can speed it up, slow it down, or even run it backwards. Use the *mcActionPlay* action in a call to *MCDoAction()* to accomplish this.

The user of a program may want to play only a section of a long movie. You can constrain movie play to a user-selected portion by using *MCDoAction()* and the *mcActionSetPlaySelection* action.

You learned about looping in the previous chapter. Here, you've seen how to use palindrome looping to continuously run a movie back and forth.

Appendix of
QuickTime Products

his appendix lists a brief description of a number of QuickTime products—many of them covered in this book. Also listed is the address, phone number, or both, for each distributer.

Audio and Video Clips

America in Motion

Jasmine Multimedia

(800) 798-7535

A set of over eighty Americana clips. None of the clips have sound, but there are dozens of sound files of American music.

Baseball's Greatest Hits

The Voyager Company

(310) 451-1383

A collection of QuickTime clips of historic moments in baseball.

Deep Voyage

Aris Entertainment

(310) 821-0234

A collection of QuickTime clips, a hundred photographs for backgrounds, and a hundred sound and music files.

Great Cities of the World, Volume I

InterOptica Publishing Company

(415) 788-8788

A number of QuickTime movies of cities throughout the world.

Image Bank CD Collection

The Image Bank

(212) 529-6700

A solid collection of over 300 QuickTime video clips. Videos are silent, but the collection also includes dozens of music and sound files.

Multiware

Beachware

(619) 492-9529

A collection of over a hundred QuickTime movies. Also included is a hundred color backgrounds and over one hundred sound and music clips.

Proclaim!

Compact Designs

(301) 869-3919

Proclaim! is a varied collection of over 250 silent QuickTime clips, 50 color backgrounds, over 150 PICT drawings, and over 50 sound clips.

Hardware

ComputerEyes/RT

Digital Vision, Inc.

270 Bridge Street
Dedham, MA 02026
(617) 329-5400

An external video digitizer that connects to the Mac's SCSI port. Capable of capturing single still images or making QuickTime movies from video input.

MacRecorder

Macromedia

600 Townsend
San Francisco, CA 94103
(800) 228-4797

An external sound digitizer. Plugs into the printer or modem port of a Macintosh. Captures live sound from its built in microphone. Also captures sound from audio sources such as the audio output of a VCR or stereo. Comes with SoundEdit Pro—sound-editing software.

VideoSpigot

SuperMac Technology

485 Potrero Avenue
Sunnyvale, CA 94086
(800) 334-3005

An internal video digitizer. This digitizer is on a card that plugs into one of the internal slots of the Macintosh. Capable of capturing single still images or making QuickTime movies from video input using the ScreenPlay software bundled with the digitizer.

Software

ClarisWorks

Claris Corp.

5201 Patrick Henry Drive
Santa Clara, CA 95052
(408) 727-8227

Integrated software package that combines the features of graphics, word processing, and more. Creates video presentations that can include QuickTime movies.

ComputerEyes/RT

Digital Vision, Inc.

270 Bridge Street
Dedham, MA 02026
(617) 329-5400

Software to capture still images from video sources. Comes bundled with Digital Vision's ComputerEyes/RT video digitizer. Additionally, the digitizer comes bundled with Apple's Movie Recorder software to capture QuickTime movies from video sources.

Director

Macromedia

600 Townsend Street
San Francisco, CA 94103
(415) 442-0200

Software for creating multimedia presentations and interactive applications.

MacDraw Pro

Claris Corp.

5201 Patrick Henry Drive
Santa Clara, CA 95052
(408) 727-8227

Graphics software that allows you to add movies to its documents. Can be used to draw graphic images to be converted to a QuickTime movie using utilities such as Apple's Movie Converter or the MovieMaker software included with this book.

MacWrite Pro

Claris Corp.

5201 Patrick Henry Drive
Santa Clara, CA 95052
(408) 727-8227

Word processing software that allows you to add movies to its documents.

Microsoft Word

Microsoft Corp.

One Microsoft Way
Redmond, WA 98052

Word processing software that allows you to add movies to its documents.

Morph

Gryphon Software Corp.

33298 Governor Drive
Box 221075
San Diego, CA 92122
(619) 454-6836

Software that creates a QuickTime movie that displays the transformation of one picture to another—a technique called morphing.

Movie Converter

Apple Computer

20525 Mariani Avenue
Cupertino, CA 95014
(800) 282-2732

Make movies from a series of PICT graphic files.

MovieMaker

MIS:PRESS

Software bundled with this book. Makes QuickTime movies from a series of PICT graphic files.

Movie Player

Apple Computer

20525 Mariani Avenue
Cupertino, CA 95014
(800) 282-2732

Allows you to view any existing QuickTime movie.

Movie Recorder

Apple Computer

20525 Mariani Avenue
Cupertino, CA 95014
(800) 282-2732

Make movies from video tapes. You must have video digitizer hardware (not included) in order to use Movie Recorder.

MovieStartUp

MIS:PRESS

Software bundled with this book. Pick any existing QuickTime movie to be used as a startup movie. Movie will play each time the Mac boots (starts up).

MovieViewer

MIS:PRESS

Software bundled with this book. View existing QuickTime movies.

Premiere

Adobe Systems, Inc.

1585 Charleston Road
Mountain View, CA 04049

An application used to edit and create QuickTime movies. Allows easy editing and merging of video, sound, and special effects.

PROmotion

Motion Works Corp.

1020 Mainland Street
Suite 130
Vancouver, British Columbia, Canada V6B 2T4
(604) 732-0289

Software that creates animated QuickTime movies.

QuickTime Starter Kit

Apple Computer

20525 Mariani Avenue
Cupertino, CA 95014
(800) 282-2732

Contains a collection of QuickTime software utilities:

- *Movie Player*—allows you to view any existing QuickTime movie.
- *Movie Converter*—make movies from a series of PICT graphic files.
- *Movie Recorder*—make movies from video tapes. You must have video digitizer hardware (not included) in order to use Movie Recorder.

ScreenPlay

SuperMac Technology

485 Potrero Avenue
Sunnyvale, CA 94086
(800) 334-3005

Software to capture still images or QuickTime movies from video sources. Comes bundled with SuperMac's VideoSpigot video digitizer.

SoundEdit Pro

Macromedia

600 Townsend
San Francisco, CA 94103
(800) 228-4797

Software that edits and adds special effects to sound clips. Comes bundled with Macromedia's MacRecorder sound digitizer.

Theater Maker

Mark Adams

11215 Research Blvd. #2036
Austin, TX 78759

Shareware software that turns any QuickTime movie into a standalone application—the movie needs no additional software to run and view. Additionally, Theater Maker surrounds the movie with a clever screen-filling background, such as an drive-in theater.

Online Services

America Online

America Online

Quantum Computer Services, Inc.
Customer Relations Department
8619 Westwood Center Drive
Vienna, VA 22182
(800) 227-6364

Online service that lets you download sound files, QuickTime movies, and graphics files.

CompuServe

CompuServe

5000 Arlington Centre Blvd.
PO Box 20212
Columbus, Ohio 43220
(800) 848-8990

Online service that provides sound files, QuickTime movies, and graphics files for downloading.

Index

A

Adobe Premiere, *see Premiere*
Apple #includes folder, 175
America Online
    downloading files, 134, 159
    navigating in, 133
    obtaining sounds, 130, 133-134
analog video signal, 78
animation, 9, 25, 60
Animation compressor, 40
Apple QuickTime Starter Kit, 14, 36, 162
audio digitizer, *see MacRecorder sound digitizer*
Audio IFF sound file format, 121
audio track, 106

B

background for movie, 31-32

badge, 46, 50
BMP graphic files, 159, 163
built-in sound port, *see sound port*

C

ClarisWorks
    backgrounds, 53
    borders, adding of, 50-52
    fade out, 53
    Master Page, 54-56
    slide shows, 52-58
CloseMovieFile(), 182, 231
compilers, 7
ComponentResult data structure, 240
CompuServe
    downloading files, 133, 161-162
    navigating in, 131-132
    obtaining sounds, 130, 131-133
ComputerEyes/RT video digitizer
    brightness adjustment, 83

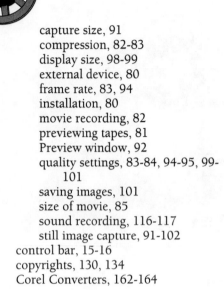
capture size, 91
compression, 82-83
display size, 98-99
external device, 80
frame rate, 83, 94
installation, 80
movie recording, 82
previewing tapes, 81
Preview window, 92
quality settings, 83-84, 94-95, 99-101
saving images, 101
size of movie, 85
sound recording, 116-117
still image capture, 91-102
control bar, 15-16
copyrights, 130, 134
Corel Converters, 162-164

D

daisy-chained devices, 79
database software, 58-59
digital devices, 78
digitizing, 25, 77-78
digitizers, *see video digitizer or MacRecorder sound digitizer*
Director, 60
DisableItem(), 261
DisposeMovie(), 190, 242
DisposeWindow(), 190
DragWindow(), 263
DrawPicture(), 281
dynamic data, 8

E

E-mail messages, 59
EnableItem(), 261
enabling keystrokes, 240-241
EnterMovies()
EPS graphic files, 158, 164
ExitToShell(), 173
Extension folder, 1-2
extensions, 1
external device, 79

F

file formats, 121-122
file system specification, 177-179
FileMaker Pro, 58-59
filters, 154-157
Fixed data structure, 282-284
For Both folder, 2
For Nonprogrammers folder, 14-15, 23, 30
frame rate, 35
frames, 9
frames per second, 35
FSMakeFSSpec(), 177-179, 227
fsRdPerm global constant, 179, 232
fsRdWrPerm global constant, 232
FSSpec data structure, 177-179, 227, 231
fsWrPerm global constant, 179
function prototypes, 178, 202

G

Gestalt(), 172-174
GestaltEqu.h header file, 172
gestaltQuickTime selector code, 172
GetDItem(), 210
GetHandleSize(), 281
GetIndString(), 194, 205, 210
Get Info menu item, 3
GetMovieBox(), 183, 234-235, 278
GetMovieDuration(), 279
GetMoviePict(), 280-282
GetMovieTime(), 280-281
GetMovieTimeScale(), 279
GetNewCWindow(), 183
GIF graphic files, 158, 164
graphic files
conversions, 162-164, 167-168
downloading, 159, 161-162
formats, 158-159, 163-164
movies from non-PICTs, 164-165
PC format, 157
graphics, object vs paint, 29
graphics world drawing environment, 187-188

H

header files, 175
Header Files folder, 175
HiWord(), 264
HLock(), 281
HUnlock(), 281

I

image compression dialog components, 225
image compressors, 10, 34-35, 40
image track, 106
include files, 202
Initialize_Toolbox(), 174, 204
Inside Macintosh books, 7
integrated packages, 49
internal device, 79
IsMovieDone(), 189

J-L

keystroke, handling, 262-263
KHz, 111, 117
looping, 240, 286-287
LoWord(), 264

M

MacDraw Pro, 26-32
MacRecorder sound digitizer
    connecting, 114-115, 128
    KHz, 117
    music recording, 117-118, 128
    sampling rates, 117
    Sound control panel, 114-115
    sound port, versus, 116
    source settings, 116
    voice recording, 117
    volume adjustment, 117
MacroMind Director, 60
mail messages, 59
mcActionGetPlaySelection global constant, 286
mcActionPlay global constant, 283
mcActionSetFlags global constant, 276

mcActionSetKeysEnabled global constant, 241
mcActionSetPlaySelection global constant, 285
MCClear(), 243-244
    MCCopy(), 243
MCCut(), 242
MCDoAction(), 240-241, 276
MCEnableEditing(), 241
mcFlagSuppressStepButtons global constant, 276
mcFlagSuppressSpeakerButton global constant, 276
MCGetControllerBoundsRect(), 235
MCIsPlayerEvent(), 237-239
MCPaste(), 243
MCSetVisible(), 277-278
MCUndo(), 244
mcTopLeftMovie global constant, 234
MenuHandle data structure, 260
menus
    adjusting, 261
    handling, 264-266
metamorphosis, see Morph
Microsoft Word, 47-48
MIS QuickTime folder, 2
modal dialog box, 207
moov resource type, 179-180
Morph
    end image, 65
    point pairs, 65-67
    purpose, 64
    saving movies in, 68
    start image, 65
    Storyboard, 65
    transition images, 67-68
motion video, 9
Motion Works PROmotion, 60
mouse event, handling, 263-264
movie
    badge, 46, 50
    borders, adding of, 50-52
    color, 41
    compression, 10, 34-35
    controller, 15-16

creating, 9
current selection, 20
documents containing, 4, 46
editing, 20, 38
files, 8
grayscale, 41
image quality, 19, 40
looping, 20
naming, 34
normal, 22
playing, 15-24
poster frame, 21-22, 46
preview, 17-18, 21-22
rate of play, 20, 41
reports containing, 5
resizing, 19, 43
saving, 22
self-contained, 22
size, 10, 43, 85
special effects, 151-154
standalone, 69
tracks, 106
transferring to disk, 47, 64
unsupported applications and, 61-
64
uses of, 4-8
MovieController data structure, 237
movie controller programming
buttons, 225
changing features of, 239-241
enabling keystrokes, 240-241
event loop, 236-239
hiding controller, 277-279
hiding controls, 276-277
looping, 240, 286-287
Movie Converter
naming movies, 37
previewing PICTs, 37
purpose, 36
using, 36-44
Movie data structure, 180
movie editors, *see Premiere*
MovieFileType global constant, 230
MovieMaker
purpose, 9, 15

using, 32-34
Movie Player
purpose, 9
start up movies, 23
using, 21-23
movie programming
closing, 182
copying frame, 280-282
displaying, 169
disposing, 190
editing, 241-246
loading, 179
opening file, 176-179
playing, 188-190, 213-216
rate of play, 282-284
saving, 246-247
selection playing, 285-286
sizing, 183-186
window for, 169, 182-187
movieScrapOnlyPutMovie global constant, 242
Movies.h header file, 175
MovieStartUp
playing movies, 23-25
purpose, 14
MovieStartUp Folder, 24
MovieStartUp.Movie, 24
MoviesTask(), 188-189
Movie Toolbox
defined, 171-172, 224
initializing, 174-175
MovieViewer
purpose, 13-14
using, 17-21

N-O

naming movies, 37
networks, 59
NewCWindow(), 183, 233
NewMovieController(), 234
NewMovieFromFile(), 179-183, 231,
247
noErr global constant, 173
OffsetRect(), 183

online information services, 130
  see also America Online
  see also CompuServe
OpenDeskAcc(), 265
OpenMovieFile(), 176, 179, 231-232, 247
operating system, 1

P

palindrome looping, 286-287
parent directory, 177-178
pathnames, 176-179
PCC graphic files, 163
PCX graphic files, 163
permission level, 179
PicHandle data structure, 281
PICS file format, 36
PICT files
  background, 31-32
  creating, 25-32
  converting to movie, 32-34, 35-38
  defined, 26
  format, 158
  opening, 30
  PICT2, 26
  saving, 27-30
  series of, 29
  Snowman example, 27-31
  uniform size, 26-27
  viewing, 30
PIM, 48
plug in modules, 48
poster frame, 21-22, 46
Premiere
  Clip window, 150-151
  Construction window, 145-146
  cutting video, 150
  editing clips, 148-149
  filters, 154-157
  importing clips, 146-147, 154
  movies, creating, 150
  previewing clips, 148-149
  Project window, 145, 148
  purpose, 118, 137, 145
  special effects, 151-154

  thumbnail, 146
presentations, 52-58
programs
  MovieFeatures, 287-311
  MovieViewer, 247-272
  OneShot, 170-171
  QuickTrivia, 190-221
PROmotion, 60
psychotherapy, 174
PutMovieOnScrap(), 242 { clipboard, copying to }
PutScrap(), 281-282

Q-R

QuickTime
  availability of, 3
  extension, 1, 7, 8
  installing, 2-4
  interface to, 17
  programs, *see programs*
  trivia game, 6
  versions, 3
  see also movie
QuickTime programming
  initializing, 174-175
  introduction, 5-8
  presence of, 172-174
QuickTime Starter Kit, 14, 36, 162
Random(), 209
RCA connectors, 108
ResEdit, 217-220
result variable, 173
RLE graphic files, 163

S

sampling rate, 111, 117
ScreenPlay digitizing software, 87-90
SCSI port, 79, 86
SetDItem(), 210
selector code, 172-173
SelectWindow(), 263
sequence grabber components, 225
SetMovieBox(), 185-186
SetMovieGWorld(), 187-188, 233

SetRect(), 234
SFTypeList data structure, 230
Show Preview checkbox, 17-18, 21-22
ShowWindow(), 186, 235
SizeWindow(), 186, 235
slide shows, 52-58
SnowMan PICTs folder, 30
Snowman movie, 31
sound
    compressed, 130-131
    copyrights, 130
    downloading, 130
    editing, *see SoundEdit Pro software*
    file formats, 121-122
    input sources, 109-110
    KHz, 111
    music, 111
    obtaining, 129-135
    port vs digitizer, 112
    previewing, 112
    samples per second, 111
    track, 106
    voice, 111
    volume settings, 112
sound digitizer, *see MacRecorder sound digitizer*
SoundEdit Pro software
    amplifying, 123-125
    amplitude, 125
    Audio IFF sound, 121
    commands, 123
    Control Palette, 118-120, 128
    cue points, 138-142
    document window, 118
    file formats, 121-122, 141-142
    Input Level Meter, 118
    Input Level Test button, 118-119
    insertion point, 141
    insertion point, 141
    labels, 142-144
    multiple-sounds, 123
    playing sounds, 120, 141
    purpose, 118
    opening sound files, 122

recording sounds, 119
reverb, 125-126
saving sounds, 120-122, 128, 141
selections, 123
smoothing, 125
SoundEdit Pro sound, 122
special effects, 123-126
System 7 Sound, 121
video tape source, 129
waveforms, 119-120
SoundEdit Pro sound file format, 122
sound port
    connections, 108-109
    digitizer, versus, 112
    Macintosh models, 108
special effects
    sound, 13-126
    video, 151-154
standalone movies, 69
standard compression settings, 38-44
standard compressor dialog box, 35
standard controller, 15-16
StandardFileReply data structure, 230-231
StandardGetFile(), 228
StandardGetFilePreview(), 228-231
Starter Kit, 14, 36, 162
StartMovie(), 188
Startup Items folder, 24
still image capture, 91-102, 103-104
strings
    defined, 205
    resource, 194, 210, 217-220
    working with, 205-206, 209-212
StuffIt compression software, 130-131
Symantec C++ compiler, 7, 175, 192
System 7 Sounds
    compatibility with Premiere, 121
    downloading, 133
    file format, 121
    Sound control panel, 122-123
SystemClick(), 263
System file, 1
System folder, 1, 2

T

TheaterMaker
    backgrounds, 69-71
    compressing, 72-75
    memory usage, 75
    purpose, 69
THINK C compiler, 7, 175, 192
TIFF graphic files, 158, 163
time-based data, 279
TimeRecord data structure, 280
TimeScale data structure, 280
time scales, 79
TimeValue data structure, 280
Toolbox, *see Movie Toolbox*
tracks, 106
trivia game, 6

U-V

UpdateMovieResource(), 247
VCR connections
    audio, 108-109
    video, 80, 86
video digitizer
    capture rate, 78-79
    video sources, 79
    see also ComputerEyes/RT video digitizer
    see also VideoSpigot video digitizer
VideoSpigot video digitizer
    brightness control, 89, 154-56
    compression, 89-90
    installation, 86
    internal device, 86
    movies recording , 87
    quality settings, 88-89
    ScreenPlay software, 87-90
    sound recording , 113, 117
    still image capture, 103-104
volume, 176-178

W

WaitNextEvent(), 237
waveforms, 119-120

Wild Magic
    distributing, 64
    installing, 61
    testing, 63
    transferring documents, 64
    using, 61-63
WordPerfect Office, 59

Z

ZeroScrap(), 281
ZIP files, 159

About This Disk

The enclosed disk contains source code for programmers and software utilities for programmers and nonprogrammers alike. It also contains a copy of Apple's QuickTime. These programs run on all newer Macs. Make sure you have any version of System 7 on yours—all new Macs come with. Owners of older Mac models can upgrade to it. The programs run on black-and-white or color systems, and run on a Macintosh with any size monitor. You need no additional software—except the included QuickTime program—to run the programs.

The one 1.4Mb disk contains one self-extracting compressed file. When expanded, this file gives you the MovieMaker, MovieViewer, and MovieStartUp programs and the THINK C source code for the three example programs listed in this book. Self-extracting means that you need no additional software to decompress these files—everything you need is right here on this one disk.

This disk is a Macintosh 1.4Mb high-density disk. All newer model Macintosh computers come with the SuperDrive—a 1.4Mb high-density floppy drive. If you have an older Macintosh with an 800K double-density floppy drive, you won't be able to use this disk. You can, however, if you know a friend or coworker who has a Mac with a SuperDrive. That person can extract the files and copy them to 800K disks for you.

To get the software from this disk on to your hard drive, follow these simple steps:

1. Insert the disk into your 1.4Mb floppy drive.
2. Copy the single file, named **QTstuff.sea**, to your hard drive.
3. Double-click on the **QTstuff.sea** icon that is on your hard drive.
4. A dialog box opens. Click the **Extract** button.

For more detailed instructions on how to decompress the software, and how to use it, read the section titled "Extracting the Disk Contents" at the start of this book.